T0271673

SHOULDER TO SHOULDER

SHOULDER
TO
SHOULDER

A Queer History of Solidarity, Coalition and Chaos

Jake Hall

First published in Great Britain in 2024 by Trapeze
an imprint of The Orion Publishing Group Ltd
Carmelite House, 50 Victoria Embankment
London EC4Y 0DZ

An Hachette UK Company

1 3 5 7 9 10 8 6 4 2

A CIP catalogue record for this book is
available from the British Library.

ISBN (Hardback) 978 1 3987 1859 3
ISBN (eBook) 978 1 3987 1861 6
ISBN (Audio) 978 1 3987 1862 3

Typeset by Input Data Services Ltd, Bridgwater, Somerset

Printed in Great Britain by Clays Ltd, Elcograf S.p.A.

MIX
Paper | Supporting
responsible forestry
FSC® C104740

www.orionbooks.co.uk

To Nan, for always being my number-one fan

SOLIDARITY

/ˌsɒl.ɪˈdær.ə.ti /

(noun)

To show support for each other or for
another group, especially between
political or international affairs.[1]

A feeling of unity between people who
have the same interests or goals.[2]

CONTENTS

Introduction

'No freedom without solidarity.'
— *Solidarity* (Polish trade union)

In 1919, physician Magnus Hirschfeld flung open the doors of his research institute, the Institut für Sexualwissenschaft.[1] This opening marked the realisation of a lifelong dream; the dream of dedicating an *entire* institution to the then-budding field of sexology, the study of human sexuality. The building itself was palatial, nestled on the edge of Berlin's leafy, picturesque Tiergarten — incidentally, now a renowned gay cruising spot.[2] Inside this building, Hirschfeld was one of the first known doctors to treat what we'd now describe as LGBTQ+ patients.

It took decades of work, sweat and passion to build the Institute. Hirschfeld himself was gay and Jewish, born in the seaside city of what's now known as Kołobrzeg, Poland. Early on, he followed in his dad's footsteps and became a general medical practitioner, but after four years of practice, Hirschfeld moved to Berlin in 1896. It was here that he started seriously studying homosexuality — not just as a medical professional, but as a young gay man, too. In 1904, Hirschfeld published a book whose title translates to *Berlin's Third Sex*.[3] As well as advocating for gay rights, he took readers on a thrilling underground tour of Berlin's gay scene, detailing clandestine bars, drag nights and even little-known cruising spots. Yet the daily realities of his medical work were more sombre, and after years of treating suicidal gay men, Hirschfeld set about dedicating himself to the practice of sexology. Through this work, he hoped, he could fight for the fair treatment of sexual minorities.

When Hirschfeld was finally ready to start laying the foundations for his fabled institute in the 1910s, he reached out to two frequent collaborators: Arthur Kronfeld, a psychotherapist, and Bernard Schapiro, an andrologist. Their combined expertise meant the Institute could operate as a multi-faceted organisation.[4]

Slowly, Hirschfeld began assembling a small but dedicated staff. He recruited clinicians, therapists and medical practitioners; between them, they offered everything from psychological treatment to sex and marriage counselling, their work always informed by principles of safe sex and zero judgement. Progressive politics underpinned the Institute more broadly, even by today's standards: as well as a zero-tolerance approach to stigma, there was a sliding-scale pricing policy, meaning poorer patients could be treated at lower costs and nobody would be turned away for lack of funds. The Institute had a handful of clinical treatment rooms, where gender non-conforming people could speak to specialists about their desire to start hormone therapy. Hirschfeld later coined the term 'transsexual' in 1923, and went on to make more key breakthroughs in what we'd now describe as gender-affirming healthcare. In fact, some of the world's earliest gender-affirmation surgeries might never have happened were it not for him laying the blueprints.

Arguably, Hirschfeld's goal as a sexologist was rooted in solidarity. His politics were far from flawless – more on that soon

– but he did seemingly fight for other marginalised groups, at least to some extent, and he used his knowledge to dispel discriminatory myths. In 1918, he co-authored an international pamphlet with his sister, Franziska Mann, the title of which loosely translated to: 'What Every Woman Needs to Know About the Right to Vote' *(Was Jede Frau vom Walrecht Wissen Muß)*.[5] When Hirschfeld started to flesh out his concept of 'transsexualism' in the early 1920s, he used his authority to issue 'transvestite passes' to trans people. If these people were harassed or threatened with criminalisation by police officers, these passes would – at least in theory – protect them.[6]

Unsurprisingly, it didn't take long for the progressive doctor to be brutally targeted by Nazis; in 1920, he was beaten so badly by German ethno-nationalists[7] that police arriving at the crime scene initially declared him dead. Yet perhaps the biggest blow of all came on 6 May 1933, when Nazi-affiliated youths broke into his beloved Institute. Not only did they smash up the building, the young Nazis also rifled through drawers and flung X-rays, photographs and classified documents out of the windows. They tore pictures from the walls, decimated Hirschfeld's bookshelves and seized decades of research papers, including some of the earliest recorded cases of trans people undergoing medical treatment. Days later, the Nazis made a public spectacle of setting these documents ablaze – and as a symbolic nail in the coffin, they fed a life-sized bust of Hirschfeld into the bonfire, too.[8]

It took a lifetime of work for Hirschfeld to build the world's largest archive of sexual minorities. It took just hours for that archive to be destroyed.

Hirschfeld's story is depressingly, infuriatingly timely in to-day's era of renewed censorship and widespread moral panic.

It's taken queer trailblazers decades to prove that we've always existed, by writing histories which trace the contours of pre-colonial cultures and paint truly global pictures of our ancestry. Queerness isn't some newfangled invention, and there's more evidence than ever to prove it.

Today's puritans might not be smashing up libraries, but they *are* launching full-scale attacks against queer culture, creating smear campaigns designed to get progressive books pulled from shelves. Incidentally, my own first book, *The Art of Drag*, has been swallowed into this so-called culture war. I've seen evangelicals slip bookmarks stamped with 'PRIDE = SIN' between its pages; when I was nominated for a teen readers' choice awards, campaigners scoured my online history and screen-shotted sex-positive articles in the hopes of cancelling my nomination, all because I occasionally tweet in support of sex workers and write about sex.

It's not just queer books, either; writing about race, gender, socialism – or, god forbid, all of the above – will have pearl-clutching parents frothing at the mouth, like rabid new incarnations of the iconic *Simpsons* 'think of the children' meme.

While we're fighting to preserve existing stories, queer researchers worldwide are *still* recovering the traces of activists whose findings, research and reputations have been erased, often violently. In the grand scheme of history, we're still in the early stages of that recovery process, dusting off the details of biographies like Hirschfeld's. As a result, plenty of us feel protective of the pioneers who came before us. It can be tempting to put these innovators on pedestals, to overstate their queerness or to use terms like 'non-binary' to describe them – despite the fact that they may not have self-identified that way, even if they *did* have today's language.

As more of us now understand, history is messy and complicated. It's also plural: there are *histories*. The ones we read are usually written by those with the privilege and resources to write and publish without fear. These are narratives from the perspectives of colonisers, often middle-class scholars shrouded by the armour of whiteness, cis-ness and straightness. This creates a sort of pressure when it comes to writing marginalised histories, an urge to omit crucial context and paint unblemished portraits of heroes through the lens of their marginalisation, and that lens alone.

It's always worth digging deeper – and further excavation of Hirschfeld's past has complicated his legacy. Especially in recent years, the broader spectrum of his work is being interrogated and called into question. A 2022 book, *Racism and the Making of Gay Rights: A Sexologist, His Student and the Empire of Queer Love*,[9] homes in on his relationship with Li Shiu Tong, a Chinese sexology student four decades his junior, as well as the complex nexus of race and power dynamics embedded within it. Of course, it's not just a book about Hirschfeld's personal life. Author Laurie Marhoefer also examines the physician's later published work on racism, drawing a handful of seemingly contradictory conclusions. 'His racism is very complicated,' Marhoefer explained in a 2022 interview with *Xtra Magazine*.[10] 'He does say repeatedly that he's against racism, and he does have some really inspiring moments where he denounces racism. I think people got thrown by that. But he's against *scientific* racism. He's against some kinds of racism and not others.'

Then there was Tong, Hirschfeld's student. In the wake of Tong's death in 1993, a handful of surviving documents indicated that his scholarship had actually gone further than Hirschfeld's, by examining what we'd now describe as bisexuality, or sexual fluidity. Tong's manuscript was never published, which begs the question: why? We may never know the specifics, but his lost contributions to sexology exemplify the wider whitewashing of queer histories.

Even historical figures who made game-changing advancements in their fields have never been perfect – and nor should they be. Hirschfeld described himself as anti-racist, and he indisputably showed political solidarity with other marginalised groups, a stance which set him apart from other experts of the time. Yet he also bought into a handful of racist and eugenicist theories popular in the early 20th century, and – at least according to Marhoefer – perpetuated some forms of racism with his later writings on the subject. Rather than viewing these critical readings of queer legacies as attempts to smear past heroes, it's worth viewing them as opportunities to learn. Usually, the stories of LGBTQ+ historical figures are syphoned off, examined through the lenses of gender and sexuality alone. As a result, it often goes unacknowledged that some groundbreaking activists were complicit in the marginalisation of other groups, and, of course, that plenty of LGBTQ+ people are *also* people of colour, they're working-class, they're trans or disabled.

This tendency to varnish over nuance has led to countless missed opportunities to write flawed, complicated histories, the kind which could form the blueprint for broader, more effective coalition-building today. Similarly, there's scope to write wider-ranging political histories, tales which look across various sectors of marginalisation to examine shared experiences, identify common enemies and chronicle historical attempts to come together.

That's where *Shoulder to Shoulder* comes in. The aim of this book is to weave together new tapestries of activism, fusing human stories with archival research and critical thinking. This won't be a book full of statistics and data, and that's largely because marginalised groups rarely get the privilege of being humanised. We're described as numbers and percentages all too often, and – as we saw in the case of Hirschfeld – it's rare that our stories get told in depth, if at all.

Shoulder to Shoulder is ultimately a book about solidarity. It's a concept that dates back to 19th-century France, but today it's an ethos beloved of trade unions, left-wing thinkers and working-class organisers. It's a mentality rooted in shared struggles, collective activism and mutuality, the idea that coalitions are more effective at making change than individuals.

The term has mutated through history, but in the late 1970s and early 1980s in particular, it became synonymous with workers' rights. In August 1980, a Polish crane operator named Anna Walentynowicz scoured through a shipyard in Gdańsk to collect candle stubs.[11] Her hope was to create a makeshift memorial for workers who had been shot years earlier by government soldiers in a series of riots driven by poverty and skyrocketing food prices. The story of Walentynowicz scouring through dirt and rubble made its way to the desk of her employer, and she was promptly fired, just weeks before she was due to qualify for retirement. Her unjust dismissal sparked the creation of a trade union called Solidarity, whose premise was simple: banding together as maligned workers was the best strategy to topple exploitative bosses.

Committee reps created an Inter-Enterprise Strike Committee, whose demands were wide-ranging: as well as the right to strike and protest, they called for the release of political prisoners and improvements to national healthcare.[12] These demands galvanised a mass movement; according to the *Guardian,* the Solidarity union had 10 million members, a third of Poland's working-age population, within just a year, representing myriad occupations. Ultimately, their aim was to improve life for *everyone*. It helped that the union had a catchy, memorable slogan, too: NO FREEDOM WITHOUT SOLIDARITY.

Unions and workers' rights are embedded in histories of solidarity, but the definition I'll use in this book is about more than just picket lines. It's about activists building relationships across lines of marginalisation, to advocate and continuously fight for one another.

In 1983, Barbara Smith – founding member of the Combahee River Collective, a trailblazing Black feminist collective – edited an anthology entitled *Home Girls*. Inside, there's a visionary essay on coalition-building by Bernice Johnson Reagon,[13] which sums up the meaning of solidarity. It's a pragmatic manifesto which acknowledges that coalitions rarely come easy. To quote Johnson: 'You don't go into coalition because you like it. The only reason you would consider trying to team up with somebody who could possibly kill you is because that's the only way you figure you could possibly stay alive.'

Home Girls was published almost a decade after the Combahee River Collective issued their joint statement on identity politics.[14] Linked by firmly anti-racist, anti-sexist beliefs, these women came together on the grounds of shared experience to speak on issues which specifically shaped their lives. 'Our politics initially sprung from the shared belief that Black women are inherently valuable,' they wrote, 'that our liberation is a necessity not as an adjunct to somebody else's, but because of our need as human persons.' It was a collective born of mainstream, second-wave feminism's tendency to speak over and disregard the specific struggles of Black women, as well as the value of their scholarship. The authors alluded to this in their statement: 'No other ostensibly progressive movement has ever considered our specific oppression as a priority or worked seriously for the ending of that oppression.'

8

Since then, identity politics has become a right-wing scape-goat.[15] Its definition has been twisted beyond recognition by bigots, who bemoan today's cultural landscape as 'political correctness gone mad'.[16] We see one-note think-pieces about 'woke' leftists and the Oppression Olympics; in these essays, 'identity politics' is described as a notion which flattens individual nuance, painting marginalised groups as monolithic.[17] This is a wildly unfair and wilfully ignorant appraisal of the concept, *especially* as one of the founding principles of the Combahee River Collective was a commitment to 'continual examination of our politics as they develop through criticism and self-criticism'.

In this sense, identity politics and solidarity can go hand in hand. Marginalised people with lived experience can be at the forefront of revolutionary change, but they can also build co-alitions and show solidarity with other communities, without trying to dictate the terms of their battles.

Some of history's best-known queer activist groups have followed these principles, taking a radical, inclusive – and often mischievous – approach to protest. In 1987, a group of New York-based activists came together to form ACT UP, the AIDS Coalition to Unleash Power. They staged 'die-ins' inside churches and outside government buildings, lying motionless en masse to illustrate the AIDS-related deaths caused by the US government's inaction.[18] They knew how to make a splash, and piss off the establishment. They once famously draped the house of Republican politician Jesse Helms in a giant condom, an act of protest so memorable it was later recreated in the award-winning series *Pose*.[19] They made powerful art to com-municate with the masses – itself a tactic inspired by feminist consciousness-raising groups of the late 1960s.

ACT UP has gone down in the annals of queer history as a

revolutionary group, but their emphasis on solidarity is often overlooked. In a chapter published in the 2014 book *Against Equality*,[20] American author and activist Mattilda Bernstein Sycamore writes:

ACT UP meant making connections – between government neglect of people with AIDS and structural homophobia and racism; between the ever-increasing military budget and the lack of funding for healthcare; between misogyny and the absence of resources for women with AIDS; between the war on drugs and the abandonment of HIV-positive drug addicts and prisoners.

The most groundbreaking examples of queer activism have never been solely in the service of LGBTQ+ people. To ignore this fact does us all a disservice.

Minimising these stories of queer solidarity has an effect on people – myself included.

I was born and raised on a council estate in South Yorkshire, educated in a school whose career advice boiled down to 'take an apprenticeship' or 'don't bother'. I knew from the first time I laid eyes on David Beckham's Armani-clad bulge that I wasn't straight; yet I also knew, from the slurs hurled across the playground, that being gay was something to shut up about, unless you wanted your head kicked in. The AIDS crisis still loomed heavy throughout my childhood, and Section 28 – a law which forbade the 'promotion' of homosexuality' – had only just been repealed.[21] As a result, the only time I saw or even heard about people like me was through the media.

This LGBTQ+ representation – and let's be real, it was mainly ripped, cis white gay guys – was almost *always* middle class, dominated by 'gay best friend' stereotypes and standard gay bar scenes, in which hunky young men get drunk on swanky mimosas (arguably the most overrated drink in history) and grind with go-go dancers. Gay *culture* was perceived as hyper-sexual, but the gay characters themselves were rarely shown kissing, making out or fucking – too much of that would alienate straight viewers.

The 1990s saw ad executives target affluent LGBTQ+ people as potential consumers, and they weren't exactly subtle about trying to win them over – at one point, Subarus were basically *the* lesbian car.[22] So we got *some* visibility, but vast swathes of queer culture were defanged. There was no mention of groups like ACT UP, the Gay Liberation Front and quirky protest groups like drag nun troupe Sisters of Perpetual Indulgence. Instead, we got a distinctly polished era of gay visibility, one in which we were either tolerated or *very* occasionally celebrated – when we could be profitable or teach hapless straight men how to dress, introducing them to basic skincare.

It's not just queer communities whose histories of activism have been sanitised, painted over with a glossy, commercial sheen. The first time I saw the face of Che Guevara, a Marxist revolutionary, it was printed on a £20 T-shirt. Artist Frida Kahlo was a die-hard socialist who lived with physical disabilities and was openly bisexual, yet her legacy is often reduced to nothing but her eyebrows. You might hear about the Black Panthers, but it's unlikely you'll hear about the Rainbow Coalition, built in collaboration with working-class activists from various demographics, who were all being trampled by systems of capitalism, imperialism and discrimination.

The most radical moments in activist histories either get erased entirely, or they're stripped of their thorns and packaged as commodities to be bought and worn without context. Especially in today's era of social media and platform capitalism, there's unlimited potential to monetise activism. As Emma Dabiri writes in her incisive, book-length essay *What White People Can Do Next: From Allyship to Coalition*,[23] 'Much of the present "anti-racist" conversation is . . . devoid of class or capitalism, which it seems to have largely replaced with interpretations of interpersonal "privilege".'

We can apply similar critiques to recent discussions of so-called 'queer issues', which leave little to no room for nuance. For the last two decades in particular, mainstream media has homed in on various topics, from same-sex marriage and military 'transgender' bans to 'queerbaiting'[24] (a term which describes apparently straight celebrities pandering to LGBTQ+ fanbases for profit), along with the endless question of which public toilets trans people should be allowed to use. These discussions are usually packaged in clickbait, incendiary opinion essays by the same revolving door of identikit, middle-class columnists who churn out divisive rhetoric to fan the flames of a so-called culture war. As a result, we rarely get critiques filtered through the lens of anti-imperialism or anti-capitalism; instead, we get today's cruel media landscape, which forces trans people to 'debate' people fighting to strip them of even basic human rights. It's an approach which perpetuates harm against us, while simultaneously denying us the right to meaningfully engage in wider political discussion.

Reductive framing makes a difference to how we see ourselves, too. I only *really* realised I was working-class at university, when I was surrounded by middle-class people for the first time. I policed myself all the time about my accent and annoyed by the fact that I had to work to pay my way while everyone else could afford not to. I struggled to articulate my queerness. I had internalised so much homophobia, much of which stemmed from the fact that I couldn't afford to buy all the shit I felt I needed to be the right kind of gay – the palatable, visible, fit kind. Meanwhile, because I *did* leave South Yorkshire and move to a relatively big city, I started to internalise classism, too. I bought into the idea that working-class queer people were fundamentally doomed if they didn't achieve social mobility, and it fucked me over. I became self-conscious all the time, constantly dialling down my personality in order to 'pass' as middle class.

It might sound trite, but learning about queer solidarity changed my life. I was sitting outside a pub, licking gravy off my fingers, when my grandma first presented me with our family tree, which showed that *all* the men in my family – bar one lone milkman – had worked as miners. A month later, I saw an exhibition in Sheffield which made brief mention of Lesbians and Gays Support the Miners, a solidarity group which built bridges between queer and working-class communities, united against the common enemy: a brutally right-wing government, determined to strip miners of their income, their livelihoods and their dignity. Gradually, I started to realise that the parts of myself I had compartmentalised weren't so incompatible after all.

To go back to Dabiri's essay, the change-making potential of solidarity is hugely under-emphasised within pretty much all marginalised histories. When harnessed effectively, it's a threat to those in power. As Dabiri explains, 'whiteness' as we know it today was created to destroy any hopes of collaboration between indentured European workers and enslaved Africans. They had a shared enemy – the mega-rich landlords working them into the ground, for next to nothing in return – and soon understood they could work more effectively in coalition. Those in power got wind of this news, thus creating the category of 'whiteness' to differentiate the European workers from their African counterparts. In this newly formed hierarchy of race, the white Europeans were elevated enough to turn their backs on the enslaved Africans, meaning that today's construction of whiteness is literally rooted in supremacy.

Like race, sexuality is also a construct; the words 'heterosexual' and 'homosexual' didn't exist prior to 1868.[25] As they trickled into everyday language, societal views of sex and sexuality began to shift. Initially, sexuality was thought of as something you *do* rather than something you *are,* a view made evident in the language of law, which criminalised acts like 'buggery' and 'sodomy' – anal, basically. In fact, lawmakers at the time wrote such broad definition of these terms that acts like bestiality – having sex with an animal – were punished under the same laws as gay sex and, in some cases, adultery. Historically, Western missionaries took these laws with them on their brutal colonial enforcement trips. Not only did they destroy and then colonise countries, they imposed these anti-gay laws. Homosexuality is still criminalised in more than 60 countries worldwide, many of them former colonies.[26] In some cases, rich cultural histories of gender non-conformity were forcibly erased.[27] Since then, heterosexuality has become a deeply ingrained cultural norm, a presumed default state of being. Anyone who deviates from this norm is punished, through social marginalisation and increased criminalisation.

Different forms of discrimination can't be directly compared – they're too nuanced, and by trying to draw false equivalences, we flatten these nuances. Marginalisation impacts us all differently, and some of us are marginalised across multiple lines: we might be queer and working-class, queer and people of colour, and so on. But there *are* key commonalities which, filtered through the lens of solidarity, could form the basis of a fight rooted in shared struggle.

This is the thread that links the stories in *Shoulder to Shoulder*. Whether it's trans women leading abortion rights movements, Black Panthers pooling their resources to feed disabled protestors, or HIV activists in South Africa building continent-wide coalitions to fight for access to healthcare, these are tales of coalition-building first and foremost.

What *Shoulder to Shoulder* won't do is provide a splashy how-to guide for today's activists. It's all too tempting to package these stories solely as lessons and blueprints, but that would be disingenuous. Anyone involved in day-to-day advocacy knows it's hard and often boring work. It's arranging endless planning meetings, navigating *yet another* WhatsApp group chat, spending long and usually unpaid hours putting together strategies, protest routes and mutual aid projects. It's not glamorous, and it's increasingly difficult, at least in the UK – the current right-wing government seems ever-more determined to criminalise protest.

Fundamentally, histories of activism are histories of *people* – and we all know how difficult it can be to work with others. People are messy, flawed and complicated. We have egos and agendas. Sometimes, we exhibit shitty behaviours – and sometimes, these behaviours cause irreparable rifts.

Arguments and disagreements aside, there are other factors which lead to activist collectives disbanding. In some cases, activists get criminalised, targeted and even killed for their work. This risk varies hugely based on location – in Latin America and South East Asia in particular, environmental activists have been murdered for their advocacy.[28] In the last few years, we've seen the deaths of human rights defenders like Marielle Franco, a Black, Brazilian queer socialist, who was killed under mysterious circumstances in Rio de Janeiro.[29] In 2022 alone, more than 400 human rights defenders – the majority of whom were Indigenous – were targeted and killed.[30] Especially in countries outside of wealthy, Western bubbles, activism can be a question of life or death. Yet marginalised activists continue to do this work, because opting out isn't an option for them.

Although *Shoulder to Shoulder* will look to worldwide examples, there are obvious barriers to writing a truly global history: language is a big one (for that reason, the book is limited to English, Spanish and French-language resources), and cultural context is another. Telling worldwide stories is one thing, but telling them respectfully, expertly and sensitively is something entirely different; in many cases, the stories simply aren't mine to tell.

When it comes to writing about groups like the Black Panthers, and Black and marginalised histories more broadly, the scope of this book is to highlight that coalition-building has *always* happened. There were collectives like the White Panthers, an anti-racist group formed as a result of Black Panthers calling on white people to stand in solidarity with them. In the case of activists like Simon Nkoli, their immense contributions to queer history are erased solely because queer histories have been so thoroughly white-washed. Even now, we see widespread racism and ableism within queer communities, yet we also see pissed-off protestors screaming chants like 'Black Trans Lives Matter'[31] and 'No TERFs, No SWERFs', loud and proud.

There are tales of coalition-building across lines of race, gender, class, sexuality, disability and more that have yet to be told. The hope is that *Shoulder to Shoulder* will help in some way to get more of these histories written.

A critique I've come across often while researching this book is that the movements spot lit in these pages have failed. Sex workers in 1970s France, for example, set out to achieve decriminalisation. Fifty years later, only a handful of places, including Belgium, New Zealand and some Australian territories have decriminalised sex work.[32] Does that mean the sex workers' rights movement has *failed*?

Arguably, no. We're seeing the emergence of sex work unions,[33] and a gradual shift in cultural attitudes towards sex and sex work. There's an increased sense of solidarity among these communities, as well as increased awareness among the general public of *what* they want and *why*. It still happens too rarely, but some sex workers are having their voices heard. The movement didn't achieve decriminalisation worldwide, but it has arguably improved the lives of sex workers around the globe, even though they do still, undeniably, experience discrimination. Does this sound like a failed movement to you?

It's worth asking what we mean when we say movements have failed, and why we say it in the first place. Here, I can't help but think of Jack Halberstam, a queer theorist with decades of experience and an influential back catalogue of academic work, which includes books like *Female Masculinity, Gaga Feminism* and more. In 2011, he published an undeniably academic but brilliantly tongue-in-cheek book called *The Queer Art of Failure*,[34] which deals in 'low theory', a term which Halberstam adapts from the work of cultural theorist Stuart Hall.

Instead of combing the archives for the works of revered philosophers and academics, Halberstam deals in more accessible subject matter, like the films *Finding Nemo* and *Dude, Where's My Car?* The book is wide-ranging, but its core thesis is that we should interrogate what failure means, and who sets the terms of what societies call 'failure' and 'success'. Halberstam references lesbian performance group LTTR, who describe failure as a 'practice'. It is, in his words, a book about 'failing well, failing often and learning, in the words of Samuel

Beckett, to fail better', which has since become a pretty popular idea. Failure can be productive, revelatory and, in a queer
context especially, subversive.

Switching back to 'success' in the context of activism, we're
often reminded that political victories can be ripped from beneath us. The US abortion rights movement, for example, led
to the passage of Roe v. Wade in 1973, which decriminalised
abortion nationwide. Yet these rights turned out to be built on
beds of sand; because Roe v. Wade was never codified, it was
repealed in 2022.[35] Currently, abortion is outlawed in many
US states,[36] but does that mean the US reproductive rights
movement is a failure? Absolutely not. Really, I'm convinced
that the desire to brand movements as 'failed' stems from an
urge to grind us down, to tell us there's no point even trying.
Calling movements 'failures' sends the message that no amount
of direct action, collective organisation or continued protest
will ever actually help us.

It seems to me – and you might disagree, of course – that
telling us past coalitions have failed is a tactic employed by
those with vested interests in the status quo being maintained.
It's a rhetoric used to depoliticise us – and whose interests does
that serve? To be apolitical is a luxury in an unequal world, and
it's a luxury many of us can't access.

Shoulder to Shoulder aims to reframe these conversations. It's
loosely chronological, a choice made to highlight that even in
the shittiest of times, hope has been maintained. It's a book
about trying, fucking up and then trying again, all with the
help of like-minded co-conspirators.

The story begins in the early 1960s, a decade as well known
for free love and mini skirts as it is for anti-war activism. We'll
travel through the earliest days of the gay rights movements,
the formation of global disability coalitions, and the rise and

subsequent persecution of the Black Panthers. There's a pitstop in Thatcher's Britain, a glimpse at the tongue-in-cheek hedonism of the Pits and Perverts benefit gig for striking miners, followed by a series of lesser-known HIV histories rooted in campy safe-sex messaging, continent-wide coalitions and the harm-reduction work of sex workers. As the tales unfold, we'll see radical art as a vehicle for fat liberation activism, the vital work of Indigenous environmentalists, and the recent coalition-building work of trans activists across Argentina, whose inclusive messaging and headline-grabbing acts of solidarity have galvanised a historic movement. As time ticks on, the legacies of past greats will become evident; today's revitalised unions, direct action groups and community organisations stand on the shoulders of giants, finding hope and solace in the stories of past coalitions.

It's easy to be nihilistic, to convince ourselves that nothing will change – and if it won't, then why bother? For plenty of us, modern life is a blur of doom-scrolling and disillusionment, working shitty jobs to keep our heads above water in an increasingly unliveable world. Yet there *is* hope. History is cyclical and, even in the worst of times, coalition-building can be life-saving; the power of community is a balm when all else feels hopeless. Not to be all 'we are the world' about this, but there *is* joy to be found in the chaos. Fighting for change can feel tiring and thankless, but it's the small victories that matter the most; maybe it's putting on a fundraising gig with your best friends or the momentary thrill of screaming your heart out at a protest. Maybe it's as simple as building new friendships, collaging old zines and finding local communities.

It's clear that 'the work' – whatever that means to you – is ongoing and, in some ways, it's never-ending. As we continue to push forward, the goalposts will always be shifted, whether we like it or not. *Shoulder to Shoulder* is about crystallising those moments of past potential, and telling the human stories behind them in order to preserve the hopes of today's coalitions.

Fighting a Working-class War

'There is no such thing as a single-issue struggle because we do not live single-issue lives.'

– Audre Lorde

In early April, the cherry blossom trees lining Washington DC's Tidal Basin begin to bloom. Tourists from across the world flock to the city's picturesque parks and gardens, a rite of passage so popular that it attracts an estimated 1.5 million visitors each year.[1]

As 1964 drew to a close, the national campus activist organisation Students for Democratic Society (SDS) decided these famed blossoms would make the perfect backdrop for a peaceful mass protest. For months, their fury had been growing steadily at escalating US involvement in the Vietnam War. Although ongoing since 1955, public support of the war began to waver in the early 1960s. Images of unimaginable horror were being circulated in newspapers globally and civilian death tolls were rising with each brutal airstrike. By early 1965, SDS had scheduled a large-scale march on Washington for 17 April, a blaze of righteous anger amid the serenity of the city's most beautiful season.

Although organisers had chosen the date tactically for maximum efficacy, nobody could have predicted the mammoth

turnout: it's estimated that between 15,000 and 25,000 protestors marched on that fateful day, making it the largest peace
protest ever recorded in America at the time.

It's hard to say precisely why the march was so huge but
there were a few key contributing factors. The first was the
recent momentum of the civil rights movement, which scored
high-profile victories in the early 1960s. Acts of peaceful resistance were making front-page news and, behind the scenes,
seeds of solidarity were being sown between campaigners
of all races and demographics. SDS members were often the
children of Second World War veterans, growing up in an era
when systemic oppression and racist degradation were being
challenged and spot lit. The threat of nuclear warfare loomed
heavy throughout their adolescence. It's no surprise that many
were vocally anti-imperialist by the time they hit their late
teens, and effective at spreading the word of revolution, especially across SDS chapters.

Music played a key role in youth involvement, too. Black
artists were busy pioneering and popularising rock 'n' roll
throughout the fifties, and by the early sixties, a new wave of
protest music was further raising youth awareness of injustice,
led by artists like Bob Dylan and J.B. Lenoir, famed for his
heartfelt epic, 'Vietnam Blues'.

This period of US activism has become iconic – even now,
it's hard to think of solidarity and activism without thinking
back to anti-war protestors lined up in front of police cars,
brandishing flowers and wreaths to symbolise peace. It's easy
to see why. There was national coordination amongst activist
movements, no mean feat in a pre-social media world. Protestors were ballsy in their commitment to pacifism, determined
to create memorable visuals rooted in peace. They marched
en masse, drawing record-breaking crowds and spreading

messages of international solidarity. As a relatively new country, the US offered fertile ground for these activist movements
to further their causes and make worldwide impact.

SDS undeniably made its mark. The 17 April march began
with those in attendance staging a demonstration on the White
House lawn, waving placards which demanded: BALLOTS
NOT BOMBS IN VIETNAM! Next, they marched through
the streets and congregated on the grounds of the Washington
Monument, where they were serenaded by folk singers Phil
Ochs and Joan Baez, both early, high-profile supporters of the
anti-war movement. (Baez was later arrested at a Vietnam War
protest in 1967). Throughout the afternoon, crowds listened
intently to passionate speeches by civil rights leaders, peace
activists and anti-poverty campaigners, who highlighted links
between the Vietnam War, systemic racism and the high US
poverty rates, which led to the enlistment of disproportionately
working-class soldiers. In a galvanising speech, Paul Potter – a
founding SDS member – asked: 'What kind of system is it that
justifies the United States or any country seizing the destinies
of Vietnamese people and using them callously for its own purpose? What kind of system is it that disenfranchises people in
the South, leaves millions upon millions of people throughout
the country impoverished and excluded from the mainstream
promise of American society?'

These broader analyses of imperialism were reflected in descriptions of Vietnam as a working-class war.[2] It's now common
knowledge that troops were disproportionately working-class
– an estimated 80 per cent – and men of colour. Chants such as
'WAR ON POVERTY, NOT ON PEOPLE' reflected these
discrepancies, framing the Vietnam War as a mass killer of marginalised populations. Civil rights leaders were among the first
to underline these talking points and campaigners listened.

Gradually, a coalition movement was strengthening, coming together to point out that the war was disastrous, specifically for those without power.

It wasn't just marginalised people from the US who were rising up against this war; already, there had been smaller-scale anti-Vietnam War demonstrations across the globe. In Australia,[3] there are online records of solidarity marches as early as 1962, when the first Australian troops were deployed to Vietnam. In March 1965, just a few weeks before the SDS march, black-and-white photo[4] was taken of a young woman in Germany. It is labelled only as an image from a ban-the-bomb demonstration against US military intervention held in Frankfurt. The woman is evidently distressed; she's being escorted by two stern police officers, all the while clutching a sign whose message translates to NO BOMBS IN VIETNAM. The nuclear disarmament campaigns of the 1950s had launched the pacifist 'ban the bomb' movements, international protest collectives which regularly held solidarity marches on historic anniversaries like Hiroshima Day. According to reports, these anti-nuclear campaigns were fading in prominence by the early 1960s, but the horrors of war – not just the Vietnam War, but the Korean and Cold Wars too – were deeply imprinted on the minds of young campaigners.

As well as media coverage and the grassroots work of peace activists, photography played a key role in showcasing these atrocities, further fuelling an activism that shaped a decade. In the springtime of 1963, a photographer named Malcolm Browne stationed himself in Vietnam and found himself fascinated by a group of Buddhist monks promising 'something spectacular by way of protest', he recalled, in a 2012 interview with *TIME* magazine.[5] 'Monks were telephoning the foreign correspondents in Saigon [now known as Ho Chi Minh

City] to warn them that something big was going to happen,' Browne continued.

By this time, the correspondents were 'bored' by these sporadic threats and refused to take them seriously. So when a group of monks and nuns gathered at a Saigon pagoda, Browne was the only Western photographer in attendance. He followed the procession as they sidled out onto the city's busy streets, a group of monks circling an intersection. Within minutes, a car had pulled up; out of it stepped three monks – one older, sombre-looking man and two younger men, who proceeded to drench the older man in an unidentified liquid. As they pulled out and lit a match, it became evident that the liquid was gasoline. This is the story of the so-called 'Burning Monk', a martyr who self-immolated in order to raise awareness of the bloody, lethal war. His aim was successful. Two years later, in March 1965, an 82-year-old peace activist named Alice Herz followed his lead in Detroit, where she declared: 'I have chosen the burning death.'[6]

These stories are grisly and awful, a far cry from the flower headbands and peace symbols we see trotted out at sixties-themed fancy-dress parties, but they exemplify how solidarity blossomed and spread across nations before social media even existed. When I think of the 1960s, I see it through rose-tinted lenses. I think of the civil rights movement, of gay liberation, of radical communes filled with self-proclaimed hippies, having steamy, communal sex and dropping acid in the mountains. It's easy to forget that this protest was in response to something; that it wasn't all shagging and floral wreaths; that people were willing to burn themselves alive to alter the course of history, to stymie the body count of imperialism.

We've been conditioned to see these movements throughout a single-issue lens, forgetting that they're all interconnected. As a result, we miss out on nuance and opportunities to learn from these shared histories.

While there is evidence that anti-war movements were largely straight and white – more on that later – the anti-Vietnam War coalition brought activists of different stripes together in one broader, communal fight, against exploitation of the lower classes. Even just at the SDS march, there were representatives from Women Strike for Peace and the Student Nonviolent Coordinating Committee (SNCC), a Black, student-led organisation with a visible presence in civil rights demonstrations throughout the 1960s. At that record-breaking march on Washington, they all gathered to voice their collective outrage at what SDS organisers called a 'hideously immoral war'.

This coalition-building is an under-discussed factor in the success of political movements throughout the 1960s, which often originated on university campuses. Vast activist networks were spread across countries, with different local chapters who communicated directly with one another. They shared their knowledge and coordinated their struggles, and SDS activists were no different; throughout the 1960s, they attended civil rights protests and watched in awe as Black campaigners across the US protested segregation, driving interracial Freedom Ride buses through segregated areas and staging sit-ins at lunch counters whose staff refused to serve them.

Teach-ins were an adaptation of these peaceful protest strategies, and played a vital role in anti-war activism. In essence, these were political lectures designed to tell the truth about what was truly happening in Vietnam, and to offer practical advice to students wanting to get involved. Teach-ins were led by infuriated university professors who'd been warned by higher-ups against 'politicising' their students. This vague and patronising language ordered educators to gloss over the horrors

of wartime, to keep their mouths shut and avoid ruffling feathers. Obviously, students weren't burying their heads in the
sand anyway – they had already been politicised. Throughout
1964 and 1965, campus activist movements like SDS, the SNCC
and the Berkeley Free Speech Movement were engaging with
these curious students, telling the truth about the ever-mount-
ing death tolls of the Vietnam War.

Not only was there student demand to learn more, academics were ready and willing to speak, despite being ordered
to keep quiet. It was in 1965 that anthropologist Marshall
Sahlins proposed a 'teach-in' at the Ann Arbor campus of the
University of Michigan. In a 2017 article for *The Nation*,[7] he
recalled making a pivotal statement: 'They say we're shirking
our responsibilities. Let's teach in instead of teaching out. We'll
take over the buildings after classes and talk about Vietnam all
night. A teach-in.' Historian Bill Zimmerman described these
teach-ins as 'remarkably successful',[8] part of a wider strategy to
first educate and then organise potential protestors. According
to Zimmerman, these efforts of anti-war campaigners in 1964
and 1965 led to activists gaining 'a deep knowledge of Vietnam
and the war', whereas 'protests, while still small, did normalise
opposition despite accusations that they were un-American.
Seeds of doubt planted in the press and the public would
flower later.'

By the mid-1960s, it was apparent that the messages of anti-
war activism were trickling across borders, sparking a mass
resurgence of anti-nuclear movements. In fact, just two days
after the SDS March on Washington, London's iconic Trafalgar Square was swarmed by an estimated 50,000 protestors,
who took part in the Easter March for Peace.[9] The following
year, 1965, marked a particular turning point, a perfect storm
of protest. Together, the civil rights, anti-war and anti-nuclear

movements were coalescing, planting the seeds of worldwide resistance that would have lasting impact.

Despite being rooted in solidarity and anti-imperialism, none of this is to say the anti-war movement was perfect, diverse or even welcoming to marginalised groups. Here, caveats are important: by the mid-to-late 1960s, the anti-war movement was spreading globally, and it's clear that no movement is monolithic. However, leftist activism has long had a reputation of being led largely by straight white men, and it's understandable that some marginalised communities would feel like they had other, more pressing issues to rally against than the war.

Still, the anti-war movement was the starting point for a handful of seriously influential Black feminists. Barbara Smith and her fraternal twin sister Beverley grew up together in a largely maternal household in Cleveland, Ohio. Born in 1946, they were raised in a segregated United States, and during their early teenage years especially, lunch-counter sit-ins led by civil rights activists were dinner-table talk. 'There was a great habit of discussing politics,' recalls Beverley, in an interview with Keeanga-Yamahtta Taylor, published in the 2017 book *How We Get Free.*[10] 'I realised that it always seemed like the grown-ups were talking about race.'

In 1965, Barbara moved to Mount Holyoke College in rural Massachusetts, a 'pretty conservative, middle-of-the-road institution in many ways', she explains, also in *How We Get Free.* Yet even in her relatively suburban university, Barbara couldn't help but watch as anti-war protests spread across the United States and, especially in the latter half of the 1960s, the world.

After completing her junior year at Mount Holyoke, Barbara transferred to the New School for Social Research, a famously progressive institution. She recalls being awed by an early assembly in the autumn of 1967: 'I looked around this auditorium and I thought, "Wow, these are some of the most dissident students in the entire country! And I'm with them!"' Barbara wasted no time in getting involved with the anti-war movement, but she found herself as one of the few Black women to do so. As a result, 'You faced the racism of the predominantly white anti-war movement,' she explains, 'but you also experienced a lot of censure from the Black community.' Although she says Black communities 'finally took heart when Martin Luther King spoke out about the war' in a series of anti-war speeches given between 1966 and 1968, she faced backlash for her anti-racist critiques of the war. As Barbara summarises: 'I cannot tell you the amount of grief that I experienced because I actually thought that ending a war against people of colour – that was fought predominantly by poor young men, who were disproportionately people of colour – was important. They thought that was irrelevant. That was a white thing to do.'

Meanwhile, Barbara was beginning to understand her life experiences not just through the lens of being Black but of being a Black woman. When she tried to buy an electric typewriter on credit, she wasn't allowed to do so in her own name – at the time, it had to be attached to the name of your husband. She was denied opportunities for career progression and patronised by men around her, and she found herself constantly battling gendered expectations, especially as, at this point in her life, Barbara explains, she was 'trying to be a heterosexual'. Yet, as a Black woman in the anti-war movement, she was uniquely placed to add new depth and nuance to the existing calls for peace; it was during these years that she developed analytical frameworks that she would go on to expand, alongside other Black, lesbian activists, like Audre Lorde and Cheryl Clarke.

There had been vocal opposition to the Vietnam War by influential Black leaders and organisations throughout the 1960s. Malcolm X[11] was one of the first to speak out in opposition to the war in 1964, marvelling at the courage of Vietnamese 'peasants' and their resistance efforts; by January 1966, the Black student activist group SNCC had issued a scathing condemnation[12] of the US military, writing: 'Our work, particularly in the South, has taught us that the United States government has never guaranteed the freedom of oppressed citizens, and is not yet truly determined to end the rule of terror and oppression within its own borders.'

As mentioned earlier in the chapter, there were peace campaigners – even in the earliest years of the movement – who took a multi-issue approach to anti-war activism, who connected dots along lines of multiple oppression. But it's no coincidence that the anti-war movement became an incubator of sorts for a handful of influential Black American socialist activists, including Smith, who later became a founding member of the Black, lesbian-led Combahee River Collective, the first feminist group to thoroughly articulate the concept of 'identity politics'. In 1967, abolitionist, scholar and revolutionary Angela Davis joined the SNCC, furthering its distinctly anti-racist critique of the Vietnam War; in 1968, Bobby Seale, co-founder of the socialist, liberationist Black Panther Party (of which Davis was also a member), was one of eight activists arrested at a violent anti-war protest held outside Chicago's Democratic National Convention.[13] He was tried separately to the other seven anti-war activists, all of whom were white.

Comb back through these histories and you'll find evidence that marginalised groups of all kinds were mobilising against the war, claiming it as their fight too. Black activists in particular made it clear that working-class soldiers of colour and countless

Vietnamese civilians were being treated as collateral damage by an imperialist government, and they forged solidarity with other activists to make their case. Building these relationships wasn't always easy but there's a level of global collaboration inherent to the success of the anti-war movement, which is often forgotten.

Especially towards the latter half of the 1960s, transnational solidarity was a key part of the movement's impact. One of the most chaotic protests unfolded on 17 March 1968 in London's famed Trafalgar Square, led by actress Vanessa Redgrave. Brandishing an anti-war petition, she played pied piper to approximately 10,000 demonstrators; the closer these crowds got to the United States Embassy, the more chaos unfolded. 'A hippy who tried to offer a mounted policeman a bunch of flowers was truncheoned to the ground,' recalls left-wing activist and historian Tariq Ali in his 1987 autobiography, *Street Fighting Years*.[14] 'Marbles were thrown at the horses and a few policemen fell to the ground, but none were surrounded and beaten up. The fighting continued for almost two hours.'

This was one of countless landmark protests in 1968. Leftist collectives from Germany and Italy to Cuba and Japan were taking to the streets, creating communications networks and circulating pissed-off flyers to draw numbers in a pre-internet world. They were agitating for an end to the Vietnam War first and foremost, but they led with a broader anti-poverty, anti-imperialist stance. Among the most memorable demonstrations were those held in France. In May 1968 – just two months after a *Le Monde* journalist accused French students of being 'too bored' to mirror the protests of their global counterparts – students in Paris led a series of mass demonstrations, which quickly fired up the country's workers and led to a historic general strike.

The earliest rumblings had begun at Paris Nanterre University, a prestigious institution in the city's western suburbs, in March 1967. Again, context is key. The introduction of the birth control pill in 1960 and a series of erotica obscenity trials had sparked debate around sex, giving rise to wider arguments for sexual freedom and liberation. Young people in particular were realising there's nothing inherently wrong or sinful about being horny and acting on those impulses. Free love movements were blossoming; fashion designers like Mary Quant were slashing mini skirt hemlines to new, butt cheek-grazing heights, and whispers of queer underground cultures were bubbling up in global consciousness.

Yet France remained – at least in the eyes of 1960s youth – behind the times, to the extent that women studying at the University of Nanterre weren't allowed male visitors, lest they end up fucking. In response, a mixed-gender group of students occupied the women's-only halls. When the police inevitably showed up, students left peacefully.

This small rebellion sowed seeds of dissent, which blossomed over the next 14 months and finally came to a head in early May 1968. Now, activists weren't just protesting specific university policies, they were taking a broader, more general aim at repression in France. 'Everything was patriarchal,' recalls Josette Preud'homme, interviewed by *NPR*[15] about her experiences of protesting in May 1968. '[It started] in the family, where you couldn't speak at the dinner table unless spoken to. You couldn't go out with friends, and never with boys. Everything was forbidden everywhere . . . We were suffocating. There was this enormous need to talk and share. Everyone was fed up.' Meanwhile, European student movements were gaining notoriety for their willingness to protest, to disrupt and condemn issues, not just in their own countries but around the world – and especially in Vietnam.

Activists weren't just advocating for their right to fuck freely or work without bosses breathing down their necks. According to a Smithsonian retrospective, young leftists saw US involvement in Vietnam as a 'continuation of France's own violent imperialism in Southeast Asia'. They were frustrated by a government which readily allowed its workers to be overstretched and exploited, and it rapidly became clear that workers themselves shared these frustrations. In early May 1968, violent clashes between students and French police officers made headlines. The brutality of these conflicts escalated sharply within just a few days; by 10 May, images of students ripping up the cobblestones of Parisian streets and launching them at police officers had made headlines. In response, they were clubbed with batons and pelted with tear gas.

As the chaos intensified, France's two largest unions called a general strike in solidarity with the young activists; within days, millions of workers were either on strike or occupying their workplaces in protest. The unrest was brief but fruitful. According to the earlier-mentioned *NPR* article, as a direct result of the disruption, 'workers got higher salaries, better working conditions and stronger unions'. The summer that Paris burned still serves as unequivocal proof that solidarity works.

What's interesting about the Vietnam War is that it served as a kind of global lightning rod, an issue which jolted people into action. If the smug *Le Monde* journalist's words are anything to go by, there was an assumption of complacency by the French government: an assumption which was promptly torched when activists started ripping up paving slabs and hurling them at cops. Although the anti-war movement was a peace movement first and foremost, it lit the fire under dissidents of all stripes, resulting in the kind of anarchic, revolutionary spirit that loomed heavy in the late 1960s – the same spirit that set the tone for the birth of gay liberation.

No matter your level of familiarity with queer history, you've probably heard at least something about the Stonewall Riots of June 1969. The riots were a days-long series of battles between the New York Police Department and patrons of the Stonewall Inn, a mafia-owned gay bar on the city's Lower East Side.

Before we continue, let's clear up a few myths. The Stonewall Riots have been written about endlessly, mythologised to the point that entire books have been dedicated to figuring out what actually happened. Depending on which sources you read, patrons being rounded up by the police first retaliated against police brutality by either throwing bricks, battering cops with their high heels or screaming at the crowd to fight back. Some say it was Judy Garland's funeral that sparked the anger on that fateful night, that grieving gays had been pushed to the limit by the death of a bonafide gay icon. There's so much discussion of who 'threw the first brick at Stonewall' that it's become a popular meme format. Despite what Hollywood wants you to believe, it probably wasn't a cis white gay with washboard abs.

The first, most obvious fact is that marginalised queer communities have long spent their lives navigating constant police surveillance and, especially by the late 1950s and early 1960s, there's documented evidence of violent resistance. In May 1959, a group of drag queens and hustlers – gay sex workers – pelted cops with cups of coffee, donuts and paper plates at Cooper's Donuts, known as a queer hangout in the 'gay ghetto' of Main Street, Los Angeles.

In 1965, groups of largely homeless, sex-working queer people came together in San Francisco's Tenderloin district to form Vanguard, the first known queer youth organisation in the United States. As well as literally sweeping the streets of the yuppies lured into their neighbourhood by expansion and gentrification, they published the words of anti-Vietnam War campaigners like David M. Shoup in their *Vanguard* zine, archived by the Digital Transgender Archive. In Issue 7, he was quoted as saying: 'I believe that if we would keep our dirty, bloody, dollar-crooked fingers out of the business of these nations, so full of depressed, exploited people, they will arrive at a solution of their own, that they design and want.'[16]

In the mid-1960s, Vanguard members rallied against the staff and owners of Compton's Cafeteria, an all-night café in the Tenderloin district, for discriminating against 'street queens' – homeless queer and trans folks, mostly femme-presenting and often sex workers. At the time, plenty of local gay bars had explicitly anti-trans policies, so Compton's became one of the only options available for gender non-conforming sex workers in particular; after a night of hustling, they could meet at Compton's. According to Vanguard members, staff were quick to call the police and ask them to throw out the street queens, with the police often arresting them for the crime of 'female impersonation' in the process. As American historian Susan Stryker explains in *Transgender History*,[17] one hot, summer night in 1966 saw the all-night cafeteria become the scene of a violent riot; when cops tried to arrest a trans woman, Vanguard members responded by throwing sugar shakers, high heels – basically anything that could become a makeshift missile – at the cops, before smashing up and vandalising their police cars.

The Stonewall Riots are well-documented, but there's a cultural tendency to zoom in on particular moments, a desire to put our finger on one neat starting point of a movement. It's peak HR allyship to write a few words about the riots and leave it there, framing them uncritically as either an act of desperation or resilience, without highlighting the broader, radical politics around them. As a result, what you don't see is the acknowledgement that queer activists were working with a broader political moment, one led by anti-war activism, the rise of socialist groups like the Black Panthers and a cultural climate defined by young people worldwide setting fire to the streets. The late 1960s were a unique moment in activist history, defined by a proto-intersectional approach that linked the tragedies of war and the sexual liberation movement through witty slogans like 'FUCK, NOT FIGHT!'. What united these late 1960s groups was a broad, multi-pronged focus, one which understood just how interconnected so many struggles truly were.

When the Vietnam War officially ended in 1975, the world looked wildly different than it had a decade earlier. During this time, marginalised communities had spent years leading influential protest movements, shifting public perceptions and advocating for their rights, all the while campaigning for an end to imperialism and a more just world for everyone.

Even today, marginalised people are told that our issues are too niche to command widespread attention. Thanks to the rise of social media and online networks, we have more tools at our disposal than ever before. There's the ever-looming threat of censorship to contend with, but making the world aware of injustice is far easier now than it was in the 1960s. Yet despite the challenges they faced, these coalitions were formed and nurtured anyway. In some ways, social media has made things harder. The internet is a marketplace, one in which we're encouraged to brand ourselves and build a following. It's an individualist landscape, one which goes hand in hand with the language of allyship and its accompanying framework of difference; covertly, the framing of allyship tells us that pro-testing issues which don't directly affect us is something to be commended.

What's powerful about the anti-war movement is that it realised the extent to which struggles are broad and intercon-nected. People of all demographics could see themselves and their families in the war's death toll, and marginalised people were able to situate themselves within this wider context of anti-imperialism, drawing insightful analyses which positioned them within broader discussions of injustice. Factor in the rising popularity of protest music and the involvement of celebrity activists throughout the late 1960s in particular, and you had a recipe for mass disruption.

In many ways, it feels like we're on the cusp of something similar today. We saw it in the Black Lives Matter protests, some of the largest in history; we see it in the climate justice networks, solidarity groups and global coalitions, which we'll hear plenty more about in this book. Legacies of sixties activism are being sustained, celebrated and referenced, used as fuel to push for broader analyses of injustice which could bring more of us together, fighting for an end to all oppression.

One of the most iconic speeches to ever grasp these com-plexities is 'Learning from the Sixties',[18] an address given by Black lesbian feminist Audre Lorde at the 1982 Malcolm X weekend at Harvard University. 'Each one of us here is a link in the connection between anti-poor legislation, gay shootings, the burning of synagogues, street harassment, attacks against women, and resurgent violence against Black people,' said Lorde to her rapt audience. 'We share a common interest, survival, and it cannot be pursued in isolation from others simply because their difference makes us un-comfortable.' Lorde painted a picture of the 1960s as a period of interconnected struggle: burning streets, the assassinations of Malcolm X and Martin Luther King, and, of course, the Vietnam War.

In her analysis, the ultimate lesson to be taken from the 1960s was simple: 'There is no such thing as a single-issue struggle because we do not live single-issue lives.'

Building a Rainbow Coalition

'You cannot fight racism with racism. You have to fight it with solidarity.'

— Bobby Seale

The opening scenes of Agnès Varda's 1968 documentary *Black Panthers*[1] are surprisingly joyful. In the summer heat, children play and dance on suburban lawns, their families clapping and singing along to lively, upbeat music. Listen closely, though, and the revolutionary lyrics paint a different picture: Time is up, we've had enough, we're taking control. 'This is no picnic in Oakland,' explains Varda. 'This is a political rally organised by the Black Panthers. On this Sunday in 1968, their purpose is to have one of the leaders, Huey Newton, released from jail.'

In 1968, the mere mention of the Black Panther Party conjured imagery of Black men dressed in leather jackets and black berets, stalking the streets in single file and wielding shotguns. These images were often weaponised by the US government; in an infamous speech, John Edgar Hoover, then-director of the FBI, called the Black Panther Party 'the greatest threat to the internal security of the country'.[2]

These stereotypes linger, especially as the stories of high-profile Panthers have found their way onto the desks of

Hollywood producers. Last year, I went to a small screening of *Judas and the Black Messiah*,[3] hosted by a radical film group in Sheffield. As the title suggests, it's a story of betrayal and heartbreak, an in-depth look into the FBI's infiltration of the Illinois Black Panthers. Yet it's also a film that does a good job of showcasing the Panthers' real-life socialist messaging, as well as the fact that it was chapter leader Fred Hampton's charisma and ability to build unlikely alliances which truly panicked the FBI.

Of course, this is still cinema. There has to be violence, drama and scandal. So although messages of coalition-building and solidarity were present in the film, they were sometimes overshadowed by action-packed shoot-out scenes, layers of filmic gloss which made the Panthers look more violent than they actually were. In one scene, cops surrounded the Panthers' headquarters and fired dozens of bullets. The on-screen Panthers responded with equal ferocity, spraying shots with vigour. This isn't representative of the actual gunfights; historical records show that Panthers fired far, far fewer bullets than the cops.

The film ended in heartbreaking, and true-to-life, fashion, when – spoiler alert! – cops battered down the Panthers' apartment door to shoot Hampton. They did so as the Panthers slept, firing almost one hundred shots, despite the Panthers being unarmed. This scene closely mirrored reality: Hampton had been drugged by an FBI informant and was killed next to his pregnant fiancé.

The screening wrapped up with an interesting discussion, a rare example of a racially-mixed audience talking frankly and openly about race. First, a white woman spoke about feeling guilty for legacies of racism, saying she felt powerless. It's an understandable sentiment, especially since whiteness means that white people don't *really* have to think about racism, at least not to any meaningful extent. We can avert our gaze because racism doesn't affect us – no, reverse racism isn't a thing – but eye-opening films like *Judas and the Black Messiah* force us to confront it head-on.

Yet pleading powerlessness helps nobody. It immobilises us, rather than jolting us into action. Taking this line of thought only cements the idea that racism has nothing to do with white people, that we should just turn away. This only perpetuates existing racism, and leaves anti-racist activism to the people most directly impacted by it.

It didn't take long for other white audience members to then chip in and speak about the importance of tangible solidarity and support, explaining that white guilt isn't helpful, but practical acts – community initiatives, protest, resource redistribution – are. Black audience members shared their discomfort at scenes of horrific trauma, and the portrayal of Panthers in the film. Some actively asked white audience members what they were doing to challenge and deconstruct racist stereotypes, and urged them to think critically. Yet the one statement that remained lodged in my mind came from an older Black woman, who shook her head quietly and summarised: 'When white people leave this film, they'll just remember the Black people with the guns.'

The real history of the Black Panther Party is rooted in solidarity, in multi-racial coalitions. The party was a survival initiative first and foremost, one which offered resources for marginalised groups and advocated for an end to *all* oppression. The Panthers built coalitions, uniting people of colour, poor people, queer people and various others, with the common goal of liberation. Perhaps most importantly, they showed the power of solidarity, and the threat that it poses to people in power.

In October 1966, students Bobby Seale and Huey P. Newton formed the earliest iteration of the Black Panthers. They had grown up witnessing day-to-day harassment of Black communities by the notoriously brutal Oakland police force. Inspired by the rise of movements like the Lowndes County Freedom Party (LCFP),[4] an Alabama-based initiative to educate and politicise Black residents in the largely Black Lowndes County, Seale and Newton co-founded the Black Panther Party for Self-Defense in October 1966, later known only by the name the Black Panther Party.

One of their earliest actions was to publish a Ten-Point Program,[5] which demanded a list of key freedoms for 'black and oppressed people'. Some of these demands were straightforward: employment, decent housing, an end to police brutality, free healthcare and 'the power to determine [their] destiny'. Others delved deeper into structural inequalities, condemning 'continued exploitation' by capitalism and calling for the release of 'black and oppressed people now held in US federal state, county, city and military prisons and jails'.

Their demands were anti-capitalist, rooted in anti-racism and pacifism, and closely aligned with the anti-war movement outlined in the previous chapter, which was gaining worldwide traction as the Panthers rose to prominence. Notably, they called for an 'end to all wars of aggression', highlighting that the country's greed and imperialism had resulted in untold global death tolls.

These were the demands; next came the strategies. Their first action was to take advantage of an open-carry law, which allowed California residents to carry weapons as long as they weren't concealed. Through lived experience, Seale and Newton knew how quickly the police force could become violent, even lethal, towards Black victims, how rapidly these altercations could escalate. They knew that, on a day-to-day level, officers were allowed to abuse their powers without consequence. So, the Panthers decided to 'police the police', following on-duty officers on the job to 'observe' them. Gradually, the Panthers recruited a kind of guerrilla self-defence patrol, recognisable by their all-black attire of leather jackets, berets and, of course, guns. The Panthers maintained a legal distance from the police, watching them carefully to ensure their routine checks wouldn't become violent. These tactics were successful and influential. Before long, local Black Panther chapters were emerging across the US.

The media and government were quick to label the Panthers as terrorists,[6] relying in no small part on the racist stereotype of Black men as hyper-masculine. Black men have long been labelled thugs, singled out as disproportionately dangerous. Police officers – 'pigs', as the Panthers called them – would trot out this stereotype after shooting unarmed Black men dead on the street, claiming they were 'afraid' of these men and that this fear made the homicide 'justifiable'. Yet the Panthers had to rely on some sense of intimidation to get their job done, to be taken seriously. This idea of the Panthers as an organisation rooted solely in machismo isn't entirely true, although there is well-documented sexism within the party, especially in its earliest years.

As the movement expanded, so did the scope of its intention. Before long, the group was as much – if not more so – about community care and mutual aid as it was guerrilla self-defence.

Back in 1966, the US government had run a pilot of a free school breakfast scheme,[7] which was deemed a radical idea at the time. It had been created by Kentucky congressman Carl Perkins, who was concerned by the number of kids in rural areas who faced long commutes to school so were often hungry and pissed-off when they arrived. The Panthers had noticed this issue in their communities, too; they knew many Black kids were too ground down to focus on their work, too busy struggling for survival to ever thrive within the school system. In January 1969, the Panthers ran their first breakfast club for kids out of a church in Oakland, a community hub with an accessible kitchen. Local businesses donated supplies, like grits, eggs, toast and milk. Kids gathered to eat, giving the occasional press interview – in one truly adorable article, one child says they haven't heard of the Panthers before but thinks they're 'groovy'.[8]

These social programmes were multi-pronged, and situated in areas where Black families disproportionately faced discrimination. There were community-led legal clinics, because Black folks were – and still are – more likely to be criminalised. Ambulance services and medical clinics[9] were put in place, as Black communities were much less likely to trust medical institutions and more likely to be abused by them. (Again, still the case – the racist 'strong Black woman' archetype, for example, is one the reasons Black mothers are far more likely to die in childbirth.[10])

Love was the driving force behind these programmes. Mutual aid has long been a lifeline for marginalised groups, forced to show up for each other when the world at large will not. This is survival work. It's low-key, unglamorous and far less appealing to a general audience than the shoot-outs and gun violence, so these survival programmes are too often minimised within the Panthers' legacy. In many ways, the Panthers were actually doing a better job than the government in protecting and caring for their communities, yet the institutional backlash was still strong. According to a woman in the Panther Party interviewed by social justice-orientated scholar Nik Heynen,[11] on the night before the first Chicago breakfast programme was scheduled to start, 'the Chicago police broke into the church and mashed up all the food and urinated on it'. FBI agents went door-to-door in Richmond, Virginia, drumming fear into parents that the party would radicalise their kids. Incidentally, these arguments are still echoed today in the racist fear-mongering around critical race theory being taught in schools.

By October 1967, party co-founder Huey P. Newton found himself caught in the literal crossfire of this violence when he was arrested after a shoot-out with Oakland police officers. Newton was accused of killing policeman John Fret, charged with voluntary manslaughter and sentenced to between two and fifteen years in prison.[12]

This was the political backdrop for the Free Huey rally depicted in Varda's *Black Panthers*, and a period which marked a key turning point in Panther politics.

The shift in focus from self-defence to socialism was due both to the Black Panther Party's expansion and to the influence of new members. In 1967, after a two-year stint of studying abroad in Frankfurt, Germany, Angela Davis decided to stop by a conference in London on her way back to Los Angeles. The theme was 'The Dialectics of Liberation', and there were two speakers in particular that piqued her interest: one was Stokely Carmichael, a civil rights organiser and a key leader of the Black Power movement; the second was Herbert Marcuse, a German-American Marxist philosopher.

Davis recounts these stories in her autobiography,[13] which details her political coming-of-age. She recalls reading *The Communist Manifesto* and having her 'mind blown' as a student, but many Black activists at the time weren't so sure. In her words, many saw Marxism as a 'white man's thing', a claim which frustrated her. In Davis's view, well-known analyses of racism at the time didn't dive deep enough; they succumbed to the 'natural inclination' to view 'the enemy as the white man', she wrote. '[It's] natural because the great majority of white people, both in the United States and England, have been carriers of the racism that, in reality, benefits only a small number of them – the capitalists.' By focusing on the interpersonal rather than the institutional, Davis felt Black activists were missing out on the opportunity to build coalitions. 'When white people are indiscriminately viewed as the enemy,' she continued, 'it is virtually impossible to develop a political solution.' Instead, she envisioned a socialist coalition made up of working-class communities of all descriptions. 'It had been clear to me for a long time that in order to achieve its ultimate goals,' she summarised, 'the black liberation struggle would have to become part of a revolutionary movement, embracing all working people.'

When Davis joined the Black Panther Party in 1967, she brought these values with her. By the time *Black Panthers* was released in 1968, these calls for solidarity were being echoed more widely. A handful of Panthers on-screen actively urged 'white radicals' to join their cause, famously articulated by Kathleen Cleaver, the Black Panther Party's communications secretary.

White radicals answered these calls. In Detroit, there was even a short-lived activist group known as the White Panthers,[14] formed in 1968. They created a ten-point programme of their own, which called for 'an end to money', 'rock and roll, dope and fucking in the streets'. The Black Panthers initially dismissed them as 'psychedelic clowns', but relations warmed considerably when the group started distributing Black Panther leaflets. A marijuana conviction spelled the end of the White

Panthers, but the minimisation of these histories indicates there could be other, lesser-known attempts by white anti-racists to show solidarity, as alluded to by Cleaver. In an interview with Varda, she says the white people reaching out to the party were 'usually very grateful', because the Panthers were able to offer 'rational', 'ideological' explanations of complex societal issues.

According to Cleaver, some white activists had seen speakers 'rant and rave' about hating white people universally, but that was never the Panthers' standpoint. 'We separate institutions from citizens,' she explained, asserting that their targets were the 'pigs' and the economic institutions which consistently starved Black communities of funding and resources. Evidently, this socialist logic – which argued that, in order to be successful, the Panthers needed analyses of class more broadly, as well as race analyses – was increasingly influential.

There were already small-scale examples of solidarity in action. In Oakland, the local Black Panther Party was mobilising alongside American Indian activists and the Brown Berets, a Los Angeles-based Chicano movement (this term was adopted by working-class Mexican Americans, similarly fighting for self-determination, liberation and an end to state violence).[15]

The Brown Berets in particular were modelled on the Black Panthers, sharing many of the same demands and initiatives.[16] Like the Panthers, they offered community-led programmes, championed by activist Gloria Arellanes. Again, her activism was intersectional: she became a prominent leader within the Brown Berets and played a pivotal role in opening the El Barrio Free Clinic, a volunteer-led service for the poor Mexican-American locals who couldn't afford healthcare. Arellanes campaigned for the rights of impoverished people more broadly; in 1968, she was one of the thousands that walked alongside

Martin Luther King Jr in the Poor People's Campaign, which called on Washington politicians to ensure justice for the poor.

In April 1969, a landmark moment came in the formation of the Rainbow Coalition, led by Illinois Black Panther Party leader Fred Hampton, the charismatic we met earlier. He believed firmly in the 'power of people', as well as the importance of 'fighting racism with solidarity'. Hampton positioned anti-racist struggle as a class struggle more broadly and, from early 1969, he became increasingly willing to build bridges with other community-led groups.

The first of these groups was the Young Lords, a group of Puerto Rican revolutionaries conceived as a Chicago street gang in 1968. They saw largely white gangs using violence to enforce redlining policies, effectively barring them from living in certain neighbourhoods. They knew how it felt to be harassed, brutalised and disproportionately criminalised by police. More broadly, the Young Lords took an anti-war stance and campaigned for the removal of US troops from Puerto Rico and Vietnam, as well as advocating for grassroots change and anti-poverty initiatives.

In February 1969, their Lord's fury at the local police bubbled over; in protest, they occupied Chicago's 18th District police station. This is when the Lords first met Fred Hampton, who set out looking for the Lords' leader, Cha-Cha Jiménez. Hampton quickly 'took the Young Lords under his wing', said Jiménez in a 2019 interview with *Southside Weekly*.[17] 'He gave us the skills that we needed to come right out of the gang and start organising the community.' This meeting laid the foundations for what would soon become the Rainbow Coalition, described by Jiménez as a 'poor people's army'.

Meanwhile, Hampton was nurturing a surprising relationship with the Young Patriot Organisation, formed in 1968.

The Young Patriots were white, working-class southerners who shared similar experiences of poverty and criminalisation, largely displaced and living in an uptown district of Chicago, known as Hillbilly Harlem. According to a brief history published on *Redneck Revolt*[18], a US coalition effort to document tales of white working-class anti-racist activism, the Young Patriots and the Black Panthers first met at the Church of the Three Crosses, when the Panthers attended a meeting after scouting the Patriots as potential comrades. After the meeting, Black Panther Bob Lee stayed behind to ask the Patriots' leader William 'Preacherman' Fesperman if the group would work with the Panthers, and if the church could be used for the Panthers' various community programmes – the free breakfast clubs, health clinics and legal aid groups. To both questions, the answer was yes. 'I had to run with those cats, break bread with them, hang out at the pool hall,' recalls Lee. 'I had to lay down on their couch, in their neighbourhood. Then I had to invite them into mine. That was how the Rainbow Coalition was built, real slow.'[19]

Establishing this trust was far from easy. With the Young Lords, it had been more straightforward: many Black and Latinx Chicagoans lived in the same underfunded projects in the city's South Side; they went to the same overcrowded schools and faced racist discrimination when trying to access certain beaches, restaurants and public spaces. The Young Patriots, on the other hand, had moved from the notoriously racist American South. At the time, they actually wielded the Confederate Flag – which, by the mid-20th century, had become synonymous with white supremacists – as their emblem. Despite this, the Rainbow Coalition between the Black Panthers, the Young Lords and the Young Patriots was officially announced at the start of April 1969, its name representing solidarity between working-class activists of different races.

During this era of the Rainbow Coalition, it wasn't unusual to see Black Panther patches ironed on to denim jackets alongside the Confederate Flag, or to see the Black Power flag and the Confederate Flag side by side at protests. Even as the Patriots became aware of the flag's history, they clung to it as a symbol of white, working-class identity; in interviews with reporters, members of the Patriots stated their aim to 'change its meaning'. But over time, after conversations within the solidarity movements, the Young Patriots 'grew politically' and eventually abandoned the flag. Young Patriots' leader Hy Thurman later denounced it, claiming there was 'no place in the movement or the world for the Confederate flag ... it symbolises a period of time when our black brothers and sisters were mere property to be sold or destroyed at the white man's convenience.'[20]

The Rainbow Coalition was violently cut short by the murder of Fred Hampton on 4 December 1969, but the FBI's ruthless erosion of the Black Panther Party showed how threatening coalition was to those in power. The Panthers battled endless obstacles, yet still managed to form vital coalitions by naming systemic oppression and offering resources – food, aid, support – that governments would not. They recognised the power of a so-called poor people's army and they harnessed it to spectacular effect, especially in the late 1960s.

Though it stalled, not even the murder of Hampton could halt this momentum – by Christmas 1969, the Panthers had found themselves a broad spectrum of new collaborators.

In many ways, 25 December 1969 was a Christmas like any other. New York was bitingly cold; families were tucked up indoors, passing around gifts and eating turkey sandwiches with lashings of cranberry sauce. The city was still, but the Greenwich Village neighbourhood was pulsing with fury. At the time, the Village – as it's known to locals – was making global headlines as a countercultural hub. Throughout the 1960s, activist movements gathered in the district's gay bars, plotting anti-war demonstrations and sowing the seeds of gay liberation.

Buoyed by the game-changing Stonewall Riots, activists set their sights on one building in particular, which towered above most others in the Village: the Women's House of Detention, an audaciously large 12-storey prison, thought to be the world's first Art Deco-inspired penitentiary. Awestruck tourists flocked to the facility, which stood roughly 500 feet away from the Stonewall Inn, taking photos and likely speculating about the crimes of the women (and gender non-conforming) prisoners housed inside.

There's a tendency to syphon off marginalised histories and frame them as disconnected, but as historian Hugh Ryan proved in his book *The Women's House of Detention*,[21] the noisy chaos of the Stonewall Riots that summer had caused ripples within the prison's walls, too. Ryan tells the story of a nurse named Arcus Flyn, who drove past the neighbouring Washington Square on her way home from work. Flyn 'noticed something strange: small points of light, flying through the sky. When she pulled over, she realised they were fires – little burning things being thrown from the windows of the House of D.' According to Flyn, prisoners in the Women's House of Detention were chanting en masse: 'Gay rights, gay rights, gay rights!' Ryan then cites author Rita Mae Brown's frustration that the prison has been written out of the gay liberation movement's history. 'The women heard the noises and started rioting inside the prison,' she wrote. '[They] burned mattresses and shoved them through the bars. This never got written up because all the accounts of that period were given by men.'

These histories – the Black Panthers, gay liberation, the Women's House of Detention – are all inextricably linked, and they converged on that memorable Christmas Day in 1969, when leftist groups came together for a week-long protest. They combined their voices to call for the freedom of Afeni Shakur and Joan Bird, the only two women arrested as part of the detainment of the Panther 21.

Like Huey P. Newton before them, Shakur and Bird had found themselves violently arrested by police officers on a mission to detain influential members of the Black Panther Party. On 2 April 1969, Shakur and Bird were among the 21 Panthers rounded up and accused of planning coordinated attacks on two police stations and an education office in New York City. After a lengthy and wildly expensive trial, all 21 Panthers were acquitted in May 1971. Throughout the trial, jury members learned that police infiltrators played key organising roles in the Panthers; essentially, they were set up. Leftist activists, who knew all too well that the Panthers were being scapegoated and sensationalised, could smell this corruption. Throughout the trial, they came to the defence of the Panthers, including on that fateful Christmas morning.

Surviving photos from the demonstration show organisers from Youth Against Fascism and the newly formed Gay Liberation Front (GLF) standing in solidarity with Bird and Shakur in front of a banner which read: THE PANTHER POLITICAL PRISONERS MUST BE SET FREE. These scenes outside the Women's House of Detention mark a key moment in queer history. Not only do they offer tangible proof that leftists across New York were embracing the power of coalition-building, but they also mark a shift in the political tide of the American gay liberation movement – one which had a global influence.

For decades prior to that 1969 demonstration, American gay liberation had an official face – organisations with a largely middle-class focus, campaigning for tolerance and acceptance – and the unofficial faces we met in the last chapter, the street queens and sex workers struggling against violence, cops and harassment on a daily basis, leading early rebellions buoyed by anti-poverty campaigners. By the late 1960s, this political splintering was impossible to ignore.

To understand why the Women's House of Detention protest was so important, it's worth zooming in on the more official faces. Perhaps the best-known example is the Mattachine Society, a gay men's group founded in a Los Angeles living room back in 1950, spearheaded in large part by former Communist Party member Henry Hay. These men described themselves as homophiles, a linguistic choice made to avoid the '-sexual' part of 'homosexual'. The '-phile' suffix, derived from the Latinate word for 'love', was intended to reorientate the focus away from sex and towards the more palatable topic of love.

The primary frustrations of the Mattachine Society were different to those of street queens and hustlers battling poverty, racism and homophobic violence. There were shared struggles, but Mattachine members were annoyed that their sexuality could see them barred from the military, criminalised indiscriminately and harassed by police officers, who saw them as easy targets. Popular cruising spots and bathhouses were monitored by undercover cops, who would 'entrap' targets by pretending to be interested in sex with them. Gay men weren't just arrested in these entrapment schemes, they were smeared, too. Their reputations would be dragged through the mud, even in cases which resulted in only mild prosecutions. This stigma could bar them from renting or buying houses, or even seeking employment. Mattachine Society co-founder Dale Jennings experienced this first-hand: after being trailed and harassed by the Los Angeles police department, he mounted a defence case, which was successful.

In 1955, the Daughters of Bilitis[22] – thought to be the first lesbian rights organisation in the United States – was formed when a woman named Rosalie 'Rose' Bamberger, a working-class Filipina, then employed at a brush-manufacturing factory, suggested forming a private lesbian social club. This led to a meeting between four founding couples: Rose and her partner, Rosemary, Del Martin and Phyllis Lyon, Marcia Foster and her partner, June, and finally, Noni Frey and her partner, Mary. The women were from different backgrounds but they shared a desire to meet and hang out with other lesbians without fearing a bar raid.

Discretion was key to their mission, so they named the Daughters of Bilitis after *The Songs of Bilitis*, a fabled book of French poetry with heavy sapphic overtones. Author Pierre Louÿs claimed to have translated the works from Ancient Greek, crediting the original poetry to a courtesan named Bilitis, a contemporary of iconic lesbian poet Sappho. This was enough to cement Bilitis into lesbian lore. It's well known that the legitimacy of lesbian couples is endlessly challenged by historians – there's even a subreddit, r/Sapphoandherfriend, dedicated to lesbian erasure memes and claims that even the most obviously horny, sapphic lovers were actually 'just friends'. The Daughters of Bilitis played into this, choosing a coded name which would be recognised by lesbians in the know, but which was discreet enough not to draw the violent surveillance of cops.

These early gay and lesbian rights groups shared a focus on respectability and assimilation, which is unsurprising given the laws and societal hostility at the time. Same-sex desire was something to be kept secret at all costs; being outed could make you a social pariah. These early organisations attracted mostly middle-class memberships and avoided disruption in favour of discretion. Throughout the 1960s, they inspired chapters across the US, but even when they stepped out onto the streets, they sought respectability and conservative aims.

At a 1964 demonstration[23] outside the US Army Building in Lower Manhattan, men and women affiliated with the Mattachine Society marched in corporate-looking black and grey suits, knee-length dresses and kitten heels. From the surviving photographs, it seems the protestors were all white, their attire chosen to prove a point: we're just like you. They were protesting the military's invasion of sexual privacy, the investigations that led to LGBTQ+ people being kicked out of the military, but among the ARMY INVADES SEXUAL PRIVACY placards were other, more general protest slogans, like LOVE AND LET LOVE. The suits and ties became a sort of Mattachine uniform, as well as a statement of intent. 'A black suit and tie works wonders anywhere,' Mattachine member Randolfe Wicker explained in a 2019 *TIME* magazine interview.[24] 'If you wear a black suit and tie, people will stop and listen to you, and consider what you have to say.' In an era which assumed all gay men were 'mentally ill' and 'morally depraved' criminals, this cloak of respectability allowed them an entryway into discussions.

In '60s LGBTQ+ activism, there were two camps: those who could at least *appear* respectable to white America, and those who could not. Naturally, tensions emerged. The Stonewall Riots and the Black Panthers exposed this ideological splintering. In the days following the summer stand-off, self-taught photographer Diana Davies[25] – herself a member of the burgeoning GLF – took snapshots of the eerie calm after the storm. One of her images is of the Stonewall Inn window. After the chaos subsided, the Mattachine Society had graffitied a message there, pleading with their fellow 'homosexuals' to 'maintain peaceful conduct' in Greenwich Village.

By Christmas 1969, some members of the Mattachine Society – Randolf Wicker included – had joined the growing GLF, whose members viewed the riots as a clear sign that disruptive protest worked, while it's likely that the more conservative members of early LGBTQ+ groups took a backseat from activism more broadly. There are clear parallels with anti-racist movements, too: throughout the mid-to-late 1960s, the rise of the Black Panthers marked a departure from the peaceful tactics of the civil rights movement, instead opting for direct action and a clearly political, socialist stance.

As the decade came to a close, activists were focusing on coalition-building, direct action and mutual aid, building bonds of solidarity rather than campaigning for tolerance. It was only a matter of time before the GLF and the Black Panthers, united by their socialist views, came together in pursuit of a shared aim: liberation.

Prior to December 1969, there were already local gay groups showing solidarity with the Black Panthers. In an article for the *Journal of Social History*,[26] scholar Jared Leighton opens with a story about an Oakland Black Panther rally in July 1969, where members of the Committee for Homosexual Freedom (CHF), a gay rights organisation based in San Francisco's Bay Area, passed around leaflets detailing case studies of lethal police brutality.

The first was Frank Bartley, a 33-year-old white gay man, shot dead by a plainclothes policeman in April 1969. The second was Howard Efland, a Black gay man. In March 1969, he checked into the Dover Hotel, a kind of early bath house designed for cruising, a frequent target for the infamous vice squad. Eyewitness reports reveal that police officers 'claimed that Efland groped them'. Their response? They brutalised him, arrested him and then dragged him naked and screaming into the streets. Here, reports differ: some claimed he was beaten to death there and then; others reported that Efland had fallen out of the car on the way to the station, his body careening down the Hollywood Freeway. Whatever the precise details, these barbaric murders showed just how disposable gay lives – especially Black gay lives – were to the police.

The CHF handed out leaflets detailing these horrific stories, explaining that LGBTQ+ communities had been scapegoated and abused by police departments nationwide, largely without consequence. They underlined that they had something in common with the Panthers: not only a common goal of liberation, but a common enemy. 'The Homosexual Revolution is part of the whole street revolution fighting fascism in the U.S.,' the leaflet concluded. 'By locking arms with our brothers and sisters in the movement, we can ALL win our freedom. POWER TO THE PEOPLE!!'

Forming nationwide coalitions proved trickier. There was – and still is – undeniable racism within the gay rights movement, but especially as more radical groups emerged in the late '60s, there was broader support for the Black Panthers. Angela Davis spoke of these more radical sectors in a 2022 interview with *The Advocate*.[27] Although she didn't talk openly about being a lesbian until later life, she was an early supporter of 'those sectors of the gay movement that were anti-racist and anti-capitalist', she explained. 'I've always supported those radical sectors of the LGBTQ+ movement that called for the abolition of marriage

57

as a capitalist institution and the dismantling of the military.' There were some Panthers willing to align themselves with gay groups, but the Black Panther Party wasn't exactly seen as gay-friendly; in his prison memoir, *Soul on Ice*,[28] prominent member Eldridge Cleaver wrote homophobic critiques of James Baldwin, souring potential solidarity in the process.

The real catalyst for queer solidarity on a broader scale was the Free Huey campaign, which had been gathering momentum. Newton was arrested in 1967 and, as we saw in Varda's *Black Panthers*, rallies were ongoing throughout 1968. Fury continued to grow. By 1970, long-standing support for Newton was palpable. The Panthers were in turmoil at the time. Fred Hampton had been assassinated. Funds were depleted, key party members had been arrested and the Panthers were nearing total collapse. So, they broadened their scope.

The aim was to draw attention to Newton's trial. To do so, they reached out to Jean Genet, a French novelist, playwright and activist. Genet had been criminalised repeatedly throughout his life, beginning at age 15. He spent his childhood moving between foster families and periods of homelessness; when one set of foster parents, an elderly couple, asked him to drop off some money on their behalf, he allegedly pocketed it and went on a night out instead.

Genet was openly gay from a young age and was regularly arrested for wearing make-up, engaging in sex work and committing the apparent crime of being homeless. In prison, he wrote about his life. The result was a novel entitled *Our Lady of the Flowers* (*Notre-Dame-des-Fleurs*), equal parts lyrical, scandalous and deliciously horny. Famed existentialist philosopher Jean-Paul Sartre called it 'the epic of masturbation',[29] in reference to the hardcore sex scenes Genet wrote to get off in his jail cell. Genet was in his late fifties by the time the Black

Panthers reached out, but he happily accepted their invitation to attend Newton's trial. He ended up staying in the Bay Area for three months in total, delivering lectures and penning impassioned pro-Panther speeches, some of which haven't exactly aged well. In one, he said: 'I am a Black whose skin happens to be white, but definitely a Black.'[30] Genet's early works veer into racial fetishisation, as did some of his comments, like the fact that he claimed he 'supported Algerian independence due to his sexual relations with Arabs'.[31] Genet's racial politics left much to be desired – although, of course, cultural and scholarly awareness of racism and racist tropes has evolved exponentially over the last few decades. Regardless, as a gay man well-versed in being punished by the law due – at least in part – to his identity, Genet understood the power of standing in solidarity with the Panthers.

Press latched onto the visual incongruence of Genet, a 'short, squat, bald figure' dressed in 'an old suede jacket, black turtleneck sweater, corduroy pants and tan moccasins', alongside the Panthers. In a 1970 news report, the *New York Times*[32] framed the French author not only as an unlikely comrade but an unexpected 'idol'. Genet spoke about witnessing 'many incidents of racism' while travelling with the Panthers, 'some of which have been subtle, but they happened constantly, constantly. Others have been so overt they stuck me in the throat.' The centring of Genet in the press coverage proves a salient point: when Black people speak out about racism, they're often disbelieved, dismissed as biased or oversensitive. When white people speak about it, it's more likely to be viewed as 'objective'. In this case, it made the *New York Times*.

By August 1970, Huey Newton had been freed, thanks in no small part to the campaign for his release. He wasted no time calling on leftist organisations to come together, to write and advocate for a Revolutionary People's Constitutional Convention, a kind of broad, unifying constitution intended to bring radical leftist factions onto the same page. On 15 August 1970, he gave an interview which urged Panther members to 'unite' with the women's and gay liberation movements in 'a revolutionary fashion'. Newton acknowledged that building these coalitions wouldn't be easy, that doing so would mean resisting the instinctual urge to 'hit a homosexual in the mouth' or to 'want to shut a woman up, because we're afraid she might castrate us'.[33] Yet he rallied members to 'have respect and feelings for all oppressed people', to put aside personal bigotry to pursue the wider goal of collective liberation. Newton went a step further, acknowledging the Panthers' previous silence on gay liberation. 'Maybe [homosexuals] might be the most oppressed people in the society,' he argued.

Seemingly, the speech worked. A few weeks later, in early September, a three-day Revolutionary People's Convention was held in Philadelphia. Estimates of exact attendance numbers vary from 6,000 to 15,000, but one thing for sure is that activists from a broad spectrum of movements – anti-war, pro-Palestine, 'Third World' liberation, women's liberation, gay liberation – gathered to join the Panthers' calls for constitutional protections. Not everything was smooth sailing. In Leighton's aforementioned research, he explains that there was divided reception of the Panthers at the conference, especially among white gay and lesbian groups. Activists accused the Panthers of 'refusing to respond to the concerns of lesbians at the convention' and described the party's theories of liberation as being rooted in 'sexist mentalities'. The conference wasn't a universal success, but it did lay foundations of solidarity which lasted far longer than just three days. Newton continued this advocacy, reiterating frequently that anybody could be a radical, no matter their gender, race or sexuality.

Momentum continued to build through the autumn of 1970. Shortly after the Philadelphia convention, Black Panthers called for radicals to join them in Washington, DC in late November 1970, where they would actually write up the Revolutionary People's Constitutional Convention. This coalition-building was panicking the government; according to a federal document, republished in a 2021 *Harper's Bazaar* article,[34] there was internal concern about 'a connection between the homosexual movement and the Black Panther Party'.

Increasingly, members of the Gay Liberation Front were following the Panthers' directives to unite as part of a broader, revolutionary coalition. The *Harper's Bazaar* article is an in-depth interview with five gay liberation activists – two of them Black, three of them white – who travelled cross-country to Washington, appealing to local gay groups for solidarity at every step of the way. They met with leftist organisers in textile mill towns; they spoke to the owner of a shelter for abandoned gay teens; in Dallas, they were pulled over and arrested. 'It had nothing to do with anything other than that we were two Black men in that car with those white boys,' explained the activist named Joel. They dropped acid, slept in the geodesic domes of a countryside commune, danced to Mick Jagger and Diana Ross. By the time they reached the convention, Joel described a 'fantastic experience'; other activists on the trip say they have no memory of it whatsoever.

This was also the year that Sylvia Rivera, the trans revolutionary who co-founded STAR (Street Transvestite Action Revolutionaries) alongside fellow trans activist Marsha P. Johnson, met the Puerto Rican Young Lords Party. In East Harlem, New York, Rivera drew up a STAR banner and went to stand alongside the Young Lords in a protest against police repression. 'I became one of them,' she later recalled in an interview with author and activist Leslie Feinberg.[35] 'Any time they needed help, I was always there for the Young Lords. It was just the respect they gave us as human beings. They gave us a lot of respect. It was a fabulous feeling for me to be myself – being part of the Young Lords as a drag queen – and my organisation [STAR] being part of the Young Lords.' This solidarity was reciprocated, as the Young Lords took a vocal stance in supporting LGBTQ+ communities, fighting sexism and calling bullshit on gendered myths. In a forward-thinking statement, published in the party's newspaper *Pa'lante*, the Young Lords' Minister of Information Pablo Guzman described gender as 'a false idea, merely traits that have been attributed through the years to a man or woman'.[36]

These interactions and moments of community-building give insight into the promise of widespread coalition that came in 1970, especially after Newton's release. The rise of the Black Panthers coincided with a revolutionary moment in activism, which saw conservative organisations replaced instead by leftist groups united in their fight for collective liberation.

A lesser-acknowledged fact is that this revolutionary spirit trickled across international borders. In 1969, K.D. Wolff, who had served as chairman of the German Socialist Students' Union (SDS) in 1967 and 1968, travelled the US for a six-week speaking tour, during which he met Black Panther leader Bobby Seale.[37] Wolff was 'moved by the self-help programs of the Black Panther party in American inner cities', as well as their focus on self-defence. Galvanised by his personal experience with the Panthers, he founded the Black Panther Solidarity Committee, which led to the creation of other local committees across Germany and Europe more broadly. The aim was both

to educate German students about the Panthers and to offer
material support, raising funds to cover the Panther's bail and
legal costs. Wolff founded his own publishing house, Roter
Stern, in 1970, and set about translating and releasing the
writings of Black revolutionaries. He even made a point of
reaching out to GIs stationed across Germany, hoping that a
coalition of 'black GIs, poor whites, as well as other minorities
in the military' would mobilise the movement globally.

Eventually, differing views (mainly on the use of violence)
and the weakening of the Panthers meant the solidarity committee was short-lived, but student revolutionaries worked
alongside Black soldiers to highlight racism within the military
and to dispel the framing of racism as an imported 'American
problem'. If nothing else, the committee galvanised anti-
racist action among German students, prompted press coverage
of previously-ignored issues and underlined racism rooted in
Germany's own history.

There was even a British chapter of the Black Panthers. In
1968, Nigerian playwright Ogi B. Egbuna founded the British
Black Panthers[38] in Notting Hill, an epicentre of Black life in
London and a key site of racist discrimination. Ogi had come
to the UK in the 1950s, the same decade that saw the birth of
a British youth subculture known as the 'Teddy Boys', young,
working-class, largely white rock-'n'-roll devotees, who mim-
icked the gelled quiffs and zoot suits of their idols. In September
1954, *The Londonderry Sentinel*, an Irish newspaper, described
them as young men with 'coloured velvet collars and cuffs,
trousers that were so tight they couldn't sit down in them, belts
on the back of their jackets, long narrow ties like bootlaces'.[39]

But it wasn't their style that was dominating news headlines,
it was their behaviour. 'They went around in gangs,' continued
the article. 'Soon their exploits branded them as hooligans, and

Edwardian clothes became the uniform of a new generation of gangsters.'

Before long, the Teddy Boy movement was synonymous with violence. There's a tendency to glamourise them as working-class warriors, especially as they clashed regularly with police forces, stashed razor blades in their crepe-soled shoes and, to all intents and purposes, characterised themselves as subversive. Quickly, they became feared – one newspaper article of the 1950s describes the Teddy Boys as 'feral youth'.

In an in-depth look back at the Teddy Boy movement, an article published on rs21[40] – a British revolutionary socialist organisation, made up of labour activists who often write for the website – highlights the need to remember this as a 'working-class phenomenon', saying the media reaction to the Teddy Boys was inflamed by a sense of 'moral panic'. It paints the Teddy Boys as maligned radicals, a characterisation which glosses over some pretty key nuance. As the 1950s went on, Teddy Boys were rapidly becoming a symbol of white nationalism. Not only were they forming gangs, they were affiliating themselves with 'Keep Britain White' groups, such as the far-right White Defence League. The rs21 article points to racist media coverage at the time, as well as racism within the trade union movement, perhaps overlooking the fact that as well as upholding racism, Teddy Boys were rebranding it as something young, rebellious and radical. 'Teddy Boys were racist and took part in attacks, but equally, many were not,' the rs21 article reads, before describing the 1958 Race Riots in Notting Hill as 'their worst press,' accusing 'lazy journalists' of 'using the term Teddy Boy to describe any young working-class person involved in a fracas'.

This statement reads as wildly dismissive, an attempt to distance the Teddy Boy movement from its wilful deepening of racial divides, which set the scene for the aforementioned Race

Riots. Newspaper cuttings[41] about the riots depict milk bottles being hurled at non-white families, who barricaded themselves inside their homes for fear of being attacked. Even their homes weren't safe; a petrol bomb was launched at the house of one family, briefly setting its roof ablaze. Black citizens spoke of fearing for their lives and being brutally beaten as crowds gathered to watch. The full extent of the violence wasn't made public until internal police files were shared with the press in 2002,[42] which stated that 'teddy boys armed with iron bars, butchers' knives and weighted leather belts' went on the prowl for Black victims in Notting Hill over the August Bank Holiday, sparking the Race Riots.

It doesn't help anyone to #NotAllTeddyBoys the narrative, and it's retrospectively clear that these riots – and, by extension, the violence that Teddy Boys played a part in inciting – were the key catalysts for the founding of the British Black Panthers.

Throughout the 1960s, visits from US Black activists like Malcolm X and Stokely Carmichael continued the rise of the Black Power movement. By the time Egbuna founded the British Black Panthers in 1968, there was clear demand for an organised response to racism in the UK. Slum landlords regularly took advantage of Black tenants, leaving them to live in squalor. Police discrimination was rife and long-standing 'sus laws'[43] were used as justification to stop, search and harass anyone perceived as suspicious – a term which, inevitably, ended up being disproportionately weaponised against people of colour.

The British Black Panthers emerged in this political context. Like the US chapters of the Black Panthers, they emphasised the importance of solidarity – both national and international. As an article[44] published by the British Library points out, many key members had links with other marginalised groups worldwide. Egbuna was an anti-colonialist, who had visited Ghana to support then-president Kwame Nkrumah in his efforts to end British rule. (He succeeded on 6 March 1957 – this date is now marked annually as Ghana's Independence Day.) Olive Morris, a co-founder of the Brixton Black Women's Group, had travelled to China and studied Maoist politics, while Liz Obi, another British Panther, had planned a solidarity visit to Eldridge Cleaver, an American Panther exiled in Nigeria. These were revolutionary networks, whose roots spread further than single-issue histories would have us believe.

Ultimately, repeated state attacks on the Black Panther Party weakened its foundations significantly; despite continued activity throughout the 1970s, the Black Panther Party eventually dissolved in 1982. Yet this consistent persecution was proof that coalition-building scared authorities. Cops in Illinois only advanced their pursuit of Fred Hampton when they learned he was actively seeking solidarity; the Free Huey movement fired up activists worldwide, cementing support for a party of revolutionaries.

Too often, these histories of collaboration are minimised and stripped of broader context. Gay liberation is framed as Stonewall and Stonewall only, but the revolutionary fervour of the Black Panthers and the prison abolitionist movement played a role in shaping the radical politics of the Gay Liberation Front. Leaders like Sylvia Rivera continued the legacy of groups like San Francisco's Vanguard, which mounted broad, multi-pronged analyses of oppression. In their eyes, anti-poverty couldn't be separated from gay liberation; police brutality couldn't be ignored or undermined within gay activism; especially for the most marginalised, coalition-building wasn't just a political strategy, it was a way to understand that oppression can be multi-faceted. The Black Panther Party may have been harangued into dissolution, but it does their legacy a disservice to paint its members as separatists with single-issue mindsets.

Their historical contribution is one of socialist justice, anchored in a key but often-ignored foundation of their Ten-Point Program: 'liberation for *all* Black and oppressed people.'

Making Mischief

'Workers of the world, masturbate!'
– *FHAR (Homosexual Front for Revolutionary Action)*

On 26 August 1970, a group of nine French feminists gathered underneath Paris's famed Arc de Triomphe.[1] Christine Delphy, a pioneering sociologist, led the procession, holding a giant bouquet of beautiful flowers. Delphy and the other eight women, among them forward-thinking scholars and activists, stood around a placard inscribed into the concrete below the fabled arch, which reads: 'Here lies a soldier who died for his fatherland.' This memorial is dedicated to the unknown soldiers who died fighting for France during the First World War, but the language implies that the only sacrifices made were made by men.

On that fateful day in Paris, the nine women were gathered to honour the invisible suffering of women in wartime. They waved flags scrawled with messages like *Un homme sur deux est une femme* ('one in every two men is a woman') and *À la femme inconnue du Soldat, les femmes en lutte* ('to the unknown wife of the soldier, the women in struggle'). The women had hoped to lay their bouquet atop the memorial, but were seized by police before they could do so.

These chaotic scenes marked the first public demonstration of the Mouvement de Libération des Femmes (MLF), a coalition of feminist activists active between 1970 and 1976 in France. Their Arc de Triomphe protest wasn't only a statement of public visibility, it was a show of solidarity with women across the Atlantic who were striking en masse as part of the Women's Strike for Equality.[2] These US activists weren't just commemorating the fiftieth anniversary of winning the right to vote, they were demanding free abortions, free childcare and equal opportunities in the workplace. The newly formed MLF in France took a stand alongside these campaigners, as well as building a movement of their own.

France had been in a state of near-perpetual unrest since the burning streets and mass strikes of summer 1968, which had shown that grassroots movements and direct action could spark change. In local community centres and classrooms, women who would go on to become influential French feminists – including Françoise d'Eaubonne, who went on to coin the term 'ecofeminism' in 1974,[3] and Monique Wittig, already known in the late '60s as a trailblazing lesbian feminist[4] – were starting to collaborate, laying the foundations of their own French movement.

The Arc de Triomphe protest was the beginning of what they deemed 'year zero' for French feminism, and they wasted no time in seeking out fellow marginalised activists to mobilise alongside.

The women sought potential co-conspirators[5] among the ranks of Arcadie, a French homophile organisation founded by philosopher André Baudry in 1954. Arcadie rose to prominence against a backdrop of social conservatism and, like their homophile counterparts worldwide, they advocated primarily for tolerance and acceptance. One of Arcadie's earliest statements was to publish the Arcadie literary review, which earned high-profile support from the likes of surrealist artist Jean Cocteau, who contributed his art to the publication. Yet shortly after its release, Baudry was prosecuted for 'outrage against good morals',[6] convicted and fined an eye-watering sum of 400,000 francs.

Arcadie was undoubtedly subversive in some ways, but one thing it was *not* is inclusive. In a 2005 article,[7] published in *L'Homme & La Société*, scholar Sébastian Chauvin explained that the organisation rejected anyone deemed mentally ill, gender non-conforming or 'feminine', a masc4masc policy which excluded not only feminine gay men but plenty of women, too. According to Chauvin, Arcadie was largely closed off to lesbians and women more generally: when the organisation dissolved in 1980, women made up just 2 per cent of its membership. The small number of lesbians within Arcadie were seemingly happy to team up with the MLF straight away, but it wasn't until February 1971 that gay men joined the alliance, too.

As much as I wax lyrical about solidarity, forging coalitions is anything but easy. It often takes time, plenty of convincing and endless internal struggles, usually sparked by inter-community discrimination – in this case, the misogyny of gay men, aimed at lesbians. It's no secret that early gay rights and mainstream feminist movements were led predominantly by white men and white, straight women, leaving lesbians and people of colour to form their own organisations. Yet the more radical fringes of activist movements were advocating for inclusion, for broad-strokes mobilisation, and they were doing so by causing mayhem, much like the feminists who were dragged away from the Arc de Triomphe in handcuffs, their memorial bouquet rapidly shedding petals.

The MLF formed a new coalition, which united feminist, lesbian and gay rights activists, driven by the revolutionary spirit of the late '60s outlined in earlier chapters. When it came to naming the new coalition, the chosen moniker reflected this energy: the Front Homosexuel d'Action Révolutionnaire (FHAR), or the Homosexual Front for Revolutionary Action. This wasn't the only group to emerge, either – there was also the Red Dykes (Les Gouines Rouges), another offshoot of the converging movements.

These new groups made demands across lines of sexuality and gender; increasingly, they took a tongue-in-cheek and decidedly radical approach to organising. They subverted old-school socialist slogans, reworking them into cheeky, provocative new ones, like: *'Proletaires de tous les pays, caressez-vous!'* – using a loose slang translation, this becomes: 'Workers of the World, Masturbate!'[8]

Throughout 1971, the movement gained a handful of recognisable, radical leaders, with aforementioned feminist theorist Françoise d'Eaubonne and writers Daniel Guérin and Guy Hocquenghem among them. They dragged up at protests, stripped naked at FHAR general assemblies and published radical essays, like Hocquenghem's seminal text 'The Screwball Asses',[9] which took aim at bourgeois capitalism and positioned homosexuality within the politics of sexual desire more broadly. In Hocquenghem's words: 'Our asshole is revolutionary.' The text was swiftly seized and destroyed by the French government.

There was a dialled-up, gleeful focus on chaos and solidarity, a 'fuck you' mentality which ruffled French feathers. These coalitions threw two fingers up at misogyny, forging alliances with feminist campaigners to broaden the scope of movements and wreak havoc in the process – a sure-fire way to get their voices heard.

★

Back in Britain, a British sociology student named Bob Mellors was on a serious comedown after spending his summer in the US, fighting alongside the Black Panthers. With the aid of a travel grant, he flew to New York in search of temporary work and, more importantly, fellow gay activists. Before long, he was picketing alongside other radicals outside the Women's House of Detention, liaising with the Black Panther Party and even travelling to Philadelphia, to take part in their Revolutionary People's Constitutional Convention. Along the way, he formed a close bond with Aubrey Walter, a fellow student. The formative trip lit a fire within them both, igniting their revolutionary spirits.

Returning to London, the post-holiday blues hit hard. 'I came back to the UK and it all seemed flat,' recalled Walter, quoted in an *LSE* article.[10] 'Bob had gone back to college at the LSE and we spoke on the phone. Bob booked a room and we held a meeting.' The meeting was small, attracting about 20 people in total, and yet this tiny, word-of-mouth rendezvous ended up laying the foundations for the London Gay Liberation Front, later the UK Gay Liberation Front (UK GLF).

Britain was in its post-war period, which lasted roughly from 1945 to 1979, an era of continuous and largely beneficial change. The welfare system was established[11] during these years, as was the National Health Service,[12] which offered – and still does – free healthcare to all British citizens. Industries like rail, steel and coalmining were all nationalised,[13] and trade unions had a largely strong and influential presence throughout these post-war years.[14]

Each country has its own politics and individual circumstances, but the drive to make change crosses borders. As such, activist movements are often either directly or indirectly inspired by each other – an obvious fact, but one which bears repeating. Like their US predecessors, the UK GLF wasted no time in situating themselves within a wider nexus of oppression. Their succinct list of demands did contain LGBTQ+ specific directives, like more inclusive sex education in schools (although, arguably, this benefits everyone), and the lowering of the age of consent to 16 for gay men, as it was for straight people. But many of their demands were shared and reflected by other marginalised groups, like an end to police harassment and to employment discrimination. Echoing the language of the Black Panthers' Ten-Point Program, they ended their list with 'GAY IS GOOD! POWER TO ALL OPPRESSED PEOPLE!'

The UK GLF's first large-scale protest came later in 1970, on 27 November. Although homosexuality had been partially decriminalised a few years earlier, in 1967, undercover policemen were still prowling around known 'cruising grounds' to entrap horny gay men seeking casual sex.

In November, a cop arrested a young liberal named Louis Eakes, whom they accused of cruising for sex in Highbury Fields. His crime? Asking for a lighter – which he maintained was an innocent request to light his cigarette, not some coded plea for sex. Word of Eakes's arrest spread quickly; within just a few days, UK GLF members had gathered around 150 protestors[15] for an impromptu protest. They minced gleefully around the park, lighting each others' cigarettes to highlight the absurdity of Eakes's arrest. As a grand finale, protestors made out vigorously.

Much like the radical groups making waves in France, mayhem was their modus operandi. Members wanted to cause chaos, so they ingratiated themselves with other groups who shared the same aims. Another organisation grabbing headlines at the time was the Women's Liberation Movement, whose members caused a stir in November 1970 by launching flour-bombs[16] onto the stage during the annual Miss World competition. Incidentally, it was to be a landmark year for the long-standing Miss World institution. South Africa – a country then divided by apartheid – sent one white contestant, Jillian Jessup, and one Black contestant, Pearl Jansen, to compete. To the shock of viewers, it was Jansen who earned the higher score of the two women, earning second-place position. The year 1970 also saw the crowning of the first Black Miss World, Grenadian representative Jennifer Hosten. 'Women from small countries, and particularly women of colour, like myself, really were not expected to be more than a number in the contest,' Hosten told *TIME* magazine in a 2020 feature.[17]

The elation of Hosten's historic win was overshadowed – dampened by 'less than positive' headlines and drowned out by coverage of the feminist protestors. On stage, leery host Bob Hope described the event as a 'cattle market' and blatantly objectified the beauty queens. Little did he know that members of the Women's Lib had smuggled themselves into the event, dressed up in glitzy ballgowns and fur coats, bought from local charity shops. Their flour-bombing was a statement of defiance against what they deemed the misogyny inherent in Miss World, but not everyone agreed. In fact, the protestors were arrested and made to stand trial.

For decades, media coverage has framed the Miss World 1970 competition as a stand-off between pageant queens and feminist activists. Yet when Hosten met the activists for the first time in 2010, she found they 'had more in common than they expected'. Both were using Miss World to make political statements: Hosten's was one of global representation and the Eurocentricity of beauty ideals, whereas the Women's

Liberation Movement's was one against misogyny and the reduction of women to their looks, and *only* their looks.

The trial attracted public attention, creating an opportune moment for the UK GLF to take their own stand. So, on 4 February 1971, members gathered outside Bow Street magistrates' court in central London, the scene of the trial.[18] A handful were dressed up as mock-Miss World contestants, draped in makeshift sashes with tongue-in-cheek slogans, like 'Miss Demeanour' and 'Miss Trial Competition 1971' – the official name of what the GLF had declared a 'street theatre' performance in support of the Women's Lib protestors. Demonstrators were dressed to cause a scene: one wore leopard-print underpants; one wore a glitzy, full-length robe; one drag queen donned a curly wig and a short playsuit with eyes printed on the chest, her oversized breastplate straining the fabric. They staged a campy, eye-catching performance and were planning to do so over and over again, but were pelted with rotten tomatoes by porters at the nearby Covent Garden fruit and veg market before they could repeat it. At the 1971 Miss World competition, 'trans people and drag queens' again showed up, according to British gay activist Peter Tatchell, bearing placards denouncing the exploitation of women. 'There was also a bloodied "Miss Ulster – the Irish Bombshell" to protest the war in Ireland,' he remembers.[19]

As well as aligning themselves with feminist groups, the UK GLF was pro-union, pro-working-classes and vocal in its opposition to exploitative labour laws. In February 1971, around one hundred members campaigned against the Industrial Relations Act,[20] which enforced tighter regulations on unions and cracked down on so-called 'wildcat strikes'.[21] The GLF made clear with their presence at demonstrations that gays and lesbians were workers too, and so any workers' issue was, by default, their issue as well.

In September 1971, a stuffy, evangelical group known as the Festival of Light announced they'd be staging a religious extravaganza in London. You might recognise the leader of the Festival of Light, a pageant-queen pop singer turned anti-gay evangelist named Anita Bryant. Her homophobia sparked some truly iconic moments of protest – from a cream pie to the face on national TV to a nationwide boycott of orange juice, spawned by her spokeswoman role at the Florida Citrus Commission. The planned headliner was none other than Cliff Richard, a rock singer first marketed as the UK's answer to Elvis Presley. He publicly denounced his 'too sexy for TV' persona in the mid-1960s, announcing himself as a reformed, puritan Christian, making him the perfect fit for the ultra-conservative, homophobic Festival of Light. The opportunity for mischief was too great for the UK GLF to ignore.

On 9 September 1971, the day of the event, protestors snuck into the venue, Westminster's Methodist Central Hall.[22] A central component of GLF demonstrations was 'radical drag' – one queen described it as being less about 'fake tits' and more about drag as a form of disruption. It was drag on a mission to disrupt. When the Festival of Light began as planned, the preaching of evangelical speakers was quickly, chaotically interrupted. Just minutes later, hundreds of mice were released into the hall. Gay and lesbian couples in the upper balcony began to passionately embrace. UK GLF members dragged up as 'nuns' in immaculate blue-and-white habits stormed the stage to shout gay liberation slogans, while a gay 'bishop' rallied the audience to 'keep on sinning'.

These ballsy, hilarious protests were called 'zaps', and they were beloved by GLF members in both the US and the UK. Mark Segal, one of the founding members of the stateside GLF, became known[23] throughout the early 1970s for chaining himself to railings and breaking up live TV recordings; in May 1973, Segal and a friend handcuffed themselves to a camera after producers of *The Mike Douglas Show* cancelled a planned segment on homophobia and gay issues. Together, they chanted: 'Two, four, six, eight, gay is just as good as straight,'[24] until police were called.

It was in this context of raucous activism that the first Pride parades emerged. On 28 June 1970, LGBTQ+ activists in New York commemorated the Stonewall Riots with the first Christopher Street Liberation Day March, marching along a route which spanned more than 50 blocks. 'We didn't have a police permit, so no one knew exactly what would happen,' recalls Mark Segal, in an interview with the *New York Times*.[25] 'We held self-defence classes and learned how to protect ourselves. As a marshal, I especially had to know how to react and control the marchers if we were attacked.' Simultaneously, LGBTQ+ activists in Los Angeles held a Christopher Street West parade; according to those in attendance, protestors created 'homemade floats' adorned with 'Vaseline jars' and a 'crucified queer man' – a kind of spread-eagled, gay Jesus — marching the streets in tie-dye shirts and their best drag to cheer for gay liberation.

By 1972, British activists had plans to replicate the chaos on their home turf. In an era which shamed LGBTQ+ people and encouraged them to stay hidden, organisers decided it would be a radical move to lead with the concept of pride, but not everyone was on board. 'Shortly before Pride 72, we went to Earl's Court, west London, to leaflet gay pubs and encourage customers to join us on the march,' recalls Tatchell, in the *Guardian* article mentioned above. 'We got quite a hostile reception from some of the gay men there.'

By that time, cracks in the UK GLF were beginning to show; some members were engaging in 'patronising racism' and women were being routinely spoken over. Despite divisions, Pride 72 was a success. Flanked by walls of police – whose presence scared away some potential Pride marchers – LGBTQ+ activists stomped through the streets of London as the public looked on. At Marble Arch, there was a mass kiss-in. 'The police left, because they couldn't stand the sight of it,' recalls author and activist Stuart Feather. 'Then we ended up in Hyde Park. I remember clouds of marijuana smoke, probably people tripping, and party games.' This became the after-party, where revellers made out, played their instruments and – in the case of around a dozen attendees – spontaneously stripped off, dancing naked around the park.

Looking back, the UK's first Pride parade seems to be a hedonistic success story, fuelled by collective fury, intercontinental solidarity and, of course, plenty of weed. Yet there was wider context to this chaotic landscape, and it could be traced back to the streets of London.

In 1972, a group of radical queens within the South London Gay Liberation Front suggested squatting an abandoned building on Railton Road, Brixton.[26]

At this point in the early seventies, Brixton was a known hub of grassroots activism.[27] Once seen as a prosperous area, the neighbourhood was increasingly marked by deprivation, its rows of Victorian housing damaged and over crowded. Buildings were left empty as the government struggled to refurbish in time, a problem exacerbated by a shortage of construction workers. Homes were becoming untenable and the poorest sectors of the British population were being made homeless; at the same time, the so-called Brixton Plan was being drawn up, with the aim of drawing in new, wealthy residents and displacing the largely Black families in the area. It was a perfect storm of poverty and corporate greed, state-sanctioned gentrification at a devastating level.

As a result, squatters' movements were growing in popularity – and among their members were seasoned radical organisers, such as Olive Morris. A dedicated anti-imperialist, she played a key role not only in the squatters' rights movement but in the British Black Panthers, the Organisation of Women of African and Asian Descent, the Manchester Black Women's Cooperative and many more. Her activism was unwaveringly grassroots, and a core tenet of her ethos was a belief in 'squatting as politics'.[28]

In late 1972, Olive Morris and Liz Turnbull found themselves strapped for cash and in need of a place to live, so they scoured the streets of Brixton and decided to squat a property above a disused laundry, at 121 Railton Road. Before long, they had opened it up to radical Black organisations. The building became an anarchist centre first, and then a Black bookstore named Sabaar. Their tenancy wasn't exactly peaceful. In January 1973, the women were illegally evicted by the agent of a private landlord. They broke back in before being violently dragged out by five police officers. Morris managed to escape the scuffle and occupy the roof, as a crowd of protestors gathered outside in support. Morris stayed put and found herself becoming a central figure of the squatters' rights movement. Most notably, she graced the cover of the *Squatters' Handbook*[29] in 1979 – dressed in black jeans and a grey, woollen jumper, she's photographed scaling a wall to climb through the window of an abandoned building.

When the queens of the South London GLF found a suitable squat, it was just a stone's throw from Morris. They wasted no time moving in, transforming it into the Brixton Gay Centre.

The name might give an air of seriousness and formality, but don't be fooled — behind closed doors, budding activists were throwing raucous parties in church crypts and other squats, bonding with future comrades while having cheap, hedonistic fun. Squatting a venue long-term allowed them to turn it into a makeshift coffee shop and drop-in advice centre, as well as a community hub with sporadic basement discos and parties. Some of the GLF's more conservative members dropped off, repelled by the decision to squat. Shagging in a church crypt was apparently fine, yet squatting was a step too far for some. The decision to squat weeded out the more conservative members, and established the Brixton Gay Centre as a distinctly leftist hub, which created space for other leftist groups. In a 2013 documentary, *Brixton Fairies: Made Possible by Squatting*,[30] one former South London GLF member recalls there was even a gay wrestling group. 'The political purists didn't approve of wrestling,' he says, explaining that the die-hard, self-identified fairies were against anything remotely 'macho', even if the aim was to subvert it. 'They were all queens! They were just getting their hands on each other, it wasn't really aggressive wrestling,' he clarified. The 'purists' were outvoted, and the gay wrestlers met happily and often in the basement, grappling on dirty mattresses laid out on the floor.

Word spread quickly that activists – gay, people of colour, working-class, largely anarchist activists – were squatting empty buildings in Brixton, which drew other marginalised, political people to the area in search of squats of their own. Along Railton Road alone, there was the People's News Service – a grassroots, anti-capitalist news service – as well as two feminist women's centres, one located just next door to the Gay Centre. There was a food cooperative further down on Atlantic Road, where food was freely distributed; around the corner, on Shakespeare Road, was the headquarters of Race Today,[31] a collective of Black radicals. Garden walls were knocked down and hot summer days were spent drinking cheap booze, drumming up plans for political demonstrations and debating with each other.

Yet there was still separation. These squats and centres were largely made up of white gay men; further down Railton Road, Pearl Alcock – hailed in a 2021 *gal-dem* article[32] as the 'Black bisexual shebeen queen of Brixton' – ran a 'shebeen', a type of illicit, underground bar known as a clandestine haven for marginalised people, usually run by women.

The history of the shebeen can be traced back to countries like Ireland and South Africa; the latter established a Liquor Act in 1927, which barred non-white South Africans from any licensed premises which sold alcohol and from selling alcohol themselves. So-called 'shebeen queens', true icons dedicated to keeping spirits high even in the most repressive of circumstances, thrived underground, brewing their own liquor and forming communities. As apartheid laws continued to be enforced, these shebeens grew in popularity; in 1960s Soweto, there were reportedly more than 10,000 shebeens, many of which also hosted gigs by local jazz artists.[33] Alcock's Brixton shebeen flourished in the late 1970s, becoming a sweaty, euphoric refuge for Brixton's Black LGBTQ+ communities, likely due to racism within gay communities and a growing cultural perception that 'gay' was a 'white identity'.

Despite this fracturing of communities, Brixton's squats and Alcock's shebeen were distinctly radical in their willingness to create space for marginalised people. There's long been unchecked racism and classism within gay and lesbian activism, yet those who made Brixton a hub of community-led organising were working just minutes away from each other. They may not have seen it then, but they were largely being trampled by the same systems. They were mostly working-class, united by the rebellious act of squatting, occupying buildings which remained empty while homeless people died on the streets.

Throughout the early '70s in particular, there were moments of hope that long-term coalitions could be built. In France, the FHAR united queer and feminist activists in acts of collective mischief-making, but infighting, lesbian exclusion and state censorship led to the collective's disbanding in 1974. The UK GLF splintered that same year and, although marginalised communities were building momentum in close proximity on the streets of Brixton, a fully-fledged coalition of marginalised groups seemingly never emerged. Put simply, the main factor breaking up gay liberation groups in the early 1970s was exclusion – and it wasn't just happening in the UK and France.

In 1973, the Homosexuelle Aktion Westberlin (HAW), or the Homosexual Action Group West Berlin held a meeting in Germany for international gay activist groups, drawing campaigners from around the globe.

What they didn't expect is the presence of drag queens from France and Italy, who drew eyes to the demonstration with their 'eyeshadow and blue fingernails'. According to *Love at First Fight!*,[34] a 2023 art exhibition at Berlin's Schwules Museum, their appearance led to what was known as the *Tuntenstreit*.[35] The Schwules' catalogue translates this to the 'drag queen debate', but the word *tunte* has the same connotations as terms like 'pansy' and 'fairy', and has historically been used as a slur – although, like the term 'queer', radical activists have reclaimed it as a term of defiant pride. The debate splintered the HAW: some members saw drag as a radical, even revolutionary artform, whereas others saw it as a distraction, a potential thorn in the side of future working-class coalitions. The members who sided with the drag queens quickly decided to strengthen their bond with the German feminist movement, self-identifying as feminists.

This drag queen discrimination is a logical evolution of the old-school 'masculine' focus of early homophile groups, who protested in three-piece suits, preaching mantras of tolerance and respectability. Drag flies in the face of these tame tactics. As an artform, it's a 'fuck you' to traditional gender norms, a rejection of the notion that LGBTQ+ communities must be silent and palatable in order to be respected. It's an art which embraces chaos, using subversive tactics to draw attention to political issues, much in the same way that groups like Just Stop Oil do today.

Especially in the early 1970s, the mantra seemed to be: fuck it, have fun. Activists were riding high on the fumes of their 1960s progress and, in a pre-AIDS climate, not following the rules was widely encouraged. Even today, we have limited definitions of activism: marches, petitions, lobbying governments. Zoom in and you'll find rich histories of social change rooted in playfulness, community spirit and a distinctly queer desire to fuck with the status quo, one 'zap' at a time. Plenty of these liberation movements were short-lived – arguably, a key downside to these chaotic protest tactics – but that doesn't mean their members abandoned the pursuit of justice, they just shifted their focus. Looking back, this brief but mischievous chapter in queer and feminist histories is exciting; these stories of kiss-ins, broadcast hijinks and dragged-up nuns provided memorable blueprints, inspiring today's rabble-rousers to wreak yet more political havoc of their own.

No TERFs, No SWERFs

'When prostitute women aren't safe, no woman is safe.'
— *English Collective of Prostitutes*

The first time I wrote about sex work activism was before I'd ever done sex work myself. Before long, I was marching through the streets of London's Soho with hundreds of protestors, brandishing signs with slogans like NO BAD WHORES, JUST BAD LAWS and SEX WORK IS WORK. It quickly became clear to me that sex work activism is inherently anti-carceral, anti-borders, pro-decriminalisation, but there was one chant in particular that fascinated me: 'No TERFs, no SWERFs.'

These acronyms stand for Trans-Exclusionary Radical Feminists and Sex Worker-Exclusionary Radical Feminists respectively, but they're misnomers: there's nothing 'feminist' about their politics. Their goal is to police who deserves access to safety and human rights, punishing so-called 'bad' women in the process. Here, a caveat: not all trans people are sex workers. Yet, as the, No TERFs, no SWERFs, chant highlights, pearl-clutching campaigners often hate trans communities just as much as they hate workers selling sex for survival. As

84

a result, there's a truly radical history of solidarity that's ripe for excavation.

Here, let's travel back in time to 1970s Marin County, a picturesque pocket of Northern California surrounded by sprawling, verdant redwoods. The area had made national headlines at the beginning of the decade, when a high-profile courtroom shoot-out made it a key battleground for the Black Panthers. Already, radicals had built tight-knit communities in Marin County, with feminist, anti-racist and queer campaigners often living in close proximity to each other. Yet one woman in particular was laying the foundations for an early sex workers' rights movement.

Margo St James, born in 1937, spent her childhood driving tractors and milking cows on her father's dairy farm in rural Washington,[1] but she fled the rural life in her mid-teens, leaving behind her husband and to set up a new life in San Francisco. St James initially worked in after-hours clubs to make ends meet, but she had never actually sold sex when she was arrested in 1962. Despite this fact, she was charged both with 'soliciting in prostitution' and 'keeping or residing in a house of ill fame'. Famously, she defended herself by telling trial judge that she had 'never turned a trick in her life'; in the judge's eyes, St James's knowledge of sex workers' lingo – which she'd gained through interactions with sex workers in the clubs where she'd worked – was enough to justify conviction on both counts.

Never one to be defeated, St James enrolled in night classes at a law school; before long, she'd learned enough to successfully appeal her conviction. However, this of injustice sparked a political flame within St James, which eventually led to a lifetime dedicated to activism.

When St James moved to Marin County in 1970, she found herself surrounded by like-minded activists. 'I socialised with the housewives who were participating in consciousness-raising groups,' she wrote, in the foreword for 1989 sex work anthology *A Vindication of the Rights of Whores*.[2] 'Elsa Gidlow, a lesbian poet, lived next door and used to push feminist literature under my door.'

The fight for sex workers' rights has always been linked to the struggles of other marginalised groups. Its core message is that nobody should be criminalised for the work they do to survive when their alternatives are so shitty. Don't abolish sex work, abolish the conditions – poverty, discrimination, precarity – that continue to make it a viable lifeline for those who rely on it. When whorephobic campaigners rally to shut down strip clubs, they argue that sex workers should get another job. Let's think critically about this: how many jobs in the world are *good* jobs? The kind which offer childcare to single mothers or flexible hours for anyone struggling with chronic fatigue or long-term health conditions? What about if you don't have formal education under your belt, or you don't want to contend with potential ableism, racism, misogyny and transphobia? What then? Talking about sex work means talking about criminalisation, migration, structural injustice. Unsurprisingly, it sits within a wide nexus of leftist activism.

This is especially true of sex worker activism and trans rights. As we have established, not all trans people are sex workers, yet trans communities – trans women in particular – are over-represented in sex work, largely because a lack of healthcare means paying extortionate prices to go private. Sex work can be a means to make that cash quickly, all the while cashing in on society's fetishisation of trans bodies. St James was seemingly aware of these links, and set about making her activist efforts queer-inclusive from the get-go.

St James was specifically inspired by – and played a key role in – an organisation named WHO (Whores, Housewives and Others). '"Others" meant lesbians but it wasn't being said out loud yet, even in those liberal bohemian circles,' she explained.[3] At the time, St James was cleaning houses and getting to know the local housewives. 'I saw the way all these [marginalised groups] were treated,' she said in a 2013 interview with Bitch Media.So, she brought them together. 'The housewives, especially, were really excited to meet the whores, so I invited them all over for a little meeting,' she recalled. 'A couple of the women even traded places for a few days. I thought it went really well!'

At the time, marginalised groups across Marin County had come to trust the newly appointed sheriff, Richard Hongisto, known locally for his liberal values. Ironically, St James actually became a sex worker after being wrongfully charged; she began seeing clients periodically in order to pay her bills. Yet she'd also gained plenty more first-hand experience in the way sex workers were criminalised and, over the years, she'd been appalled by the so-called 'prostitute stings' she saw on a regular basis. In late 1972, she saw an upscale brothel raided by policemen decked out in riot gear. '[They seemed] high, really up, turned on, their eyes sparkling, nostrils flaring,'[4] she wrote in an account of that night, which ended with the brothel's madam either falling or being pushed out of a third-storey window onto a cement courtyard. Street sex workers weren't safe either; they were seen as a scourge on the landscape, so laws sought to push them underground, into dangerous working conditions. St James raised these issues with Hongisto when she bumped into him at a party. In her words, she 'cornered him in a hot tub' and asked what would need to be done to protect sex workers. He responded bluntly: 'Someone from the victim class has to speak out. That's the only way the issue is going to be heard.'

St James took his words to heart. On May Day 1973, she announced the formation of COYOTE, an acronym for Call Off Your Tired Old Ethics, inspired by a 'coyote hunter' nickname given to her on a wild mushroom-hunting trip. St James debuted a COYOTE letterhead featuring a howling dog alongside spiky, aggressive text, and vowed to support sex workers – especially marginalised sex workers, who faced the double bind of whorephobia combined with racism, transphobia and other forms of prejudice. Two weeks later, on Mother's Day, she announced a bail fund and the recruitment of COYOTE members, who offered legal assistance and self-defence classes to sex workers in need.

COYOTE had a huge queer presence. Not only was St James directly inspired by the queer and trans activists that had long stood in solidarity with sex workers, these communities often shared 'beats' – spots to solicit, either for cruising or for street sex work. In 2021, Carol Queen, PhD – an influential sex educator affiliated with San Francisco's iconic sex store, Good Vibrations – said of St James: 'Because I've been involved in the sex-positive movement, the queer movement *and* the sex workers' rights movement, I think about Margo as an inspirational figure in all three.'[5]

In their authoritative book *Revolting Prostitutes*,[6] co-authors Juno Mac and Molly Smith flesh out a timeline of this shared marginalisation. They specifically look back to the Second World War archetype of the 'disease-ridden prostitute', scapegoated as a symbolic enemy of the state, an impure succubus looking to ensnare her victims. According to the authors, she was often depicted as an 'archetypal femme fatale' with a 'cigarette between her lips, a tight dress, and a wicked smile'.

Smith and Mac draw parallels between 'these questions about the duplicity of the sexualised body' and wider discourse around 'queer and gender non-conforming people':

Trans women are often questioned about their 'biological' status: a demand that invariably reveals an excessive focus on their genitals. A trans woman is constantly targeted for public harassment; at the same time, if she is 'read' as trans, she is seen to be threatening as a man – accused of trespassing into bathrooms to commit sexual violence. Conversely, if she can pass for cisgender, she is regarded as dangerous, liable to 'trap' someone into having sex with her unawares.

This fascination with gatekeeping the status of 'womanhood' has been prevalent throughout feminist history. It's been a question of identifying the 'good' women – predominantly cis, white, straight, middle-class and 'ladylike' – who seemingly deserve protection, alienating other women in the process. The British suffragettes, for example, won the right for women to vote in 1918. However, the law only applied to property-owning women over the age of 30; it therefore excluded vast swathes of working-class women, including the most marginalised. By this logic, queer, trans and sex-working women have long been lumped into the same categories and discriminated against in similar ways. In the eyes of puritans, they're all 'bad' women.

Given this context of shared prejudice, it's unsurprising that St James set out to create an inclusive and collaborative organisation. Within a few months of its inception, COYOTE had become a powerhouse of grassroots activism, with St James as the charismatic leader of this new, glorious revolution. 'We got support from the street all the way up to the top,' she recalled in the aforementioned interview. 'Even some of the rich liberals liked the pretty women and invited us up to their mansions on

[San Francisco's] Nob Hill.' Gay and lesbian activists threw their weight behind COYOTE, as did cannabis decriminalisation campaigners, Chinese-American organisations, progressive lawyers and even the White Panthers, the short-lived anti-racist group which emerged in Detroit and later spawned chapters across the country, including in San Francisco.

In 1974, after befriending Reverend Cecil Williams, pastor of Glide Memorial Church, St James began sowing the seeds for a hedonistic extravaganza, The Hookers' Ball, planned for the same week as Halloween. Williams – a truly game-changing pastor, known for opening up the church to Black Panthers, social justice campaigners and leftist activists – allowed St James to use the church, which had also offered safety and resources to the homeless queens of San Francisco's Vanguard in the mid-1960s, as the location for the ball. With Williams's blessing, St James transformed the institution's hallowed halls into the scene of one of the world's most memorable parties, repeated annually until 1979.

A newspaper report, published in the *Berkeley Barb* and archived by the Digital Transgender Archive,[7] offers a glimpse into the chaos of the inaugural Hookers' Ball. The salacious report details 'decadence and bare asses', as well as 'leotarded whores, panama'd pimps, and transvestites festooned with feathers, glitter and satin'. Tickets to the Hookers' Ball were $10 a pop, and all proceeds went straight to bail funds for incarcerated sex workers. Lack of funds was no reason to be turned away, though – those who were poor or unwaged were allowed free entry. The queer presence at the event was enormous. There were drag queen brides with their cocks hanging out of their dresses, porn stars dressed as lion tamers and renowned erotic artists having X-rated fun with guests in the corners. Banquet tables filled with dishes of liver pâté were stationed next to a mammoth champagne bar, and the decoration brief was camp, camp, *camp* – think vinyl tiles strewn with glitter and paper streamers hanging from the ceiling.

Drag queens worked security on the door, teased guests with comedic stripteases and entertained the revellers with crass jokes and cheeky winks. Not everyone was happy with their presence, though; some sex workers thought the drag artists were stealing their spotlight. 'You camera people have got to stop giving all your attention to the queens,' said one sex worker to documentary maker Max Scherr. 'This is a hookers' ball!' But these were minor squabbles in what was otherwise a memorable show of solidarity.

Presiding over the debauchery was St James herself, who vowed the Hookers' Ball would be the 'social event of the year for heterosexuals, bisexuals, transsexuals, asexuals . . . I guess that about covers it!' A vision in burgundy silk, she rounded off the night with a speech about 'the incredible amount of tax dollars vice squad arrests cost San Franciscoans', and she extensively praised two Black sex workers who had helped to organise the event. St James's speech concluded with a call for the full decriminalisation of sex work, met with a roar of support from the crowd. That first year attracted around 300 attendees and established an annual tradition which got wilder and more impressive with each year that passed. In 1978, 20,000 people attended, resulting in profits of $60,000, all of which were sunk back into COYOTE.[8] New staff members were employed and their efforts to destigmatise sex work continued.

When St James passed away in 2021, a flood of high-profile obituaries were released in the press, which praised her as a formidable activist. One of her greatest achievements was the St. James Infirmary,[9] a service based in the Tenderloin District which offered a vital community hub for 25 years, before closing in 2023. The infirmary was a place where trans folks could find shelter, access harm reduction services (such as syringe exchanges and STI testing and seek out key mental health services. It's a lifeline for trans people and sex-workers alike, and a living, breathing testament to the interlocked struggles of trans and sex working populations. COYOTE recognised these shared experiences from day one, advocating broadly for reproductive rights, bodily autonomy and an end to discrimination.

The Hookers' Ball wasn't only a raucous annual fundraiser for the ages, a place where drag performers rubbed shoulders with strippers and proud whores draped in their most magnificent finery. Above all, it was the glamorous, hedonistic emblem of an anti-carceral movement led by marginalised people, one which deployed iconic fundraising tactics and built a deeper ethos, rooted in solidarity and shared struggle.

COYOTE wasn't the only feminist movement gaining traction in the 1970s. The decade is hailed as the 'decade of women' – and, increasingly, activists were questioning and challenging exactly *who* was included within that category.

This meant spotlighting the 'whores, housewives and others', fighting for poor and working-class women, advocating for lesbians, sex workers, disabled women and women of colour, whose nuanced needs were so often ignored. It was a decade of *socialist* feminism, one which recognised that socio-economic justice and an intersectional framework would be key to ensuring the liberation of *all* women.

In the US, Black women led the welfare movement, and they were demonised as a result. Linda Taylor – nicknamed the 'welfare queen' by press and politicians – became a scapegoat, when, in reality, she was simply spotlighting endless unpaid 'women's work.' Political figureheads held her up as an example of laziness, and racist caricatures led to her widespread vilification. In response, Taylor said: 'I'm a Black woman. I'm a poor woman. I'm a fat woman. I'm a middle-aged woman. And I'm on welfare. In this country, if you're any one of those things, you count less as a human being. If you're all of those things, you don't count at all.'[10]

Lesbians were demanding their voices be heard, too. In 1970, a lesbian collective known as the Lavender Menace – a reference to lesbians being described as a 'lavender menace to the women's rights movement'[11] by Betty Friedan, president of the National Organization of Women – stormed a feminist conference in New York, hand-delivering a powerful manifesto which described a lesbian as 'the rage of all women condensed to the point of explosion'.[12]

Globally, women were demanding wages for housework and challenging the assumption that domestic labour wasn't *real* labour worth paying for. There are knock-on consequences to housewives not having their own income; if they're being abused by a husband who controls their finances (still not uncommon today), they risk extreme poverty if they leave. In countries which don't offer free abortions, poor women are forced to carry babies to term – if, of course, abortion is even legal in the first place.

This collective action was widespread, synchronised and effective. In Iceland, women across the country took a meticulously planned 'day off' on 24 October 1975. They stopped cooking. They refused to clean. They didn't go to work. Not everyone participated – although an estimated 90 per cent did[13] – but the strike still brought the country to its knees, both personally and professionally. It lit a fire under Iceland's feminist movement, ultimately leading to the election of

Vigdís Finnbogadóttir in the summer of 1980. As a divorced single mother, her presidential success was historic – and in a 2015 BBC interview,[14] she attributes it partly to the shift in perceptions sparked by the 1975 'Women's Day Off'.

Meanwhile, the impact of COYOTE was being felt and replicated outside of the US. Between 1971 and 1974, sex workers in Lyon, France, were being found murdered in increasingly barbaric ways, their bodies tortured and mutilated. In May 1974, a woman named Chantal Rivier – a 'newcomer' who worked 'mostly on the streets' – was found dead, her body stuffed into a sack.[15] These were just the murdered sex workers whose stories made it into the newspapers; it's likely that many others' stories didn't. Terrified for their lives, sex workers had no choice but to watch other sex workers get murdered. Then, they had to watch those murders go unsolved by the same police force that routinely harassed and criminalised them. Unsurprisingly, their fury mounted.

In June that year, around 50 people – mainly sex workers, but also lawyers, journalists and activists – gathered to draw up a statement calling on authorities to protect sex workers. They created a list of demands: sex workers wanted to be able to work together in shared premises for their own safety, without being prosecuted for 'pimping'. They wanted an end to fines, which were handed out frequently and arbitrarily, under a law that allowed police officers to fine anyone for 'behaviour likely to encourage debauchery', a deliberately broad definition. Bars could be shut down if officers suspected that sex workers regularly solicited there, which then caused owners to visually stereotype and ban sex workers from entering. The demands weren't wholly dissimilar to those of COYOTE.

Naturally, because sex work in Lyon was criminalised, sex workers couldn't formally join a union or conduct any kind of legally recognised strike. That didn't stop them. These women held clandestine meetings, plotting ways to make their voices heard. This was a rarity, as disclosing their sex work could see them barred from future jobs and housing opportunities, alienated by their families and friends, and potentially reported to social services and robbed of their children. Anonymity was a prerequisite to safety, but it meant that the vast majority of discussions about sex work happened without their input. These discussions branded them as 'harlots'; they insinuated that these 'bad' women were somehow tarnishing the reputations of 'good' women by merely existing. The subtext was clear: sex workers were a moral scourge, deserving of the violent, often lethal treatment they received.

A key component of sex worker activism is humanising these workers, so often forced into anonymity by the threat of persecution. Perhaps the most in-depth glimpse into the lives and minds of sex worker activists in Lyon in the 1970s is the book *Prostitutes, Our Life* by Claude Jaget. In an introductory essay, written by Margaret Valentino and Mavis Johnson, it becomes clear that many of these women had already been organising for their rights in other jobs. 'They had perhaps been workers sitting in, or students in school occupations,' they write. 'They might already have been on the game and were financially supporting relatives on strike.' Most importantly, sex workers knew their experiences of oppression weren't unique to France. 'The women who are speaking are French,' wrote Valentino and Johnson, 'but their experience is as international as our profession.'

The coalition group of sex workers, lawyers, activists and journalists met frequently in the months following June 1974, often with a fresh murder to discuss. They tried inviting two policemen to a meeting in autumn of that year, which proved

'useless', according to Jaget, 'apart from reinforcing the solidarity of the prostitutes already mobilised'. Instead of listening,
police officers were actively stepping up their repression in
response to the flourishing activist movement.

As months rolled by, the coalition decided they needed to
take action. In April 1975, they began contacting journalists
to spread word of the harassment and criminalisation they faced,
but the rare press appearance – usually conducted by the group's
spokesperson, who called herself Ulla – seemed to scandalise
the French public. Occupation was deemed their best shot at
being heard. It took some brainstorming, but eventually they
decided to occupy Lyon's Saint-Nizier church. There were a
few justifying reasons, some practical, some symbolic. The first
was that 'many of the women were already due to go to prison,
and in church you are supposed to find sanctuary even from
the police', write Valentino and Johnson. The second was that
churches are deemed sacred, moral centres. By occupying a
religious building, the activists were demanding that religious
moralists become outraged by the murders of sex workers.

Protestors knew they would have to drum up some kind of
public support, to encourage people to stand in solidarity with
them, no matter what. On Monday 2 June 1975, around 100
prostitutes entered the church.[16] They occupied the building
quickly and quietly, climbing the steeple to drape a protest
banner, which read: OUR CHILDREN DO NOT WANT
THEIR MOTHERS TO GO TO JAIL. A handful of mem-
bers discreetly handed out statements to the press: 'We're here,
and we're not moving.'

Encouragement came from unlikely places. The church's
priest was interviewed by the *New York Times* soon after the
occupation. He refused to call the police. 'It would not have
been an evangelical act,' he asserted. 'We decided instead

to close the church.'[17] Journalists were granted access to the women, which resulted in their messages being spread worldwide. In the aforementioned article, Ulla is described as a 'tall, freckle-faced, fast-talking blonde', and she makes a powerful statement: 'Prostitution is a product of society, and it cannot be changed by a truncheon.'

In letters distributed to media, the occupants stressed that the vast majority of sex workers were merely women working to financially support their children. This line of argument was meant to address the dehumanising media coverage of sex workers in the media, but it was also intended as an invitation to solidarity. Fundamentally, they were working-class people like any other. Their circumstances weren't unique; people across France knew what it felt like to be exploited by capitalism, to struggle to pay bills despite working full-time jobs, to struggle to secure employment at all. They understood that women were treated as second-class citizens, and – thanks to welfare rights campaigners, and activists reframing perceptions of housework – they were increasingly aware that women's work was valuable, yet poorly compensated, if at all. According to Valentino and Johnson, the public response was one of surprise. 'A lot of people hadn't realised that prostitutes are mothers,' they write. 'Once they did, they understood that prostitutes are just women, not so exotic, not so different, not so bad!'

News of the occupation travelled far and wide. According to Jaget, it became *the* news story in France at the time, and press coverage was – for once – informed and led by the voices of prostitutes themselves. Meanwhile, sex workers inside the church were settling into a cosy, communal living situation, pooling their resources to create sleeping areas, cook big, hearty meals and speak to journalists, who were allowed entry into the church only if they could show their credentials to sex workers stationed at the door. The rule was that 'nobody leaves', which was tricky to say the least. Some sex workers had come last-minute, unable to secure long-term childcare arrangements or to reschedule planned surgeries. Luckily, they were not short of supplies. The general public regularly showed up for the striking workers, bringing them drinks, hot meals, coffee and newspapers. Women living in Lyon 'felt solidarity with the prostitute women', bringing crates of croissants and strawberry cakes to stock up the otherwise basic food supplies within the church. Local musicians came down to play live sets, to liven up the evenings.

In the days that followed, sex workers in other French cities followed suit. Some of them journeyed to Lyon with supplies and messages of support; others staged occupations of their own in the churches of French cities like Toulouse, Grenoble and Montpellier. The protestors took advantage of their moment in the spotlight, holding impromptu educational summits in the form of meetings. The Saint-Nizier churchyard was transformed into a semi-permanent meeting space, where locals could come to pick up educational leaflets, listen to speeches and mingle with local feminist groups, many of whom showed solidarity with the sex workers. Other meetings were held in cinemas, theatres and halls, and organised by the Collective of Prostitutes (known internationally as the French Collective of Prostitutes). Six days into the occupation, Parisian sex workers managed to enter the St Bernard Chapel in Montparnasse.[18] Now, the sex workers' strike was national.

This mobilisation of prostitutes across France sparked the rage of police departments. In Lyon, after ten days of occupation, police officers stormed the church at 5.30am, brutally dragging the women out of the building by their hair. According to reports from the women there that day, officers were 'punching and kicking' them as they hauled them into police vans, as well as liberally beating the women with their police batons. They later learned that the priest, who had been unwavering in his solidarity, had been assaulted by plainclothes police officers.

Historically, religious institutions haven't been quite so welcoming. Evangelicals have long tried to either criminalise or 'rescue' sex workers, offering aid and resources only if they pledge to exit the industry. The organisations offering this conditional help aren't really helping at all; they're modern-day missionaries trying to convert vulnerable sex workers to their religious viewpoints by threatening to withdraw potentially life-saving aid. Yet this religious intervention has galvanised sex worker activism; some sources date the modern sex workers' rights movement back to 1917, when Reggie Gamble, a brothel madam in San Francisco's Tenderloin district, led hundreds of sex workers to the door of a church minister who had been campaigning to close down her business.[19] Sex workers have long been framed as enemies of the church – it's why there's still so much debate around whether Mary Magdalene, a disciple of Jesus, was *actually* a sex worker.[20] Even today, evangelical Christians launch high-profile campaigns to shut down the porn industry, weaponising sex trafficking victims in what is essentially a war on morality.[21]

Still, there *are* progressive churches and ministers, who have come to the aid of sex workers on numerous occasions. It was the Lyon priest's decision not to call the police which kept the sex workers' strike alive for longer, allowing the activists more time to evade capture and spread the word. When sex workers in Soho, London, had their brothels violently ransacked by police in 2013, a local parish priest later made headlines for condemning police behaviour as 'unacceptable and at times unlawful', outlining that pushing these women out of premises and onto the streets would leave them 'more vulnerable to abuse, attack and rape'.[22]

In Lyon, the violent suppression of the occupation may have proven the indiscriminate brutality of the police force, but it didn't succeed in crushing the sex workers' spirits; a few weeks later, they occupied the château of the president of the Republic, hanging a protest banner over the entrance gates and holding an impromptu meeting on the lawn. 'We've come from all over France to visit the château [he] has been able to buy for himself with the money from our fines and our taxes,' said the sex worker spokespeople.

The Saint-Nizier occupation was a landmark moment. It showed how widespread support for sex workers actually was. Gay men – who shared cruising 'beats' with sex workers in red-light districts – took to the streets, handing out pamphlets detailing the activists' demands. Trans women in French-speaking parts of Canada joined the fight, highlighting that trans sex workers were doubly susceptible to arrest, thanks to soliciting laws and police crackdowns on so-called cross-dressing. According to the *New York Times* article mentioned above, there had been 'telegrams of support from women's branches of France's two biggest labour organisations', as well as feminist activists worldwide and 'homosexual militants in France'. Across the country, cars filled with protestors drove past open strip clubs in red-light districts, encouraging the strippers to join them on strike.

Global media took notice of this political stance; even now, the legacy of this strike lives on in the form of International Whores' Day, celebrated annually on 2 June.

Ultimately, the church occupations didn't achieve decriminal-isation in France. Nowadays, the country legislates sex work under what's known as the 'Nordic model', as it was first adopted in Sweden back in 1999. Since then, it's been adopted in other countries such as Ireland, Norway and, more recently, France. In a nutshell, this model – which is vehemently opposed by sex workers[23] – criminalises the *purchase* of sex but not the sale of sex. Criminalising one side of a transaction doesn't exactly help sex workers; clients can leverage their potential prosecution to force workers into accepting bookings under riskier, more clandestine circumstances, and if a sex worker is harmed, either deliberately or accidentally, during a booking, clients risk being criminalised if they call for help.

Yet the occupations did achieve some key gains. The first is that they raised awareness of the harassment of street-based workers and stymied murder rates in Lyon. More importantly, they established sex workers as a political force to be reckoned with, and solidified their budding rights movement in France.[24] Soon afterwards, international prostitutes' collectives began to emerge: there was the English Collective of Prostitutes, established in 1975,[25] and the Prostitutes of New York (PONY), founded in 1976.[26] Increasingly, these groups were acknowledging the importance of solidarity. Soon after its formation, the English Collective of Prostitutes became part of the International Wages for Housework campaign in 1975, galvanised by the prospect of 'building an international network', not only with other sex workers, but with feminist activists more broadly. Through this international campaign, they allied themselves with the likes of Black Women for Wages for Housework and Wages Due Lesbians.

These global groups came together on 2 June 1976 at an event hosted to commemorate the one-year anniversary of the occupations, at the Mutualité cinema in Paris. Wilmette Brown, a prolific activist and member of the Black Women for Wages for Housework campaign in the USA, travelled to France for the event. Brown is known for her belief in coalition politics: throughout her life, she's been active within Black, lesbian and feminist groups, repeatedly underlining the shared oppression meted out by white supremacy and the military-industrial complex. In her rousing speech at the Mutualité, Brown explained that the 'struggle of prostitute women in France' was also the 'struggle of Black women in the USA',[27] who were routinely scapegoated by police officers as potential prostitutes, arrested and charged under anti-loitering laws. Whether or not these women were sex workers was besides the point; the scope of anti-sex work legislation was broad enough that policemen could weaponise it however they saw fit. (In 2021, New York's law – known as the 'Walking While Trans' law, due to the work of activists like Ceyenne Doroshow, was repealed.[28] Prostitute arrests dropped sharply as a result.[29])

In the decades that followed, sex workers worldwide looked back to Lyon for inspiration. In the early '80s, London police officers embarked on a clean-up mission, which invariably involved the increased targeting of sex workers. This increased attention was particularly keenly felt in the city's red-light districts – not only in Soho, the best-known district, but in Westminster and King's Cross, too. In 1982, the English Collective of Prostitutes decided to mimic the occupation of Saint-Nizier, setting their sights firmly on the Holy Cross Church, nestled away in St Pancras, just next to King's Cross.[30] Donning black masks to hide their identities from press, photographers and police, dozens of sex workers filed into the church with sleeping bags and, in some cases, their children in tow. For twelve days, they bedded down to protest criminalisation and to call for the legal rights of sex workers across the country.

Activists were crystal clear on the fact that police

discrimination was a common experience among marginalised groups. In particular, they drew parallels between kerb-crawling laws, which allowed the indiscriminate arrest of anyone suspected of prostitution, and the corrupt 'sus laws' of the time, which empowered officers to stop and search people on the streets who looked 'suspicious' – mainly young Black men.[31] To this day, the Met police remain disproportionately likely to use force and brutality against Black communities in particular.[32] Protestors inside the church drew out these parallels and repeatedly used the language of solidarity in their list of six demands, which included 'an end to police threats, blackmail, harassment and racism'. In media interviews, the sex workers regularly cited the slogan: 'When Prostitute Women Aren't Safe, No Woman Is Safe.'

In 1983, Wages for Housework founder, English Collective of Prostitutes member and pioneering activist Selma James wrote an in-depth account of the occupation, entitled 'Hookers in the House of the Lord'. It's in James's coverage – published in the anthology *Sex, Race and Class*[33] – that we glimpse the extent of queer solidarity on display. When protestors were stuck with no food, they were served regular deliveries of hot meals – one pot for meat-eaters, another for vegetarians – by the employees of LGBTQ+ bookshop Gay's the Word. Gay men set up crèche facilities to care for the sex workers' children as they gave media interviews and negotiated with authorities. Lesbian anti-nuclear activists occupying the RAF's Greenham Common base came out in force, too. James recalls an enthusiastic message sent by a 'Greenham friend', which read: 'Lesbians and whores have taken over a church. Things are really moving!' Activist organisations also lent their support to the occupation; Jackie Forster, founder of lesbian organisation Sappho, came to show support for the sex workers. 'The English Collective of Prostitutes goes back a long way with Jackie and Sappho's Tuesday evenings,' reads James's essay. 'Each time Jackie invited us to speak there, there were always one or two lesbians who gave us a special welcome, making it clear they worked as prostitutes.'

These protests are still held in reverence, inspiring art and activism even today – *The Service*[34] by Frankie Miren is, a gripping novel which centres the experiences of sex workers and features scenes which call back to the famed Lyon occupation. Decades later, queer communities and sex workers continue to protest alongside each other, with increasing acknowledgement that their struggles are – and always have been – interlinked.

Misogyny plays a key role in the shared discrimination between women, whether they be housewives, sex workers or trans women, and queer communities. There's a genre of homophobia rooted in the deliberate feminisation of gay men, which equates femininity with weakness and punishes gay men as a consequence. It's why homophile organisations of the pre-1970s donned a sort of respectable businessman drag – there's a belief that gay men are more attractive, palatable and tolerated if they conform to ideals of masculinity. If gay men are deemed to have 'failed' at masculinity, they're punished. Lesbians face the same excessive gender policing if they're perceived as even slightly butch or androgynous; if they *do* perform femininity in a way that's deemed conventional (the so-called 'lipstick lesbian'), then their queerness is often erased as a result. Trans women are held to punishingly high standards of femininity to prove that they're 'really' a woman (an obvious transphobic dog whistle), and if they *do* perform this hyper-femininity, they're framed as either a danger or a pornographic imitation of a woman. As for trans men, they're viewed patronisingly by TERFs as 'lost lesbians' engaging in a kind of Shakespearean 'man' drag to escape the trappings of misogyny.

Sex workers are similarly forced to navigate society's farcical gender games. According to statistics[35] collated by the English Collective of Prostitutes, around 70 per cent of sex workers are mothers, largely working-class mothers struggling to navigate societal misogyny. Women have long been sexualised whether they like it or not, but when they monetise that sexualisation, they're criminalised and blasted as promiscuous.

This label is weaponised against queer communities, too. Society is obsessed with our sex lives in a weird and intrusive way, asking us about our favourite sex positions (if I hear 'Are you a top or a bottom?' from a stranger once more, I will actually scream) and probing us for details about our genitals without a second thought. Yet somehow, queer people and sex workers are seen as the *real* sexual deviants.

From historical witches burned for promiscuity to today's queer sex workers, in the eyes of those in power, we're all threatening in some way. In the face of this bullshit, we've long come together; these displays of unity live on, usually through oral and otherwise undocumented histories. The Digital Transgender Archive features a protest badge reading: TRANS SOLIDARITY! DECRIMINALISE SEX WORK NOW![36] In Tbilisi, Georgia, a trans man named Bart Nikolo 'spends his winter nights gathering kindling for sex workers',[37] lighting fires to keep them warm on the streets. Especially throughout the pandemic, trans and sex worker mutual aid groups fundraised to provide financial support to sex workers hit hard by their inability to work.[38]

We're even together on the streets. In cities worldwide, gay quarters and red-light districts are either directly next to each other or they're intertwined: just look to the cruising 'beats' of

Lyon as proof. When London's Soho – the city's long-standing gay quarter – was extensively raided as part of the earlier-mentioned sting operation in 2013, scenes were aggressive and humiliating.[39] Flats were smashed up, and officers pocketed the income of migrant sex workers (destined to be funnelled back into the Home Office) and ransacked sex shops, some gay-owned. Sex workers were then herded out onto the streets in their underwear in the middle of winter and photographed without their consent. Migrants – many of whom didn't understand much English – were interrogated by police, who asked if they'd been trafficked. The aim, apparently, was to 'rescue' them. In practice, this meant confiscating their cash, filing charges against them and potentially deporting them back to countries they'd risked their lives to escape.

Soho's residents fought back. 'Soho has historically been the home of sex workers and the gay community,' said an unnamed woman at a London protest, who was interviewed by the English Collective of Prostitutes.[40] 'We made it a rich, culturally diverse place and the big businesses and would-be rich residents who like to move here should remember what gave Soho the qualities that they so admire and want a piece of.'

For decades, we've been tarred with the same discriminatory brushes, piled into the same run-down neighbourhoods and fucked repeatedly by the state. We've been shunned for failing society's weird gender games, beaten with the rhetoric of moral purity and described as inherently sinful. In response, we've come together constantly, forming coalitions rooted in anti-carceral, anti-racist and pro-trans politics, supported by the socialist feminists fighting to liberate *all* women.

These histories are rarely told. They should be — they're crucial, especially as the language of purity continues to dictate policy. There's a rebellious joy underpinning these key moments of solidarity: from the Hookers' Ball drag queens dancing with their dicks out to the defiant sex workers spilling communally into churches, we've seized opportunities to build long-term alliances. Because *we* know that we're not dirty, immoral or sinful; we're simply trying to survive in increasingly shitty circumstances. This powerful kinship between sex workers, queer communities and socialists continues today. It's why we stomp through the streets, brandishing pro-sex work signs and twerking to songs like 'Bitch Better Have My Money'. Continuously, at protests worldwide, we stand together and scream until our throats are sore: 'No TERFs, no SWERFs!'

Piss on Pity

'We were the Ungrateful Disabled. A force to be reckoned with.'

— Barbara Lisicki

In June 1976, thousands of disability professionals from around the world gathered in Tel Aviv, Israel, for the thirteenth world congress of global disability charity Rehabilitation International (RI). Yet, of these thousands, only a handful were actually disabled themselves.

For years, activists had been voicing their increasing frustration with RI. Founded in 1922 by social worker Bell Greve and orthopaedic surgeon Dr Henry Kessler, RI was first known as the International Society for Crippled Children.[1] Between the 1920s and 1970s, the organisation underwent three major name changes: first in 1939, when it renamed itself as the International Society for the Welfare of Cripples, to reflect its increasing focus on disabled war veterans, and again in 1960, when the term 'cripples' was replaced by 'the disabled'. The name Rehabilitation International finally came in 1972, driven by criticism that the term 'welfare' was borne of the charity's paternalistic approach.

The name changes reflected progressive intentions, but the 1976 world congress was an accessibility shit-show, a logistical nightmare which proved to disabled attendees that RI had a *long* way to go in terms of meeting their needs. First scheduled to take place in East Germany, RI made a relatively last-minute switch and decided to host the world congress in Poland instead. These plans were then thwarted by the Polish government's announcement of severe price increases, which would price everyday families out of basic necessities like bread, sugar and meat. Wage raises were proposed, but at nowhere near the rate of inflation, so strikers across the country mobilised and brought Poland to its knees.

This growing political unrest then forced RI to relocate yet again, this time to Tel Aviv, but barely any accessibility plans were made to accommodate the few disabled people who could actually afford to attend. (Disability benefits were – and still are – low worldwide, meaning disabled people are more likely to live in poverty.) Those who did attend were 'loaded up into military vehicles and driven around'[2] – treatment they described as 'humiliating' and especially frustrating, given RI's position as a global disability charity. Sure, the circumstances were shitty, but the chaos of the conference did little to improve relations between RI and the communities it claimed to serve.

At the closing plenary, a man named Liam Maguire took to the stage. A dedicated socialist and trade unionist, Maguire was chairman of the Irish Wheelchair Association and a committed activist, as well as a wheelchair-user himself. According to Linnéa Gardeström, a Swedish delegate, his impassioned speech was a 'very impressive protest against the arrangements'.[3] Maguire had already made progress in Ireland, advocating for solidarity between workers and people with disabilities. Later, in 1978, his union – the Federated Workers' Union of Ireland – submitted a resolution[4] to the Irish Congress of Trade Unions, demanding more accessible workplaces for disabled workers, as well as broad improvements in healthcare provision for *all* workers. Maguire's words made mention of the logistical nightmare, highlighting that even disability-specific organisations were failing to be truly accessible.

The 1976 conference sparked a wave of global action against RI, uniting disability activists – Maguire included – in a determined plan to ensure that disabled voices would be heard en masse at the next RI conference, scheduled for 1980 in Winnipeg, Canada. Ahead of the event, a Canadian collective named COPOH (Coalition of Provincial Organizations of the Handicapped) sent around 50 volunteers to the Winnipeg location, where they met with reporters and shared information with other disability activists. Swedish politician Bengt Lindqvist, a member of RI's Swedish delegation at the time, proposed an amendment to ensure that at least 50 per cent of global RI delegates would be people with disabilities. The amendment was defeated prior to the 1980 world congress.

RI *did* respond to mounting fury by providing travel grants to some disabled workers, predominantly workers in the US, which enabled them to travel to the conference. Yet COPOH remained frustrated, and members started to protest in more disruptive ways. Every day, they compiled a series of updates into a news bulletin from the world congress, *Newsline*. In the mornings, they paid a local taxi company to deliver the subversive bulletin to media newsrooms, the aim being to platform actual people with disabilities, rather than professionals with zero lived experience who were repeatedly speaking over them. RI's organisers heard through the grapevine that *Newsline* was causing ripples within newsrooms and they were nervous – so nervous that one organiser set off on an early morning expedition to intercept one of the bulletins before it reached the press. He was caught red-handed by a reporter, who told him in no uncertain terms to leave.

The final straw came when Lindqvist announced to attendees of the world congress that his proposed amendment had been defeated. Upon hearing the news that RI had essentially denied disabled people a seat at the table of a charity built *for them,* anger bubbled up quickly. Here was concrete proof that RI wasn't listening to him – and seemingly wasn't willing to listen. According to historical accounts, Lindqvist's announcement was met with a 'tremendous roar' which reverberated throughout the conference centre. 'Do I hear you say you want a World Coalition of Citizens with Disabilities?' he asked. The response was rowdy and unanimous, more like a rock concert than a professional conference. This pissed-off enthusiasm paved the way for what – within a matter of months – became Disabled Peoples' International (DPI),[5] a truly global movement rooted in transnational solidarity.

Although experiences of disabled people differ wildly based on where they live and their identities (some also had to contend with racism, homophobia and other forms of structural discrimination), they built a strong coalition. DPI's ad hoc planning committee was comprised of representatives from Canada, Costa Rica, India, Japan, Sweden and Zimbabwe, and they collectively described themselves as a cross-disability coalition, meaning they covered and advocated across a wide spectrum of disability. By 1981, the disability justice movement had gone global, but this progress didn't happen in a vacuum.

Throughout the 1960s, the Independent Living Movement[6] emerged to challenge negative and heavily medicalised views of disabled people, which were used as justification to strip them of freedom. In the US, Canada, Germany and elsewhere, disability activists were advocating for independence and challenging discrimination, including within the realm of caring for elderly people.

For centuries, disabled people were viewed through a paternalistic lens as objects of pity. They were patronised, denied autonomy and treated as sickly, helpless victims, which has always been far from true. There are darker histories, too. In recent years, evidence has shown that Austrian physician Hans Asperger – who conducted some of the earliest studies on autism and created the diagnosis of Asperger's Syndrome, now widely disowned – collaborated with Nazis, rounding up disabled children and sending them off to be euthanised.[7]

Disability has always been a wide spectrum, yet monolithic, medicalised views of disabled communities have silenced their voices, all the while taking the condescending – and sometimes lethal – attitude that they couldn't possibly dictate the terms of their own liberation. This is how the RI model, which focused on helping disabled people, but seemingly didn't view them as worthy of explaining what help they needed, was developed and consolidated: through the notion that disabled people were in need of charity. The Independent Living Movement marked a move away from these approaches, but by the 1970s in particular, views had started to change on a wider level.

One activist who played a key role in shifting these perceptions was Vic Finkelstein. Born in Johannesburg, South Africa in 1938, Finkelstein was raised by Jewish parents in a country fiercely divided by apartheid laws.[8] At 16 years old, he attempted a pole vault and broke his neck, an accident which left him paralysed. The local Jewish community came together to fundraise for his medical treatment, and after undergoing a year-long stint at a hospital in Buckinghamshire, England, he returned to South Africa, now a wheelchair-user.

Finkelstein was political from a young age and, although resistance movements were regularly tracked and banned by the South African government, he became an anti-apartheid activist. Specifically, he became a member of the Congress of Democrats, an organisation for white people in the broader Congress Alliance. Finkelstein was earmarked as an anti-apartheid campaigner, so in 1966, the home he shared with his cousin was raided by police. His cousin managed to get away, but because Finkelstein's home wasn't accessible, there was no chance of him escaping in his wheelchair. He was arrested and then detained under the country's 180-day detention laws, during which time he endured 'torture, deprivation and much hardship' before being sentenced to 18 months imprisonment. Ironically, Finkelstein later said his time in prison 'was the only time in South Africa that things were made accessible for me. In jail I was provided with a bed [political prisoners slept on a mat on the floor] and assisted with "helpers" because, of course, the jails were otherwise totally inaccessible. Somehow, when the state has a need, it *does* make things accessible!'[9]

Upon release, Finkelstein was sentenced to a five-year ban, which meant he couldn't do 'anything to further the struggle against apartheid'. Yet Finkelstein was already pretty much unable to attend activist meetings. As he recalled: 'All these premises, facilities and social meetings are inaccessible anyway.'

Finkelstein fled South Africa shortly after his release, coming to the UK as a refugee in 1968. He soon met his wife, Elizabeth Lewin, a physiotherapist who encouraged him to seek out other politically active disabled people. He became closely involved with the UK-based Disabled Income Group (DIG), which he described as 'one of the largest mass organisations of disabled people in the world'. Much like the feminists fighting for Wages for Housework, and the Black women leading the welfare movement in the US, the demands of the DIG were rooted in financial liberation. The organisation was founded by Megan du Boisson and Berit Moore, who advocated for the social rights of disabled people and drew attention to the fact that disabled housewives were ineligible for disability benefits. Their lens was wide-ranging, focused on financial and social discrimination. Yet soon afterwards, the DIG became male-dominated both in its leadership and its advocacy. Gone was the focus on disabled women or a multi-pronged stance against inequality, replaced by a focus on parliamentary lobbying for benefits.

Just as Finkelstein was growing disillusioned with the DIG, he met fellow disability activists Paul and Judy Hunt, who shared his belief that 'no single issue should characterise any new disability association'. Here, he nodded back to the anti-apartheid struggle, explaining his stance that the key question for any activist should be: 'How do you change an oppressive system rather than spend fruitless time appealing to the prejudiced to cease their discrimination?' This wider focus on systemic injustice laid the foundations for a new organisation, established in 1972: the UPIAS (the Union of the Physically Impaired Against Segregation). To avoid a repeat of the DIG's trajectory, they initially opened up membership only to disabled people. According to Finkelstein, 'this policy . . . drew on the American experience of the women's movement as well as the South African experience where, under apartheid, the oppressed (Black Africans) organised in the African National Congress, while other racial groups supported them in separate alliances.' Disabled members would play an instrumental role in organising and outlining their demands, and then alliances would be formed with solidarity groups. 'To transform society, you've got to work with others,' he explained.

The UPIAS wasn't the only organisation advocating for this reframing of disability as a social issue. In 1968, Swedish activist Vilhelm Ekensteen published a book whose title translates to *In the Backyard of the People's Home*, in which he devoted an entire chapter to sex and sexuality.[10] He condemned the Swedish government for its puritanical teachings on sex, which 'exaggerated fears of promiscuity' and intensified 'feelings of guilt and shame' among disabled people, who struggle disproportionately with isolation.

Ekensteen's critiques were game-changing – for one, they actually acknowledged that disabled people fuck, too. Rather than focusing on medical language, limitations and pity, he conceptualised disability justice within a wider framework of welfare, sexual discrimination and loneliness. Ekensteen saw the need for a new form of disability justice, so he set up the Anti-Handicap organisation in 1969; by 14 April 1970, members were slapping 'Anti-Handicap' stickers across inaccessible buildings in Lund, Sweden, an action which gathered enough traction to spawn a copycat protest in Stockholm later that day. The group released its *A.P. Bulletin* in 1970; the newsletter positioned disability as a social issue, which required a broad-strokes activism rooted in anti-capitalism and anti-discrimination more broadly.

Finkelstein's activism was integral to the later establishment of the 'social model of disability', which posited disability justice as a social issue above all. In 1975, he co-authored a 24-page pamphlet, *Fundamental Principles of Disability*,[11] which argued: 'It is society which disables physically impaired people. Disability is something imposed on top of our impairments, by the way we are unnecessarily isolated and excluded from full participation in society.'

Across the pond, US protestors spent the 1970s growing pissed off at constant delays to the implementation of Section

504, an amendment to the Rehabilitation Act which legislated against financial discrimination and a lack of welfare provision for people with disabilities. In 1977, campaigners coordinated 504 sit-ins across the country. In San Francisco, disabled lesbian activist Kitty Cone played a pivotal role in organising her city's sit-in.[12] Cone was an activist veteran; she'd protested the Vietnam War, organised within the Young Socialist Alliance and worked at the Centre for Independent Living, spearheading campaigns to cut curbs and install accessibility ramps. Throughout these years, she'd learned the importance of coalition-building, and she brought that knowledge to the sit-in.[13]

For months, she did vital outreach work, which paid dividends during the 25-day occupation of the San Francisco HEW (Health, Education and Welfare) office. Black Panthers continued their community survival programmes by bringing hot meals to the protestors, as well as publishing statements of support in the *Black Panther Newspaper*. Crucially, the messaging framed disability justice as a civil rights issue; in a media release, the Panthers wrote: 'The issue here is human rights – rights of meaningful employment, of education, of basic human survival – of an oppressed minority, the disabled and handicapped.'[14] Machinist union workers drove protestors from San Francisco to Washington in their trucks to extend the scope of the sit-ins. Dinners were donated by lesbian co-operatives, gay-owned restaurants and the Glide Memorial Church. The Butterfly Brigade – a little-known San Francisco group of self-described 'drag queen vigilantes'[15] – smuggled walkie-talkies inside, so protestors could get their messages out. When the building's water was switched off, a local lesbian bar owner started coming in to wash the hair of protestors, and those who stayed throughout the sit-in recall gay women in particular 'throwing the best parties'.

The 504 sit-ins were successful in getting the regulations signed and writing what Cone described as a 'new chapter in American history', one which eventually culminated in the 1990 passage of the Americans with Disabilities Act (ADA).

These early victories – as well as the work and words of activists like Finkelstein and Ekensteen – were essential to the 1981 creation of DPI, and they weren't earned in isolation. It took food, support and solidarity from other groups, as well as the transformative introduction of the social model of disability, which moved the needle of debates around disability justice, focusing on *structural* discrimination rather than individual people.

If the world were made truly accessible, countless obstacles would melt away; if disabled communities were listened to, we'd have a way better idea of how to accommodate their needs. The social model underlined that people with disabilities are people, too. They have personalities, opinions, sex lives and struggles, many of which are tied to broader human rights issues. This framework laid the foundations for a broad coalition movement rooted in justice for *all* marginalised communities, one built upon analyses of mutual oppression and solidarity.

DPI still exists today, and its vital advocacy for disabled communities continues, but it wasn't the only notable moment of progress in 1981, a year earmarked by the UN as the International Year of Disabled Persons.[16]

That same year, Ian Stanton became the first disabled person to be expelled from the UK's Queen Elizabeth Rehabilitation College. During his stay, he saw a never-ending series of shitty practices and documented them in his radical newsletter *The Tuppenny Terrible.* The newsletter was seemingly never digitised, so the exact details of this poor practice aren't documented online, but increasingly, Stanton's history of activism is.[17]

Stanton was born in Oldham, Manchester, in 1950 and spent his childhood dreaming of becoming a printer. His twenties were spent battling Buerger's disease; by the end of the 1970s, he was a double amputee. It was in the early 1980s, with *The Tuppenny Terrible,* that he began to gain a reputation within activist communities for his quick wit, sarcasm and use of irony to make caustic political points. As a journalist, he sought out stories of injustice and detailed them extensively, largely for the Greater Manchester Coalition of Disabled People, founded in 1983. In 1986, the collective launched a journal entitled *Coalition,* and Stanton was appointed as its editor.

As well as writing and editing stories, Stanton developed a knack for producing tongue-in-cheek lyrics about his experiences as a disabled person living in a deeply ableist world. Perhaps the best-known example is his song 'Tragic but Brave', which features iconic lyrics about 'pissing on pity', an endlessly quotable 'fuck you' to the notion that disabled people need sympathy, not rights.

Throughout the late 1980s and early 1990s, British television station ITV was one of the leading fundraisers for disability organisations, but their approach was borrowed from the paternalistic handbook: think celebrity guests and emotive video packages designed to tug on the heartstrings of guilty viewers, urging them to pledge money to those in need. To disability activists, this rhetoric was all too familiar, and it flew in the face of the work they'd done to frame societal barriers as the problem, not the disabilities themselves. ITV's telethons seemingly missed these memos entirely, from the moment they were first launched in 1988.

Each year, activists protested the broadcasts.[18] By 1992,

they'd decided to take matters into their own hands, and create a radical protest destined to go down in the annals of disability justice.

Barbara Lisicki – who, as Wanda Barbara, was a key member of the Tragic but Brave collective, alongside Ian Stanton and Johnny Crescendo, the pseudonym of her then-partner, blues guitarist Alan Holdsworth – played a leading role in organising the demonstration. 'The starting point was simple and visceral,' she explained, in an in-depth 2018 blog post.[19] 'We hated what we saw – a pity-fest, and were engulfed in rage and shame each time it was broadcast.' In a 1990 phone call with Anna Thorpe, a disabled woman, Lisicki began to realise that other disabled people shared her views. So, in March 1992, she set about contacting press outlets, reaching out to activist collectives across the country, plotting a mass demonstration outside the July 1992 telethon.

The messaging was deliberately brash and ballsy, designed to cause a stir. At a 1990 protest, police had confiscated a PISS ON PITY placard for being too offensive – clearly, it was a mantra subversive enough to stick. So ahead of the July '92 protest, 100 T-shirts were printed with this slogan. The black-and-pink tees borrowed the colour palette of the AIDS activists behind ACT UP, who used a hot pink, upside-down triangle as their symbol, a reference to the pink triangles painted on the uniforms of gay concentration camp prisoners in Nazi Germany.[20] The T-shirts were an unequivocal success. People queued to buy their PISS ON PITY merch, and cops were furious. When Lisicki was told by a police officer to take hers off, she calmly replied that she was wearing nothing underneath and that there were 99 other T-shirts being worn. She was allowed to keep it on. Press headlines decried the 'Ungrateful Disabled' – a term which Lisicki revelled in.

According to Lisicki's accounts, the protest outside the '92 telethon was a 'party, a celebration, a gathering of up to two thousand disabled people and our supporters showing that we were proud, angry and strong.' She wrote: 'We were the Ungrateful Disabled. A force to be reckoned with.' Outside, 'people gave speeches, sang, danced, performed comic monologues and poetry in sign language'. And not even a police barricade could stop a handful of the activists from infiltrating the studio. The telethon's celebrity guests were bemused, to say the least. According to attendee Elspeth Wilson, her favourite memory was of the faces of 'celeb types . . . arriving in their limos. Their faces beaming generously to the grateful masses, then, when realising we weren't the grateful masses, turning to bewilderment and possibly horror. What sort of PR disaster might this be?'

The demo marked a turning point in the history of British disability activism; from the contact list of organisers, the DAN (Disabled People's Direct Action Network) was born.[21] Holdsworth similarly described it as a turning point in public perceptions of disabled people. 'In the end, it was ridiculous for Telethon to portray us as helpless cripples when the very same people were battling with police, barging into their studios and demonstrating in their thousands against the very notion,' he wrote. 'Disability Pride had truly arrived.'

No mention of Disability Pride would be complete without mention of Mad Pride, founded in the 1990s as Psychiatric Survivor Pride Day by Lilith Finkler, a community legal worker at Parkdale Community Legal Services in Toronto, Canada. Here, she met countless ex-patients of psychiatric facilities, as well as scores of undocumented, homeless and otherwise vulnerable people.[22]

The building itself sits on Queen Street, a stone's throw from one of the largest psychiatric facilities in Canada, built in the 19th century as a 'lunatic asylum'.[23] Finkler, a queer, Jewish, Libyan woman, had been detained in psychiatric facilities herself and knew how cruel the treatment could be. Patients were routinely physically restrained; until the late '70s, lobotomies were prescribed as 'treatments' for 'insanity'. Even those deemed by these facilities to have recovered – Finkler calls them, and herself, psychiatric survivors – are released into the world with a diagnosis marred by stigma, making them vulnerable to homelessness, unemployment and abuse.

Finkler got to know these psychiatric survivors not as patients but as people. She played cards with them in the lobby of the Queen Street Mental Health Centre, as it was known in the early 1990s; she visited tenants living in boarding homes; she spoke to homeless survivors spending their nights on park benches. By 1993, Finkler had decided that something needed to change.

Instead of turning to professionals, Finkler decided to engage directly with people like herself, who had been admitted to psychiatric institutions. 'Many of us . . . have been told that we are not capable of contributing to society,' she wrote in a 1997 paper. '[We're told] that we should take our medication and stay out of the hospital if we can.' Finkler wanted to counter this narrative by proving that psychiatric survivors could build something of their own, that they could come together in solidarity and change the public image of mental illness. To do so, she looked to the mobilising histories of Black, queer and disabled movements, which led to the idea of a Pride event.

From its inception, Mad Pride was built on the understanding that marginalised communities are more likely to be impacted by medicalisation and psychiatric facilities. Throughout history, Black and disabled people have been treated as experimental subjects, or as objects of study. LGBTQ+ people have historically been forcefully detained and made to endure 'conversion therapies' – which, in some cases, involved electroshock torture and lobotomies. Like psychiatric survivors more generally, many were given the so-called choice of either submitting to detainment and treatment or being imprisoned. Finkler was clear about these links from the moment she set about rallying an organisational committee, but not everyone was on board: 'When I distributed our posters at Gay and Lesbian Pride Day, I also received negative responses. Some gays and lesbians did not want to be associated with "crazies" and felt we were "stealing" their day,' she wrote, before quoting someone who flatly said: 'Name your day something else. Don't name it after us!'

In reality, these communities are all bound by the societal notion that they aren't 'normal' – and that state interference is the only way to rectify that. It's about punitive conformity, and this is a thread that remains. We might not be hearing about lobotomies anymore, but we *are* hearing politicians seriously consider writing trans communities out of existence,[24] or making public health policies which treat disabled communities as collateral damage in the quest to 'return to normal' – in other words, to return to capitalism – in the wake of a lethal global pandemic.[25]

Finkler understood these links early on and, despite the handful of negative responses, her organising committee set about distributing leaflets, sticking up posters in subway stations, advertising through local radio stations and asking 'regulars' at the Queen Street Mental Health Centre to invite patients verbally. They had to get creative, bearing in mind that many psychiatric survivors would be homeless and living on tiny amounts of cash, and therefore unlikely to see newspaper advertisements.

Ground rules were set that 'racist, sexist, and other hurtful jokes' would be met with zero tolerance, and that the Pride events should be as accessible as possible. Reporters and media were barred from the events, which were varied: from workshops on tenants' rights and the heavy policing of survivors to clothes swaps and free meals, Finkler's 1993 Pride event sowed the seeds for what would ultimately become a global movement.

More than two decades later, there's a rich, worldwide history of the Mad Pride movement. In a 2015 video report on Paris's Mad Pride,[26] attendees in brightly coloured wigs and hats grin as they describe themselves as 'crazy and proud to be crazy'. In France, Mad Pride is usually celebrated around Bastille Day, an annual celebration which commemorates the liberation of prisoners who were jailed indefinitely and arbitrarily in Bastille, a Parisian fortress-prison stormed by French revolutionaries in 1789.[27] Mad Pride is linked to Bastille Day in the sense that patients detained and mistreated in psychiatric hospitals are often held indefinitely and stripped of any autonomy. Now, 'mad' is used by protestors as an umbrella term to unite an entire coalition of people with disabilities.

The events themselves are joyous, raucous and infuriated in equal measure. Protestors brandish colourful placards with slogans which reclaim slurs and insults. Activists of all descriptions are usually present at the event, showing solidarity with those protesting. The grand crescendo of Mad Pride is almost always a 'bed push'[28] – where Gay Pride events have decorated floats, Mad Pride events have hospital beds draped in colourful throws and spray-painted with protest slogans.

Thirty years after their inception, these protests are as necessary as ever. Better, though, is that there's an increasing public awareness of Mad Pride – and mad studies, the emerging radical study of mental health histories and discrimination – that's trickling across borders. In 2019, a group of around 50 demonstrators travelled from all across Mexico to hold the country's inaugural Mad Pride;[29] by 2023, scholars were documenting the rise of mad studies across Latin America,[30] highlighting a growing call to centre the experiences of 'mad people', whose voices are either deemed untrustworthy or excluded from conversations about their own treatment. Websites and forums are increasingly connecting these people, and offering mad studies a place to flourish outside of academia. Naturally, these online hubs are translating into more in-person Mad Pride events, which have been held over the last few years in Brazil, Argentina and Chile, and the movement looks set to keep expanding.

In 2022, following a years-long hiatus, London's Mad Pride returned.[31] As the cost of living crisis pushed yet more people into homelessness, and the UK government's response to the Covid-19 pandemic made it clear that disabled people were viewed as disposable, organisers gathered hundreds of protestors for a day filled with food, fury and a hunger for liberation. The Mutual Aid café – a London-based, pay-what-you-can initiative – 'filled [demonstrators'] bellies with warmth, love and delicious food',[32] wrote the organisers, and clothes and other resources were handed out freely to those who needed them. 'There is nothing madder, more fringe-like, more lunatic than being crazy enough to look after each other in a world which teaches us the opposite,' they continued. Solidarity collectives of all descriptions – fighting for an end to detainment, imprisonment, policing and more – gave speeches which were 'stirring, emotional, grief-stricken, rageful, joyous, beautiful, hopeful and all mad as fuck'. A hospital bed was draped in a

Palestinian flag, making a strong statement of solidarity: 'We are proud to scare off psychs and colonisers alike!' As hospital beds were pushed along the banks of the River Thames, tourists 'collectively turned with shock or confusion, the same expressions and thoughts, no doubt, that members of the public would have had when our lunatic elders first started the bed push'.

Similarly, Piss on Pity has remained a mantra for disability activists in the UK, animating yet more playful, disruptive protest. In 2019, a vacant shopping centre unit in Wakefield, West Yorkshire, played host to an exhibition entitled *Piss on Pity: Disabled Artists vs Charity*.[33] The exhibition was dedicated to Katherine Araniello, described in the exhibition's accompanying zine as a 'legendary artist and performer'.

In 2007 – after more than a decade of studying and creating art – Araniello co-founded the Disabled Avant-Garde with deaf artist Aaron Williamson, creating political, satirical and hilarious work about disability justice, all the while rallying against the more respectable corners of the disability arts movement. In 2012, she began blogging under the alias of SickBitchCrips,[34] using biting humour to parody what she saw as the condescending portrayals of disabled athletes as 'superhuman' by the Paralympics. Araniello was unapologetically punk, and never shied away from the direct-action tactics of rights movements past and present. In 2013, she took aim at *Charity*, a seven-metre-tall sculpture by artist Damien Hirst.[35] The sculpture is of a disabled young blonde girl, who clutches a teddy bear and holds a collection tin for the 'Spastic's Society' – the former name of the charity now known as Scope. Araniello dressed up as the little girl in an act of public protest, donning a blue sack dress, comically circular dabs of pink blush and a papier-mâché wig, parking her wheelchair behind a plinth painted with the words: SickBitchCrips Pity Charity. In 2019, Hirst's *Charity* made its way to the Yorkshire Sculpture Park[36] – so, in tribute to Araniello's send-up, the *Piss on Pity* exhibition was held in Wakefield.

Araniello's *Pity*, the aforementioned performance art piece, was one of the works shown at the exhibition, which came accompanied by a collage-style zine, compiled by curator Gill Crawshaw. Inside, there's a scathing manifesto which takes aim at the right-wing government's austerity policies, introduced in the UK in 2010. 'Disabled people are fighting a sustained attack on their lives and dignity under the government's austerity programme, with cuts to public services and welfare benefits,' the manifesto reads.[37] 'A last resort to many, charities are inadequate in the face of this assault.'

Even now, it remains the case that people with disabilities globally are more likely to live in poverty, to face housing instability due to a lack of accessible, affordable housing, and to be unemployed. The artists behind *Piss on Pity* are clear that their barriers are structural, that 'zombie charities' driven by a quest for 'airbrushed' public images are often established by 'billionaires who set up charitable foundations as big as their egos', motivated more by tax write-offs than benevolence. The artists underline a difference between 'well-intentioned' individual fundraisers – 'the people who are sponsored to shave off their hair, who run marathons in the memory of a loved one, the volunteers rattling collection boxes' – and the 'greedy charities' who underpay their workers while they 'willingly bankroll galleries and exhibitions'.

These critiques are anti-capitalist and reminiscent of the disability justice movement's wider, radical history: from impassioned speeches by pissed-off trade unionists to key contributions by anti-apartheid campaigners, disability justice has always been rooted in broader, global struggle.

Today's radical artists and activists continue this legacy, placing disabled people firmly at the centre of a wider, more complex web of inequality. No longer are disabled people seen as powerless victims. They're making punchy, avant-garde art; in the case of Canadian queercrip icon Loree Erickson, they're even making porn,[38] challenging the ableist stereotype that disabled people are inherently sexless. They're fighting long-standing barriers, uniting alongside other marginalised communities and, through organisations like DPI and beyond, maintaining the truly global presence of the disability justice movement, fighting for change through transnational solidarity.

Dispatches from the AIDS Crisis

'An army of lovers cannot lose.'

– Queer Nation

In June 1981, American physician Dr Lawrence Mass published a column in gay newspaper *New York Native*,[1] in which he outlined rumours he'd been hearing of an unknown disease spreading throughout the gay community.

Perfectly healthy, young gay men were being struck down with an elusive skin cancer named Kaposi's sarcoma, which causes angry, cancerous blotches to form. Simultaneously, there were reports of gay men suffering with a rare but severe form of pneumonia, typically reported in severely immuno-compromised patients. This article is now thought to be the earliest-known documentation of AIDS in America. Weeks later, the *New York Times* reported on a 'rare cancer in 41 homosexuals'.[2]

Even now, there's widespread debate around the timeline and origin stories of the AIDS crisis in the US. According to some accounts, AIDS was a 'gay plague'[3] spread through sexual deviance. In the eyes of others, the people of Haiti – the world's first free Black republic – contracted it in their homeland, bringing the disease to foreign shores through immigration.[4]

This narrative still exists; in 2021, former US President Donald Trump claimed Haitians 'probably have AIDS', describing their arrival on American shores as a 'death wish for our country'.[5] Why did he say this? To justify turning away Haitian asylum seekers, of course.

Perhaps the most commonly held view is that the earliest cases in the US showed up amongst white, middle-class gay men in coastal cities. In a 2021 article published in the *American Journal of Public Health*,[6] researchers describe Ken Horne, a 'gay sex worker in San Francisco', as the first person to be diagnosed with AIDS in the US, back in 1980. Early coverage of AIDS and HIV – the virus that can lead to AIDS – is often unsubtle in its homophobia, and it didn't take long for these stories to result in similar homophobic coverage worldwide.

In October 2014, an 'international team of scientists' made global headlines with their theory that AIDS originated in Kinshasa, a city in what's now known as the Democratic Republic of Congo. 'Their reports say a roaring sex trade, rapid population growth and unsterilised needles used in health clinics probably spread the virus,' reads a BBC report.[7] The scientists also attribute the virus's global prevalence to railway expansion, implying that Congolese sex workers became vectors of disease, passing the virus to foreign labourers.

These origin stories are steeped in the language of invasion. Especially over the last few years, we've been reminded that pandemics are always political – just look at the 2020 spike in anti-Asian racism, the result of Covid-19 being traced back to Wuhan, China.[8] It doesn't matter how heavily these origin stories are contested, how extensively they're rewritten as new details become available. Narratives carry the same rhetoric: that marginalised bodies are vectors of disease; that migration is an act of invasion. There's long been a tendency to anthropomorphise AIDS in particular, to frame it as inherently villainous, a poison that resides solely within the bodies of sexual 'others'.

In reality, there's evidence to suggest that AIDS was killing marginalised people in the US way earlier than the 1980s. In 1987, the *New York Times* ran a headline: 'Boy's 1969 Death Suggests AIDS Invaded U.S. Several Times'.[9]

The boy referred to was Robert Rayford, a 15-year-old Black teenager, whose 1969 death in St Louis, Missouri, was retroactively linked to AIDS-related complications. To date, there's plenty of misinformation and speculation around Rayford's death. In the aforementioned research report, which named Ken Horne as the 'first' diagnosed AIDS patient in the US, researchers list Rayford as an example of a 'gay or bisexual man'. In truth, little is known about Rayford. The most comprehensive account of his life, and death, was published by *The Chicago Tribune* in 1987. What we do know is that he died on 16 May 1969.[10] For nearly two years, he had suffered from frequent swelling in his lower legs and genitals. In interviews with clinicians, he described having sex with the girl next door; from an early stage, doctors treated his case as one of a sexually transmitted infection. Gradually, he started to lose weight, to grow more frequently short of breath. He was constantly tired, and his skin became pale and sallow. His chlamydia – still one of the world's most common STIs, usually easily treated by antibiotics[11] – was spreading; as his physical health deteriorated, doctors noted that chlamydia was swirling through his bloodstream. After showing brief signs of getting better, Rayford's blood cell count plummeted. He quickly succumbed to a fever and died.

Medical professionals at the time knew they were dealing with something unprecedented, so in the last two years of

Rayford's life, they took all the samples they could: of lymph nodes, blood and tissue. Yet Rayford himself was clearly untrusting of the medical system – unsurprising, given its histories of blatant racism. In interviews, scientists describe him as sullen and uncommunicative. A microbiologist, quoted by the *St Louis Post Dispatch,* said: 'He was the typical 15-year-old who is not going to talk to adults, especially when I'm white and he's Black.'[12]

Naturally, accounts describe Rayford as tired of being poked, prodded and pressed for personal information by older strangers, even if they were supposed to be working in his best interests. His admission to having sex with his next-door neighbour was reluctant, but he was never once asked about homosexuality, nor was he subjected to a rectal examination. In the *Tribune* article, it's stated that 'circumstantial evidence suggests that he may have been the recipient of anal sex'. The 'evidence' in question was that Rayford lived in the so-called ghetto of St Louis, that he had severe proctitis – rectal inflammation – and that he had Kaposi's sarcoma on his rectum and anus. None of this is concrete proof that Rayford had contracted AIDS through anal sex, but doctors speculated anyway. 'He could have been a male prostitute,' continued the aforementioned microbiologist. 'He certainly lived in the environment where that was possible.'

None of this was helped by the fact that news of the AIDS crisis first broke in the early 1980s, a period marked by consumerism and conservatism. In 1981, Ronald Reagan gave a US presidential inauguration speech which pledged a future rooted in God-fearing values. 'We are a nation under God, and I believe God intended for us to be free,' he said. 'It would be fitting and good, I think, if on each

Inaugural Day in future years it should be declared a day of prayer.'[13]

This shift to the right was arguably a backlash against the 1970s, a decade which saw all the groups I've explored in this book make bold leaps toward freedom, such as the Gay Liberation Front, the Black Panthers, COYOTE and various others. The 'free love' movement of the 1960s had born political fruits, and although the gains were minimal in concrete terms, evangelists saw the rising presence of these communities as an attack on their old-school values. On 22 March 1980, a group of Christian leaders delivered a petition to then-president Jimmy Carter's office, which demanded an end to the advancement of gay rights. 'God's judgement is going to fall on America as on other societies that allowed homosexuality to become a protected way of life,'[14] said Bob Jones III, a staunchly homophobic evangelical leader. In further remarks made to the Associated Press, he said: 'It would not be a bad idea to bring the swift justice today that was brought in Israel's day against murder and rape and homosexuality. I guarantee it would solve the problem post-haste if homosexuals were stoned, if murderers were immediately killed as the Bible commands.'[15]

It's no accident that just a year later, Reagan – a born-again Christian – was voted into office, buoyed by a campaign which advocated for family values. Meanwhile, the US AIDS epidemic was quietly bubbling up in coastal cities. Fear was trickling through conservative communities, as news of the virus then known as GRID (Gay-Related Immune Deficiency) was spreading through the grapevine. Increasingly, calls to ban blood donations from 'high-risk' donors were growing, and the US FDA wasted no time in doing so. In 1983, the FDA announced a lifetime ban on blood donations from sexually active gay and bisexual men. Other countries quickly followed suit and, to this day, a handful of countries still uphold the ban.[16]

At the time of the ban, AIDS was still a relatively new disease, but it was one tainted by stigma. Gay men had to beg to be treated with dignity, and those who *did* want to help AIDS patients were harshly stigmatised: in September 1983, New York physician Joseph Sonnabend was threatened with eviction from his office building for treating AIDS patients, resulting in the first AIDS discrimination lawsuit.[17] Meanwhile, Reagan didn't even utter the word AIDS until 1985.[18] Especially in the first half of the 1980s, research wasn't being funded; the little money that *did* come was often the result of mutual aid and LGBTQ+ fundraisers. As a result, gay men – and especially gay men of colour – were dying in their thousands; by the end of the decade, an estimated 100,777 deaths[19] were reported to the CDC, making the disease a lead killer of young adults.

Increasingly, the role played by women in these early years of the AIDS crisis – both within and outside of the US – is being highlighted. The British, BAFTA-winning series *It's a Sin* drew from the real-life experiences of Jill Nalder, who first learned of AIDS after watching her gay male friends 'leave for home and never come back'. Nalder later learned that they were going home to die, and it wasn't uncommon for families to erase all trace of their sons' deaths. Nalder is one of many activists who scrambled for information about the virus, all the while visiting and nursing friends who had contracted HIV. 'I became like a dictionary of AIDS-related infections,' she told the BBC in a 2021 interview.[20]

In the US, San Diego's Lambda Archives held a celebratory event in 2016 entitled *Heroines, Pioneers and Trailblazers* to spotlight the often-forgotten lesbians of queer history. Archive staff conducted a series of in-depth interviews with these women, but one of the most arresting collectives highlighted in the exhibition was the Blood Sisters of San Diego. Barbara Vick moved to San Diego in 1974, when she was young, free and single.[21] She was a regular at gay and lesbian bars and coffee houses, and became closely involved with the city's LGBTQ+ community as a result. But when the first murmurs of GRID began trickling out in the early 1980s, she – like many others – convinced herself it was a distant problem, as the earliest cases were largely concentrated in New York, San Francisco and Los Angeles. Vick met her long-term partner Tracy in 1981 (they eventually married when it became legal in 2008), so wasn't personally concerned about AIDS transmission, especially as lesbians were being categorised as a relatively low-risk group. But Vick, a regular blood donor, didn't like that the gay blood ban marked out gay men as a demographic to be treated differently.

San Diego had a private blood bank at the time, which operated differently to state-run banks. 'You could designate a fund,' she explained in a 2010 interview, now archived online.[22] 'An employer, for example, could have all their employees donate their blood to the company's blood bank, so if anyone got ill and needed a blood transfusion, they could use credits to withdraw it [from their designated fund].' One day, in the middle of donating, it occurred to her that she could set up one of these specially designated funds of her own.

Vick was a member of the Women's Caucus of the San Diego Democratic Club, an organisation which, at the time, was still in its infancy. Enthused by the prospect of being able to show tangible solidarity with gay men, she suggested to the other members that they start their own fund, in the name of the Democratic Club. That way, gay men – and, if the men wished, their close friends and loved ones, too – could use specific credits to access the blood supplies reserved for them. Vick recalls that other members of the Caucus weren't so enthusiastic about the idea, but they rallied together anyway. In a brainstorming session, one of the women (Vick doesn't recall who) suggested calling themselves the Blood Sisters of San Diego. Not only was it a fairly literal descriptor of what these women would do, but the idea of mentioning 'blood' in the name also struck a symbolic chord. Blood symbolises family ties. These 'sisters' were figuratively designating early AIDS patients as their kin and treating them as such.

AIDS treatment was wildly experimental at the time, driven in no small part by the US government's lack of desire to research a virus which was thought to only kill the marginalised. The conditions experienced by early AIDS patients were horrific. Some were treated like lepers, locked into hospital rooms to die alone, with no contact with others for fear of contagion.[23] In 1985, rumours of an HIV treatment drug named AZT began to circulate; by 1987, the FDA had approved it.[24] The drug was a big earner for pharmaceutical companies but, gradually, evidence started to suggest that it basically didn't work. Not only that, but patients began reporting hideous side effects. Michael Cottrell, a gay man from the UK diagnosed as HIV-positive in 1985, suffered chronic headaches, nausea and debilitating muscle fatigue. Studies have also linked AZT to a heightened risk of anaemia, and patients had to endure a seemingly endless rotation of blood tests, which similarly heighten the risk of iatrogenic anaemia. For AIDS patients, blood transfusions were increasingly vital, yet even gay men who weren't infected with HIV couldn't donate their own blood to help.

Determined to proceed with their plan, the Blood Sisters set about mocking up flyers and choosing a date – 16 July 1983 – for their very first blood drive. Their expectations were modest; at most, Vick expected maybe 50 women to show up. To her surprise, almost 200 women queued around the block to donate.

Buoyed by this early success, the San Diego Blood Sisters set about creating logos, pins and flyers to keep their momentum going. According to Vick, an early flyer was inspired by the bicep-flexing Rosie the Riveter, a cartoon icon who starred in a campaign to recruit women for factory and shipyard work during the Second World War. Dressed in a denim shirt, her black, immaculately coiffed hair tucked beneath a red polka-dot headscarf, she became a symbol of patriotic resilience. 'I think lesbians like that sort of thing,' joked Vick. Although the 1980s were seemingly a decade of power suits and corporate feminism, many lesbians still suffered extreme employment discrimination and were likely to have less money. 'I don't think [they] economically had a lot to give,' explained Vick, so blood was something they could donate instead.

The Blood Sisters of San Diego held annual blood drives in the years following 1983, but requests from lesbian activists in other cities and states, like Long Beach and Pennsylvania, came in thick and fast. Similar blood drives were held in Denver, Boston, Los Angeles, Baltimore, Memphis and Washington. Lesbian women across the United States joined the Blood Sisters to stand in solidarity with gay men, offering support, friendship and bedside care, as well as their blood.

Prior to the 1980s, GLBT was the most common umbrella term used to describe gay, lesbian and trans communities. It's thought that this term was replaced with LGBTQ+ in the late 1980s to acknowledge the vital activism of lesbians throughout the decade, much of which directly benefited gay men diagnosed with AIDS.[25] The Blood Sisters continued to hold regular drives, but they took further measures, too: they served as nurses, illegally organised clean needle projects to reduce transmission rates through intravenous drug use, and amplified the voices of those who died of AIDS.

These histories of lesbian solidarity are crucial. As we've seen in earlier chapters, one of the main tensions that splintered previous LGBTQ+ groups was the tendency to speak over lesbians, to alienate them from what quickly became predominantly white gay male movements. The Blood Sisters adopted the powerful moniker of blood, of 'chosen family' – when our families abandon us, we create our own – to imbue their activism with tenderness, a sense of intimacy and urgency. These bonds are important, especially today; more than ever, there are frequent attempts to divide the LGBTQ+ community, to pit us against each other. Stories like these are proof that these divisions are sometimes tactically exacerbated, weaponised to break potential bonds of solidarity. Clearly, even after decades of tension between lesbians and gay men, the Blood Sisters were motivated to step forward when their help was needed the most.

Of course, queer communities aren't the only ones that know what it's like to be stereotyped as 'contagious'. In Britain throughout the 1800s – this was largely before the word 'homosexual' was even coined in 1868[26] – sex workers were targeted constantly by law enforcement, particularly if they were poor. The Vagrancy Act of 1824[27] claimed that 'every common prostitute wandering in the public streets . . . and behaving in a riotous or indecent manner . . . shall be deemed an idle and disorderly person'. This rhetoric still exists today; it's why 'prostitute cautions'[28] are dished out by police officers, sometimes to sex workers who aren't even working, or street outreach workers simply offering them resources.

The streetwalker has long been framed as a vector of social contagion, a woman – and, in society's imagination, it's *always* a woman – who lures in otherwise 'good' men. But gradually, this framing of sex workers as transmitters of disease became more literal. In 1864, the Contagious Diseases Acts were passed in Britain. Later expanded in 1866 and again in 1869, the roots of these laws could be traced to other countries, like Greece and India. First and foremost, these laws were designed to prevent soldiers being infected by sex workers; the framing was that 'good' soldiers were being infected by 'dirty' women, and armies were losing colonial fighters in the process.

As scholar Kimeya Baker highlights in a brilliant article[29] on how these laws were used to control the bodies of women, the British Army was shifting to an emphasis on so-called 'moral masculinity' at the time, steeped in the evangelical language of purity and abstinence. It's a stereotype as old as time, weaponised not just against sex workers but against so-called bad women more generally, as we saw in the 'No TERFs, No SWERFs' chapter. As Baker outlines, the notion was that sex workers were slutty sirens luring in hapless soldiers with 'substandard mental facilities', so they needed to be stopped.

Again, this argument still exists, just in different guises: it's why sexual assault victims are asked to show their underwear in court[30] to see if they were 'asking for it'; it's why some schools insist young girls dress like buttoned-up matrons so as to avoid 'tempting' rabid, horny young boys seemingly incapable of self-control.[31]

The main purpose of the Contagious Diseases Acts was to create the condition that 'women suspected of prostitution' had to 'register with the police and submit to an invasive medical examination'. This is why so many sex workers campaign for decriminalisation and *not* legalisation – in countries like Germany and the Netherlands, the state keeps a close eye on sex workers and makes their work legal in only limited contexts. It also creates official records of prostitution. Given these horrible histories of state-enforced sex worker control, it's not exactly surprising that so many don't trust the authorities.

With this in mind, it was only a matter of time before sex workers became a target of HIV moral panic. In a 1990 report 'Women Prostitutes in the AIDS Era',[32] published in the journal *Sociology of Health & Illness*, the authors explain that sex workers were stigmatised when the realisation dawned that straight people could contract HIV, too. According to their research, sex workers were especially stigmatised across Africa, as 'prostitutes' were 'blamed for the rapid spread of infection in a number of Central African countries'. In Western countries, namely the US and the UK, those who already vehemently opposed sex work on moral grounds were presented with new ammunition to use against sex workers, even though same-sex transmission rates and intravenous drug-user transmission rates were the highest.

In a series of interviews, it becomes clear that sex workers at the time were not only personally afraid of contracting HIV, but they also stood in solidarity with their gay friends, whom they saw dying and falling ill on a regular basis. An interviewee known only as Sarah highlights that multiple communities were impacted by media rhetoric. 'There's been a huge link-up between the idea of the spreading of AIDS through prostitution, drug abuse and gay men,' she said. 'They've all been lumped together as a sort of group.'

These demographics were all bonded by, at least to conservative eyes, a sense of moral failure, a rejection of puritanical values. The specifics didn't necessarily matter; when it came to

HIV, these communities were banded together and treated as a joint scapegoat.

It's unsurprising, then, that in the decades since AIDS was first named in the early 1980s, sex workers – often in coalition with drug-users and queer activists – have played a pivotal role in HIV activism. These communities tend to share an approach known as 'harm reduction'. Instead of aiming to abolish high-risk behaviour, they use safety measures to mitigate potential harms.

One of the earliest examples comes courtesy of Gloria Lockett, a Black woman who started doing sex work in the 1970s to support her family.[33] Lockett was based in San Francisco, where it had long been established that 'whores and queers' were the backbone of the growing gay liberation movement. Lockett had already been mobilising for change and for sex workers' rights on a state level, but in 1982, she became deeply involved with COYOTE and a group of affiliated activists: Margo St James, Carol Leigh (the so-called 'Scarlot Harlot'[34] widely credited for coining the term 'sex work'), and another activist named Pricilla Alexander. They began holding weekly 'Bad Girls' Rap Groups', informal meetings where pissed-off women could vent their frustrations. These groups were aimed at marginalised women, and they helped to grow the cacophony of voices calling for sex workers' rights.

By 1984, a sex worker named Dolores French had similarly been welcomed into the San Francisco fold. French was already prolific in Atlanta, thanks to her appearance on talk show *The Phil Donahue Show*. She spoke alongside three other sex workers, all of whom spoke from behind semi-translucent screens. French was offered this option too, but, after much deliberation, and a carefully considered letter to her parents, which let them know for the first time that she was working as a prostitute, she chose to appear 'face-out', making her the first self-proclaimed prostitute to speak on national television. Already, French had experience in advocacy and organising – in fact, it was her advocacy for sex workers' rights that had motivated her to get into the business in the first place, equipped as she was with contacts and realistic information about the ups and downs of the industry. But French's political experience was wide-ranging.

In her autobiography, *Working: My Life as a Prostitute*,[35] French describes 'working on political campaigns in Atlanta for ten years', as well as having 'contact with at least a dozen political groups, from Gay and Lesbian Rights to the Georgia Civil Liberties Union to the Democratic National Party.'

The rise of COYOTE and the sex workers' rights movement in San Francisco was nationwide news for working women, but French decided she could live a life of comparative luxury in Atlanta compared to San Francisco, a 'high-competition city' where 'too many women were working as prostitutes', she said. Plus, sex workers in Atlanta were calling out for an organisation of their own. In 1982, French obliged, forming an organisation called HIRE – Hooking is Real Employment – as well as a genius merch collection, the star of which was a T-shirt reading: 'I'm for HIRE'. She wrote to COYOTE leader Margo St James to ask if HIRE could become a sister organisation; St James obliged and sent over the paperwork.

Lockett, French and the other key members of COYOTE knew, given the history of scapegoating sex workers, that sex workers would be blamed in some way for the AIDS crisis, and that the press would be wildly misinformed. In *Working*, French argues that official statistics were focusing disproportionately on street sex workers, and ignoring the fact that many of these street sex workers were also intravenous drug-users. French wasn't saying this to distance herself from or to stigmatise these women. Instead, she was making a key argument: that, for these workers, class, race and drug use were much more important risk factors than their occupation. 'Generally, the lower the socioeconomic level of the prostitute, the better the chance that she will not practise safe sex,' French explained. 'Safe sex requires money for condoms, the time to bother insisting that clients use condoms, and some sense of a future.' To make things trickier, clients would often – and still do – pay more for bareback sex, meaning there's a financial incentive for hard-up sex workers to take the risk. Clinical sexual health settings which offer free condoms can be a daunting prospect for sex workers, especially those also navigating intravenous drug use. The fear of stigma can be greater than the potential reward of getting free condoms and, even then, access to free sexual health products is rarely unlimited. Elsewhere in *Working*, French underlines that street sex workers are more likely to be sex workers of colour, due to generations of institutional racism.

Similarly, Lockett knew that racism would play a role in the framing of street sex workers as vectors of disease. So, in 1984, she founded and became the Executive Director of CAL-PEP,[36] the California Prostitutes Education Program. Lockett knew that state-sanctioned HIV outreach programmes would alienate anyone who distrusted the government or who wouldn't be counted in official research. CAL-PEP centred these populations – street workers, Black sex workers, drug-users – in its advocacy, using street-based and mobile rapid HIV testing clinics to not only identify potential cases of HIV but to educate sex workers and focus on getting them into treatment if they needed it.

There were obvious answers: expansive access to free

contraceptives; better sex education; needle exchanges to prevent transmission of AIDS through dirty needles; judgement-free treatment for those suffering with substance abuse and – last, but by no means least – decriminalisation of sex work, which would allow sex workers to engage in AIDS-related services without risk of arrest. While governments turned a blind eye to these actual solutions, sex workers were left to fend for themselves; according to French, at a 1984 sex workers' convention, attendees were given bottles of lubricant containing spermicidal nonoxynol-9, thought to prevent vaginal transmission of HIV. Later studies have found it doesn't – in fact, as it's usually shot into the vagina with a lube shooter, it can actually cause lesions and therefore increase transmission risk[37] – but, as with misoprostol, the so-called DIY abortion tablets, criminalisation forced marginalised communities to take matters into their own hands.

As well as HIV activism on a street and community level, some sex workers made such gains within their work that governments took notice and enlisted them to help shape HIV policies and outreach programmes.

In Thailand, the government decided to dish out free condoms to sex workers as part of its 100 Per Cent Condom Use Programme, first established in 1989. Described in a 2000 UNAIDS report[38] as a 'collaborative effort among local authorities, public health officers, sex establishment owners, and sex workers', the initiative required brothels and massage parlours to promote condom use. If they failed to comply, they were threatened with closure. The logic was that clients were refusing to frequent establishments which *did* require protection, and sex workers were losing cash in the process. But if *all* premises upheld these rules, sex workers couldn't be undercut by clients who tried to negotiate lower rates for protected sex or threatened to go elsewhere. HIV transmission rates dropped quickly as a result, and by 1992, every province in Thailand had adopted the policy. Statistics show that the programme 'increased the use of condoms in sex work from 14 per cent in early 1989 to over 90 per cent since 1992', and before long, countries such as Cambodia, the Philippines, Vietnam and Myanmar were implementing similar policies of their own.

Already, many sex workers in Thailand were politically active, thanks largely to the establishment of Empower Foundation, a sex worker organisation founded by Chantawipa Apisuk in 1984.[39] Throughout the 1980s, sex workers were forming self-help groups and sharing peer-education tips and tricks – community-led harm reduction, basically – so it seemingly wasn't difficult to get sex worker advocates on board to help with outreach. However, there were still doubts that the programme would work. As the report notes, a regional newspaper in Chiang Mai sent an undercover journalist to hire a sex worker for unprotected sex, presumably to write some salacious exposé about sex workers flouting the rules. To his surprise, none would agree to it.

There were some flaws in the policy, namely that it enforced tight regulation by increasing sex workers' exposure to police – which, as we've seen already, goes against what sex worker activists have generally called for. Seemingly, distrust of the police stemmed from common knowledge that police officers would sometimes accept bribes to ignore violations. As a result, sex workers were 'unfairly exposed to exploitation', while those exploiting them were comparatively rarely punished. That's not to mention that vast swathes of Thailand's sex industry wouldn't have met the conditions for the programme, as they weren't deemed reputable or official in any way.

But more broadly, the programme took a holistic approach,

which did undoubtedly prioritise the health of sex workers. Condoms were freely available in every hotel room, and sex workers were given vouchers to stock up on extras and to buy other sexual health supplies. Sex work activists held regular meetings to educate workers about HIV prevention; in 1996 alone, '100 meetings were held with groups of sex workers, an indication of the program's emphasis on frequent contact with sex workers'. The Thai government understood that funding sexual health would save them cash when it came to treating sexually transmitted infections more broadly – prior to 1997, 'Thailand's Public Health Ministry earmarked 50 million baht ($1.5 million) for the distribution of free condoms, not only to sex workers, but to queer communities and other at-risk groups, too.

Despite the measurable benefits of the programme, a 1997 financial crisis and the misinformed perception that HIV is no longer an important issue led to gradual defunding. Yet sex workers have continued to share resources and educate one another. Charismatic approaches have worked, too: AIDS activist and former politician Mechai Viravaidya has been so synonymous with safe-sex advocacy that he's now affectionately known as 'Mr Condom'.[40] In the past few decades, he's held condom-blowing competitions in schools across Thailand, as well as using the harm reduction method of sending mobile sex education vans through Thai provinces to raise awareness of safe sex and distribute safe-sex materials.

Especially for marginalised communities, who had every reason to distrust the moralistic messaging of government institutions, harm reduction programmes were vital – and increasingly, they're being spot lit.

In late 2022, the Ex Convento del Carmen in Guadalajara,

Mexico, held an exhibition entitled *Presentes: 40 Años de Visibi-lidad.*[41] To call it groundbreaking would be an understatement. First, there's the location: until the 1860s, the Ex Convento church was both a sacred site of holy worship *and* a symbol of the cultural dominance demanded by institutionalised religion. Now, the Ex Convento is something entirely differ-ent. Its hallowed halls have been transformed into a cultural centre, which often pays homage to the most subversive activist collectives in the country's history.[42] This exhibition fit the bill perfectly. Not only was it a tribute to the activists and groups that paved the way for today's LGBTQ+ Mexicans to enjoy greater rights and respect, but the exhibition was also a testament to the power of solidarity, as well a glimpse into the wry, tongue-in-cheek humour that activists have em-ployed when challenging the invisibility of HIV and safe-sex education.

In a room dedicated to safer-sex activism throughout the AIDS crisis, an unusual sculpture was tucked away in the corner: a life-sized, blue-painted, anthropomorphic condom. A decidedly chirpy mascot, he had a gleeful grin spread across his ribbed (for *her* pleasure!) face, accessorised by a thick black moustache. Taking centre stage on his torso was a painted, twisted red ribbon, a long-standing symbol of AIDS activism.

Humour can be crucial to the spirit of downtrodden com-munities. When the world feels bleak, pointless and nihilistic, a few shit jokes can make bitter pills easier to swallow. It's a powerful communication tool, too – increasingly, books like *A Comedian and an Activist Walk into a Bar: The Serious Role of Comedy in Social Justice*[43] are underlining the potential of comedy to make social change. In the case of AIDS activism, sex was being framed as a death sentence. But sex education seen solely through the lens of fear does nobody any favours.

It makes us bury our heads in the sand in a desperate bid to fuck without panic. As a result, we miss out on key info. So some AIDS activists set about creating witty, informative campaigns aimed at high-risk communities. In response to the governments and politicians enabling the mounting death toll, they made pissed-off artistic statements and staged disruptive, direct action protests which targeted the most openly bigoted politicians.

One of these politicians was Jesse Helms, a notoriously homophobic senator who spearheaded a 1988 legislative amendment which prohibited the funding of AIDS programmes which supposedly 'promote, encourage or condone homosexual activities'. As if that wasn't enough, to add insult to injury, he was quoted by the *New York Times*[44] as saying: 'We have got to call a spade a spade, and a perverted human being a perverted human being.' Another quote: 'There is not one single case of AIDS in this country that cannot be traced in origin to sodomy.' Of course, Helms was wrong; he was simply determined to use a public health crisis to spread his own bigotry – and HIV activists weren't about to let his rhetoric pass unchallenged.

This challenge took time. Throughout the late 1980s, the most common form of HIV protest was a 'die-in', during which activists laid on the ground playing dead to symbolise the lives lost to HIV through government inaction. But during the summer of 1991, activist Peter Staley was growing increasingly annoyed that Helms hadn't yet been a target of AIDS activist groups like ACT UP and Queer Nation. So, he began to formulate a plan. 'One of the best tools an activist can use is humour,' he wrote in a 2008 opinion piece for *Poz* magazine.[45] 'If you can get folks laughing at your target's expense, you diminish his power.'

Incidentally, it was a climate activist – Twilly Cannon, a prominent campaigner within climate justice organisation

Greenpeace, who taught new recruits how to drape enormous banners over the sides of bridges and buildings – who helped to bring Staley's vision to life. After deliberating, he came up with a hilarious plan: to encase Helm's two-storey colonial house inside a gigantic, yellow condom. Staley set about contacting 'gay spies' to track down Helms's address; he reached out to the only three manufacturers of giant inflatables in his local area and gathered a range of cost estimates for a building-sized condom, which ranged from $3,000 to $15,000. The eventual condom was bankrolled by music industry mogul David Geffen, a known philanthropist, and was made of the same material as most standard-issue parachutes, enabling it to be rolled neatly into a large duffle bag.

The ensuing scene was one of glee, rebellion and chaos. Staley and his fellow activists worked as a well-oiled machine, using electrical wires, ladders and rubber mallets to drape the condom over the house in less than five minutes, to avoid being interrupted by the police. They had rung the doorbell the night before to make sure Helms wasn't at home. 'The last thing we wanted was to spend our lives in jail for giving a senator a heart attack,' joked Staley. An infuriated neighbour – later identified as Becky Norton Dunlop, who played a key role in staffing Trump's Republican administration – was filmed screaming at cops. 'You guys don't want to tangle with these people,' she reportedly said. 'You don't want to get AIDS.'

Comparatively, the police officers called to the scene took a more relaxed approach, apparently sniggering with laughter at the political prophylactic. They gave the activists time to deflate and remove the condom; in the end, the only punishment doled out to the AIDS activists on that fateful day was a parking ticket.

Throughout the 1980s and 1990s, when the crisis was at its

peak, conservatives seized the opportunity to double down on the narrative that queer people of all descriptions are ir-responsible perverts. For decades prior to the virus's spread, laws had criminalised what governments saw as 'deviant' sex: in the United Kingdom, the legal language of the Buggery Act 1533 treated fucking an animal and having anal sex as acts of equal disgust.[46] By the 1980s, artists were re-appropriating this narrative and having a laugh with it. The gay leather sub-culture was in full force; huge, hulking men with handlebar moustaches were the illustrated mascots of the movement, sporting gigantic bulges and barely-there leather chaps. Sub-versive pioneers, like Tom of Finland, made it their mission to create hyper-sexualised parodies of conventional masculinity.[47] There were hot and horny policemen wielding their batons with glee, and homoerotic sailors in skin-tight white flares, which strained to cover their hulking dicks. Embracing smut, filth and sex became a key protest tactic for queer communities, one which showed an unwillingness to cover up and 'tone it down' (still a homophobic dog whistle today), instead flaunting their sex lives and amping them up, all to make pearl-clutching conservatives uncomfortable.

Activists looked to this imagery when creating safer-sex informational materials, many of which actually pre-dated the height of the AIDS crisis. In Denver, Colorado, a group of local activists came together to stage 'Safe Week' in May 1981. Flyers were handed out in gay bars, encouraging people to get tested for sexually transmitted infections and then to wear a 'safe' button afterwards, to urge others to do the same. The flyer even had a sexy illustrated mascot: 'Le Hunk Safe'.[48] In gay cruising culture, there was a visual language known as the 'handkerchief code'.[49] Tucking a handkerchief into your back pocket not only let strangers know you were down to fuck, it told them exactly *how* you wanted it. Within the community, it was – and still is – known as 'flagging'. Colours correspond to kinks: black means you're looking for 'heavy BDSM'; yellow signifies a desire for golden showers; red indicates that you're into fisting, and so on. Le Hunk Safe sported a handkerchief of his own. It was chequered, a pattern used by activists to indicate a preference for safe sex.

Those most likely to be affected by the AIDS crisis were gaining their own first-hand knowledge, both through research and the experiences of watching their loved ones battle the virus. Gradually, it became clear that HIV transmission *could* be prevented and that abstinence wasn't the only way. AIDS activists took the aforementioned examples of safer-sex activism and used them as a blueprint for a distinctly tongue-in-cheek form of information sharing, one which prioritised knowledge rather than perpetuating fear.

Groups like the Gay Men's Health Crisis – co-founded by Dr Lawrence Mass, the author of the *New York Native* article which opened this chapter – ran a hotline for those impacted by HIV, and experimented with different kinds of posters. In one, an aardvark-like animal – with a hint of a grin and a long snout – sits on a grassy field, its entire head and body covered in what looks like a baggy brown condom. 'Thank goodness for latex,' reads a speech bubble.[50] The Gay Men's Health Crisis took other opportunities to dispel long-held myths rooted in the initial description of a 'gay plague'. In a 1993 advertisement for their hotline, three couples are pictured: one gay, one lesbian, one straight. The words 'hot', 'young' and 'safe' are plastered across the eye-catching purple poster,[51] using the language of porn to make safe sex look sexy and to remind viewers that HIV impacts straight people too. In fact, UK statistics collated by the Terrence Higgins Trust in 2022 showed rates of HIV transmission were highest in heterosexual populations for the first time in over a decade.[52]

These community-led resources saved the lives of marginalised people when governments were more than willing to ignore mounting death tolls to politicise a virus which killed indiscriminately. The heartbreak of queer communities is hard to overstate; not only were people seeing their friends and chosen families dying from a virus which *would* have been preventable, they were being shamed for their sexuality, in some cases even told that AIDS was a punishment for their sins.

None of this advocacy was concentrated through a single-issue lens, nor was it happening solely in the UK – as we'll see in the 'Treatment Access Campaign' chapter, it sparked vital activism worldwide. AIDS activists were ballsy, witty and politically lucid, illuminating key links of marginalisation. The likes of Queer Nation and ACT UP had wide-ranging aims: they created homeless shelters for people living with AIDS, rallied against anti-immigration laws and launched multi-pronged campaigns rooted in coalition-building and solidarity. Meanwhile, sex workers were passing around spermicidal lube and educating their clients on condom usage, building harm reduction initiatives of their own.

We still don't know the full story of how AIDS spread across borders, but what we *do* know is that pandemics create scapegoats, and those scapegoats are usually often already marginalised. Rather than trying to identify a patient zero, activists have spent decades plugging the gaps in governments' lethal healthcare policies, pooling their blood, expertise and resources to survive one of the world's deadliest crises.

Pits and Perverts

'It won't change overnight, but now 140,000 miners know that there are other causes and other problems. We know about Blacks and gays and nuclear disarmament, and we will never be the same.'

– David Donovan

Before the days of corporate sponsors and splashy, rainbow-branded floats, Pride parades were grassroots efforts organised by volunteers, and often on a shoestring budget. London's 1984 Gay and Lesbian Pride almost didn't happen, allegedly because overstretched volunteers were running late with their plans. Admittedly, it wasn't unusual for plans to come together last-minute, yet 1984 was even more hastily planned than usual, leaving organisers scrambling to deliver on what was, by that point, an annual celebration. Luckily, the march was a success anyway: according to an edition of newspaper *Gay News*,[1] more than a thousand sweaty, joyous revellers gathered in the sunshine to mark what was to become a landmark year.

For context, there *were* early cases of AIDS-related deaths reported in the UK in this year, which cast a sombre cloud over the event. The first European AIDS Conference was held in 1984, and the vital HIV charity the Terrence Higgins Trust was established. Yet, death tolls in the UK were still relatively low; at year-end, 108 cases had been reported, 46 of which had been lethal.[2]

The real headline story of 1984's Gay and Lesbian Pride was the decision of activists Mike Jackson and Mark Ashton to shake buckets in the hope of raising much-needed funds for striking miners. Arthur Scargill, then-president of the National Union of Miners (NUM), called the strike in March 1984, after widespread pit closures resulted in the loss of around 20,000 jobs. What started as an industrial dispute became a bitter, protracted battle to save working-class livelihoods, exemplified by the slogan: 'Close a pit, kill a community.'[3] NUM's bank account was frozen, leaving members in dire need of solidarity from outside mining communities.

Making the decision to support the miners was far from easy. Both Ashton and Jackson were initially sceptical, yet NUM members had a presence at that year's Pride parade and, as the groups got to know each other, tensions started to ease. In the aftermath of the event, Ashton and Jackson were part of a gay lobby group who met with a striking miner to hear more about the community's hardships. 'I had this semi-antagonistic attitude towards the organised labour movement, trade unions, macho het bully boys,' recalled Ashton, quoted in the research of scholar Diarmid Kelliher.[4] Yet he soon realised that miners were 'thinking about things that we'd never actually expected [them] to think or talk about'. This meeting became the catalyst for a more permanent solidarity group, known as Lesbians and Gays Support the Miners (LGSM).

Ashton was already involved in political organising, as a member of the Young Communist League (he went on to become the general secretary), so he called an impromptu get-together in his ramshackle south London flat for anyone who wanted to get involved. He published an invitation in the local gay newspaper *Capital Gay*, yet that first meeting attracted just 11 attendees. Despite the rocky start, membership grew rapidly within just a few months.

Ashton may have ended up an activist hero, but he hadn't always been politically minded. He was born in Oldham, one of England's best-known mill towns, to a family with deep ties to the textile manufacturing industry.[5] Early in his childhood, Ashton relocated with his parents to Northern Ireland but, after grappling with his identity, he came out as gay and moved to London in 1978. Just 18 years old, he arrived in the capital in search of more vibrant, queer-friendly surroundings, and he quickly found them – within months, he was working as a barmaid at a King's Cross gentlemen's club, where he dragged up in a blond beehive wig to crack jokes and pull pints for rowdy punters. Ashton's political awakening came in 1982. His family had relocated temporarily to Bangladesh for work, so he decided to fly out for a three-month visit. The country was in a state of political turmoil at the time, its leadership sporadically and brutally upturned by military coups, including one in 1982. Ashton was horrified by the poverty and inequality he saw, and made it his mission to fight inequality from that point onwards.

Jackson was a close friend of Ashton's, raised in a 'very working-class background' in Accrington, Lancashire. He moved to London at 19 years old and called the volunteer-led helpline Gay Switchboard – incidentally, the duo actually met when Ashton later interviewed Jackson to volunteer at the switchboard. 'I was persuaded that there was nothing wrong with me,' Jackson recalled in an interview with *Tribune Mag*,[6] 'and that what was wrong was this thing called homophobia. And then the penny dropped, and I moved from being this really depressed teenager into this kind of firework of joy and anger at the same time, which is a heady mixture.' It was a game-changing revelation, one which taught him 'about other people's liberation – Black people's struggles, women's struggles, these became much clearer to me because I could see the common thing about oppression in our culture'.

Back at Ashton's flat, the 11 recruits at the first LGSM meeting started to brainstorm what the solidarity group could actually offer. Union bank accounts had been frozen, but there was a solution to be found in the form of 'twinning' with a particular mining community, a more direct way of offering support to specific communities. The decision was taken to twin with the mining community in Dulais Valley, South Wales – 'We did actually have some initial links with the area through a member of the Young Gay Socialists group, a person named Hugh Williams, who was from Swansea,' explained Martin Goodsell, an LGSM member interviewed on the *Working-class History* podcast.[7]

The work started in earnest soon afterwards, with the primary aim being to raise as much cash as possible. It was a political alliance for sure, but it was ultimately practical – mining families were being effectively starved by a ruthless government, so the simple goal was to keep food on their plates and ensure their bills were paid. Bucket-shaking remained LGSM's favourite fundraising method, so activists lined the pavements outside gay bars, bookshops like London's iconic Gay's the Word and other queer community hubs to collect donations. Some people were immediately supportive, handing over their spare cash willingly alongside words of encouragement. Some had personal ties to the mining communities – perhaps their family members were miners or they knew about the situation through friends of friends. Others were simply pissed off that the government was annihilating a predominantly working-class industry. Not everyone was so understanding. Throughout months of fundraising, one question recurred: 'What have the miners ever done for us?'

This line of questioning is understandable. Despite the partial decriminalisation of homosexuality in the UK in 1967, and the post-Stonewall efforts of radical collectives like the Gay Liberation Front, acceptance was a long way off. This was especially the case in rural, working-class communities, for a number of reasons, but without a nuanced lens it's easy to buy into the assumption – amplified by classist media – that all working-class people are inherently homophobic. I've done it myself, drilling it into my own head that I could somehow escape homophobia by fleeing my working-class village.

Spoiler alert: that's bullshit. Even as I achieved the mythical premise of social mobility, discrimination followed me, just in different guises. There's nothing inherently working-class about bigotry. Yet LGSM's detractors bought into this narrative, uncritically accepting the argument that supporting working-class miners means redirecting resources away from the LGBTQ+ community and giving cash to potential homophobes in the process.

Jackson and Ashton knew better than this. Both were born into working-class backgrounds before moving to London, so understood how it felt to grow up in an isolated, out-of-the-way town where queer people felt the need to be 'closeted' to avoid being ostracised. This lack of visibility can be alienating at best, soul-destroying at worst. It can feel like the only option is to run away to supposedly more progressive big cities, where the much larger population meant more chances to meet other LGBTQ+ people.

The catch-22 is that queer people moving away to big cities means small towns and villages are left with little representation, which then affects rural working-class communities. If we up and leave, then the people who stay in those communities start to believe they've never met a queer person in their life. So they turn to mainstream media, which has historically either erased us entirely, painted us as predators or diluted us into one-dimensional stereotypes. Then there's the news, which at the time of the Tory government wasn't exactly heartening – to say Thatcher's government was institutionally homophobic was a vast understatement.

The best-known example of this discrimination is the 1988 passage of Section 28,[8] a bill which barred the teaching of LGBTQ+ materials in school. The seeds of this legislation had been planted years earlier; in 1986, a government amendment prevented teachers from mentioning same-sex relationships in front of students, and local libraries began quietly banning books and pulling any apparently queer material from their shelves. Thatcher saw queerness as a moral contagion, and never minced her words when saying so. At a 1987 conference, she said: 'Children who need to be taught to respect traditional moral values are being taught they have an inalienable right to be gay. All of those children are being cheated of a sound start in life. Yes, cheated.'[9] Although Section 28 was technically designed to stamp out LGBTQ+ *materials*, it ended up being weaponised against LGBTQ+ school teachers, who could be flagged as suspicious and monitored if their colleagues even suspected they were gay.[10]

Thatcher's blatant homophobia sparked chaos. Lesbian protestors abseiled into the House of Lords, barged their way into television studios and handcuffed themselves to desks, all to raise awareness of and protest against Section 28.[11] Their tactics were callbacks to the early days of the Gay Liberation Front and the rabble-rousers we met in the 'Making Mischief' chapter, but their driving force was pure, unabashed rage at the erasure of queer communities and histories.

This erasure is important because every opportunity to interact with us represents a chance to humanise us; it's a chance to find common ground, to begin to nurture the bonds of solidarity.

Jackson has spoken extensively about how his experiences informed his mantra: prejudice cannot withstand proximity. In a 2015 interview[12] with *The New Statesman*, he fleshed out definitions of two main types of homophobia, the first of which he described as lazy, learned and cultural. People who fall into this kind of homophobia base their opinions of LGBTQ+ people on crude assumptions, which generally start to melt away when they come into contact with actual gay and queer people. This exposure to multi-faceted, complicated people leads to an understanding that LGBTQ+ people are more nuanced and interesting than the stereotypes suggest. In Jackson's words: 'They say to themselves: "Oh you haven't got two heads, you don't eat babies for breakfast and you actually get pissed like I do. What's the difference?" That's the majority of homophobia. But then there is this residual, tiny number of people who are toxically homophobic.'

This works both ways. Some reluctance within the gay community to support the miners was driven by suspicion that these miners were homophobic by default, but that was based on stereotypes too. Working-class communities were as much a government enemy as LGBTQ+ communities, painted as lazy, ignorant scroungers – stereotypes which persist to this day. Plus, they were – and are – disadvantaged in their own ways: priced out of elite education, starved of the vital community resources needed to thrive, and stuck in patterns of low pay, exploitative contracts and dead-end jobs, if and when they did get work.

We can broaden this out to other groups, too. It's evident in the arguments which scapegoat immigrants impossibly as both job thieves *and* benefits scroungers, trans women as sexual predators and Black men as hyper-violent. These myths are peddled to break potential bonds of solidarity, to encourage us to see ourselves as too intrinsically different to ever mobilise together. It's a tactic of oppression, and it's an effective one.

Those in power hate unions specifically because they pull different people together with a collective aim: to challenge exploitation. It's not hard to argue that Thatcher feared solidarity – the miners' union had successfully toppled her plans for privatisation in 1981, after all – and the rhetoric that frames LGBTQ+ communities and working-class communities as distinct, incompatible groups plays into the wider aim of discouraging recognition of shared struggles. The fact that so many people questioned LGSM's motives, in some ways insinuating they suspected miners were inherently homophobic, proves that these tactics worked.

Ashton kept his tongue lodged firmly in his cheek when addressing these questions. He had a wicked sense of humour, so whenever he was asked what miners did for queer people, he'd respond: 'Miners dig for coal, which produces power, which allows gay people like you to dance to Bananarama until 3am.'[13] It was a mocking answer in a sense, but it made a key point – mining was dirty, dangerous work, and so many people were reliant on the labour of miners without even realising it. Ashton's soundbite generally did the trick, encouraging even the most stubborn gay passers-by to dig into their pockets.

The Dulais Valley mining community gradually opened their eyes, too. When they first learned they were being tirelessly supported by gay activists, the general reaction was one of bewilderment, and the occasional ignorance-driven homophobic comment. On the *Working-class History* podcast, Sian James – a politician married to one of the striking miners in Dulais Valley – recalled: 'There were lots of typical working-class jokes, like: "You'll have to stand with your backs against the wall." The women just got really cross with this and said, "Oh for god's sake! We should be so far beyond this now."' Attitudes changed quickly, especially as LGSM made good on their promise to support the community; according to Kelliher, they raised thousands of pounds through raffles, jumble sales and bucket-shaking. The twinned communities built a friendship, too. Before long, miners and their families had invited LGSM to South Wales, where they bonded over pints and shit jokes at the local pubs. In return, gay activists hosted the miners in London, taking them to gay bars and introducing them to their chosen families.

None of this should be surprising; it's simply a story of people from different backgrounds coming together. In the *Tribune Mag* interview, Jackson called bullshit on the myth that these communities were polar opposites to begin with. 'That's just wrong,' he explained. 'One of our group, Clive Bradley, said that it makes it sound like we introduced them to opera and pasta. It wasn't like that at all. We learned a great deal.' He described it as 'a way the working-class is maligned, that the men are all thugs'. Yet there is something beautiful about an act of solidarity forging long-lasting friendships between communities conditioned to believe they had nothing in common.

By the end of 1984, bucket-shaking wasn't enough. The government had continued to hold strong, so LGSM brainstormed

ideas to boost their fundraising efforts – and as Ashton's
Bananarama gag implied, members agreed that queer communities know how to party. It's a fact evidenced in the annals of
queer history: from the raucous molly houses of 18th-century
London[14] to the glamorous salon scenes of Paris and Berlin,[15]
there's ample proof.

These plans to accelerate fundraising led to a momentous
benefit gig, cheekily titled Pits & Perverts – a nod to homophobic press coverage that indicated all queer people were
filthy and promiscuous, rhetoric which had intensified as news
of a so-called 'gay plague' named AIDS had begun to trickle
into public consciousness. For Pits & Perverts, a punchy black,
white and pink poster was designed[16] and later screen-printed
onto a series of fundraising T-shirts, still found in queer ward-
robes – including my own – today. The gig was to be held at
Camden's iconic Electric Ballroom on Monday 10 December
1984, and Ashton said all were welcome. 'They don't have to
be gay, that's the point,' he explained. 'It's a coming together
of all different kinds of people.

Pits and Perverts built on the lineage of solidarity-themed
extravaganzas like the Hookers' Ball, with the added bonus
of bringing the communities – by this point, close friends –
together. Tickets were priced on a sliding scale – £2.50 for
unwaged, £4.50 for waged, free for miners – to make the event
accessible, and organisers scored a huge coup by landing the gay
pop powerhouse group Bronski Beat as headliners, then riding
a wave of mainstream success thanks to their anthemic single,
'Smalltown Boy'. Dressing up was positively encouraged, and
miners travelled from across the country – some on an LGSM-
branded minibus, paid for with money raised through ticket
sales – to show their appreciation, shake their butts to Bronski
Beat, and mingle with a crowd of queer activists, drag queens

and working-class comrades, all keen to stick two fingers up to the government.

It was a raucous night filled with laughter and chaos, which managed to raise thousands of pounds to sustain the miners throughout their long, drawn-out strike. In the aforementioned podcast, Sian James recalls 'lugging' the cash back to South Wales in a 'bloody great big fake snakeskin handbag!' The proverbial cherry on top came courtesy of David Donovan, an NUM rep who gave a heartfelt speech to the tipsy, euphoric crowd. 'You have worn our badge, "Coal Not Dole", and you know what harassment means, as we do,' he said. 'Now we will pin your badge on us; we will support you. It won't change overnight, but now 140,000 miners know that there are other causes and other problems. We know about Blacks and gays and nuclear disarmament, and we will never be the same.'

The NUM remained true to their word. Although the strike was eventually forced to come to an end in 1985, the unionised miners remained steadfast in their solidarity. They showed up at Pride events to march for the rights of queer people and, as the AIDS crisis ravaged LGBTQ+ communities, they collected money and nursed AIDS patients – who were stigmatised and literally locked away by medical institutions – in their hours of need.

Especially in recent years, these stories have been documented — the 2014 film *Pride* brought them to the big-screen, with heart, compassion and a sense of urgency. Naturally, there was censorship. As Jackson recalled in his *Tribune Mag* interview, 'The American DVD covers for *Pride* actually airbrushed out the lesbian and gay elements of the movie. It was absolutely absurd. It just talked about "a group of activists" supporting the miners.' LGSM's impact has been powerful and long-lasting;

Lesbians and Gays Support the Migrants, a direct action group which protests unjust deportations and detainments, is maybe the best-known example of a collective that builds directly on these legacies.

In fact, it was LGSM that lit the fire under this book; to see the queer and working-class parts of my own identity reconciled in such a powerful story had a huge impact on my own politics.

Although capitalism has largely wrapped its clutches around LGBTQ+ advocacy – think hollow, corporate Pride campaigns, rainbow-printed T-shirts being pumped out of sweatshops – there are activist bookshops, pubs and collectives who fight to keep these histories of working-class solidarity alive, reproducing Pits & Perverts T-shirts and posters to celebrate these stories. Today, the UK is in a seemingly never-ending cost of living crisis,[17] one being exacerbated by a right-wing government whose aims aren't dissimilar to Thatcher's. We're seeing Section 28 play out again in real time, only now, it's trans communities being targeted, demonised as predators and deemed inappropriate for kids.[18]

There's solace to be found in the fact that histories are cyclical, that the widespread transphobia, classism and workplace exploitation of today will, at some point, lessen in their intensity. In the meantime, unions are experiencing a renaissance in the UK,[19] and transphobia is being challenged and met with solidarity. If there's one lesson to take from the history of Lesbians and Gays Support the Miners, it's that this solidarity should *always* cross class borders.

No Fats, No Femmes

'I am what they fear most – fat.'

– Michelle Olley

As a British teenager growing up in a village with not much more than a castle, a few takeaways and the occasional charity shop, the internet was my salvation.

The first time I saw Alexander McQueen, I fell in love. He was chubby, working-class and a little bit awkward, just like I was. Articles always mentioned that his dad was a taxi driver,[1] the implication being that the fabled world of high fashion wasn't meant for him, that he had somehow slipped through the cracks. At arguably the peak of his career, he moved to Paris for a stint at the legendary French fashion house, Givenchy. The press ripped him to shreds. In their eyes, he was an 'East End yob'[2] tearing the veil of fashion's privileged cocoon.

There was something anarchic but optimistic about McQueen's designs. He sent models storming down the runway in ripped-up dresses; in *No. 13*, spray-paint-wielding robots lurked menacingly at the side of the runway, ready to deface a lily-white gown. In his 1998 tribute to Joan of Arc, he dressed a model from head-to-toe in red lace, a veil across her face to symbolise blood, violence and so-called scarlet women.

At the show's triumphant climax, she stood, arms raised, inside a circle of flickering flames.

When I moved to Paris myself, I started suffering – for the first time – with depression. I developed patterns of disordered eating, restricting myself to select foods, mostly bananas and cereal bars. I skipped meals not just because I had no cash to my name, but because I had internalised the idea that thinness was aspirational, especially for anyone desperate – like I was – to work in fashion. In lieu of wandering the streets of one of the world's most expensive cities, I started writing a review of one of his shows every day. Those reviews earned me my dream job in fashion journalism. I don't think it's an exaggeration to say that Alexander McQueen saved my life.

Fashion sometimes gets a bad reputation as shallow, superficial and hyper-capitalist, but it can be an excellent vehicle for art as activism. Fighting for social change is about more than brandishing placards and showing up for protest marches. Art is a different kind of activism, but it's powerful nonetheless. Artists like McQueen have long amplified their queerness to piss people off, to make a statement. Over the last few decades in particular, fatness has gleefully been used in the same tongue-in-cheek way.

In late 2000, McQueen staged a runway show for his *VOSS* collection. Editors arrived promptly, but all they saw when they showed up was a giant, mirrored cube; packed neatly like well-dressed sardines into hierarchically-ordered rows, they had no choice but to sit and stare at themselves. McQueen was backstage, giggling as he watched the editors grow increasingly uncomfortable at the sight of their own reflections. He waited almost two hours to start the show.[3]

VOSS was about beauty, obsession, fragility and narcissism. When the show finally started, the four walls of the mirrored cubes fell and smashed to reveal a makeshift psych ward, again lined with mirrors. A dress made from razor-clam shells was made to be torn apart, a commentary on the transient nature of beauty. Models clawed at their faces, snatched back their skin and grew distressed as they posed in the mirror, contorting their features and examining themselves. McQueen had ordered them to 'have a nervous breakdown, die, and then come back to life'.[4]

The show ended with a reveal which had been months in the making. At the heart of the makeshift ward was another glass cube, which smashed open to reveal the fleshy, nearly naked body of Michelle Olley, stretched out on a chaise longue. Moths fluttered into the audience. Olley's only item of clothing – if you could call it that – was a metal mask, hooked up to a series of feeding tubes, like she was in some state of decay. 'My body [is] going to be so at odds with the fashion sparrows and bony old crow-people in the audience,' wrote Olley, in a series of diary entries leading up to the show. 'I am what most of them fear most – fat.'[5]

This grand finale was a tribute to artist Joel-Peter Witkin's *Sanitarium,* an exploration of beauty in the grotesque. Together, McQueen and Olley forced fashion to confront its own 'grotesque': fatness.

Beauty standards don't emerge in a vacuum, they're created – and fashion, alongside advertising and media, plays a *huge* part in that creation. Even on a broad, global scale, aesthetic ideals are Eurocentric; it's why we see worldwide demand for skin-bleaching creams[6] and diet pills.[7] In most corners of the world, thinness and whiteness are deemed aspirational.

When it comes to fatness, the punishment for not meeting these standards is moving through a world that's not made for you. Aeroplane seatbelts aren't long enough, so you're forced into the sometimes humiliating task of asking for a bright red extender. You go to the doctor with a minor illness and you're told without any further examination that you should probably just lose weight.[8] TV shows like *The Biggest Loser* – which, thankfully, are mostly relics of a past generation – drew huge audiences by showing presenters screaming at fat people until they broke down, all so they could lose enough weight to win a competition. Usually after these crash diets, fat people put back on all the weight they lost – if not more – because starvation and exercising until you puke aren't sustainable.[9] If you look fat and happy, you're told that you're 'glamourising' fatness. If you're fat and have a partner who loves you, you're told they probably have a fetish, that they're a 'chubby chaser'. If someone makes a cruel comment about your weight, they say they're shaming you for your own good.

Despite these facts, naming fatphobia on a legislative level is difficult. Increasingly, we know that fat people shy away from going to the doctor for fear of being shamed or treated badly.[10] We also know that structural discrimination contributes to fatness. If we look at fatphobia through an intersectional lens, we know that non-white demographics in the UK and US are more likely to be fat.[11, 12] Generational legacies of racism mean that people of colour are more likely to have less cash and therefore to live in areas far away from big supermarkets – known as 'food deserts'.[13] As a result, they might have less cash to spend on food and less choice in where they spend it.

Companies have capitalised on a world that fears fatness, making us pay a premium for things like gym memberships, nutritionists, and organic fruits and vegetables. Disabilities can make exercise more difficult, if not impossible, and that's hardly helped by the lack of accessibility within the fitness world more generally. Many gyms don't have adaptive facilities, and statistics have shown for years that sports aimed at disabled people are comparatively underfunded.[14] Meanwhile, LGBTQ+ communities are more likely to suffer with eating disorders, linked to the negative mental health impact of discrimination.[15] Speaking anecdotally, TV producers are often happy to platform us when we're beautiful. Shows like *Queer Eye* – although they're great in many ways, especially the more recent reboot – tell us that we're only useful when we can turn people into better consumers. Is it cynical? Sure! But it's emblematic of a wider mainstream movement which still treats palatability as the ultimate goal.

There are tangible examples of structural fatphobia – health discrimination being one of the most talked about. Yet fat activists also have the challenge of changing societal opinions, or – in some more radical cases – making audiences confront their fatphobia.

This is where art comes in. Like McQueen's beautiful, fat heroine reclined in a makeshift sanitarium, artists – many of them queer – have been using their bodies as a 'fuck you' to beauty standards for decades. In the mid-to-late 1960s, Glenn Milstead discovered an independent film director named John Waters, whose transgressive artistic vision was equally inspired by highbrow art films and sleazy, countercultural filth. Milstead described himself as a 'spoiled brat'[16] as a kid. For years, he starred in Waters' experimental films while living off his parents' credit cards. Together, Waters and Milstead conceived the idea for a drag character named Divine, an unapologetically fat, slutty drag queen with a hairline shaved back to the middle of her skull.

Divine made her debut in Waters' 1966 film *Roman Candles,* in which she performed as a shoplifting, chain-smoking nun. Gradually, the commentaries on mainstream beauty standards became more overt; in the 1968 film *Eat Your Make-Up*, Divine dragged up as American First Lady Jackie Kennedy, kidnapping models and forcing them to swallow their expensive collections of cosmetics. Like McQueen's *VOSS*, it's a commentary on the links between beauty, consumption and the idealised form of fashion, delivered with a brilliantly subversive flair.

Milstead and Waters' best-known collaboration came in the form of *Pink Flamingos*, described by Waters as an 'exercise in poor taste'.[17] Just as McQueen revelled in making the grotesque beautiful – in the case of *VOSS*, using fashion's fear of fatness as a stand-in for the grotesque – Divine's *Pink Flamingos* character more literally revelled in filth, eating a handful of fresh dog shit at the film's iconic climax. Around this time, Divine amped up her look even further, wearing super-short mini skirts and tight dresses to show off her curves.

Divine's reputation continued to grow, and mainstream audiences were given more opportunities to be shocked by what they saw as her brazen embrace of her fatness. In 1984, she performed her single 'You Think You're a Man' on *Top of the Pops*, wearing a skin-tight silk dress and a giant blond beehive wig. Thousands of complaints quickly poured in from viewers who were furious about the 'fat lady' they had seen on-screen, describing her performance as 'disgusting' and 'obscene'.[18]

Especially in the 1980s, queer people grew used to having their health constantly policed. As news of the AIDS crisis travelled, the emphasis on looking 'healthy' – read: slim and muscular[19] – grew, but a handful of performance artists pushed back. Australia-born Leigh Bowery was a mainstay on the London club kid scene throughout the '80s; his most famous art performance involved 'giving birth'[20] to his wife Nicola Bateman. The show would open with Bateman strapped to Bowery while hanging upside-down, her legs around his neck and her face in his crotch. Suddenly, she would slip out of the harness and plop onto the ground, as though he had given birth to her. To ensure maximum revulsion, the 'birth' came with plenty of stage blood and links of sausages, which would spill onto the floor alongside Bateman. Bowery's art disrupted ideas of beauty and fatness. When Lucien Freud painted Bowery, the rolls of fat on his torso were rendered in beautifully intricate detail. When Bowery staged a fashion show in 1986, he sent an anonymous fat model down the runway, naked apart from black gloves, high-heeled shoes and a string of gold chains around her neck. She held a giant sign reading 'BOWERY' over her face.[21]

Even as stigma has faded, thanks in no small part to the tireless work of AIDS activists, this preoccupation with aesthetics has continued to hit queer communities disproportionately hard, especially queer people of colour. In 2016, Korean American drag queen Kim Chi took the opportunity to speak about these pressures in her finale performance on *RuPaul's Drag Race,* performing a song called 'Fat, Femme and Asian'.[22] In many ways, Chi was an anomaly. Despite featuring on a global franchise, Chi kept both her drag alter-ego and her sexuality a secret from her parents, and continued to do so even after the show had aired. Throughout the season, she cracked jokes about still being a virgin, and about desirability politics within LGBTQ+ communities. 'Shady gays believe in no fats, no femmes and no Asians,' she said. 'As someone who is all of the above, I understand your pain.'

Historically, queer desire has been criminalised and fraught with unique challenges: from plain clothes policemen stalking well-known cruising spots[23] to the minefield of navigating the potential danger of 'coming out' as trans to a romantic interest,[24] there are plenty of reasons we might use dating apps. Location-based app Grindr, which shows users other nearby users in their area, was launched in 2009, and the uptake was quick. Initially, the app was aimed solely at gay men, but over the years, it's opened itself up to trans women, trans men, non-binary people and cis women. In 2016, the app was predominantly gay, and Chi's 'Fat, Femme and Asian' was named after an exclusionary tagline she often saw on users' profiles. Increasingly, studies[25] – which also examine HIV stigma, exemplified by the language of 'cleanness'[26] – are probing these rigid standards, but the damage has been done.

In a world which has long aired shows with titles like *How to Look Good Naked*, it's no surprise that fat activists have used nudity as a tool to provoke discussion. When we're told to get 'beach body ready', the implication is that fat bodies are too unsightly to be seen without clothes. Society encourages us to heavily police ourselves, exercising regularly and eating restrictively in order to be seen as 'beautiful'. But 'beauty' is a nebulous concept, one which has long excluded people of colour, disabled people, queer and trans people, and countless others. When bodies aren't thin, white and cisgender, they're treated as abnormal, as objects of study.

A well-known historical example of this is Sarah Baartman, the so-called Hottentot Venus, a South African woman brought to Europe as a slave in the early 1800s.[27] Despite the passage of the 1807 Slave Trade Act, Baartman was displayed as a 'freak' due to the size of her buttocks and genitalia. Rich masters brought her out at private parties, and by the time she was taken to Paris in 1814, 'her existence was really quite miserable and extraordinarily poor . . . [she] was literally treated like an animal.'[28] Even after Baartman's death in 1815, her remains were pored over by scientists.

Countless bodies which don't fit the straight, white, able-bodied ideal have been policed and punished. Intersex people are subjected to genital mutilation, as are cisgender women in countries which still permit female genital mutilation. Fat activism is about far more than just seatbelt extenders and bigger chairs in theatres; it's about societal policing of bodies, and which bodies are allowed to exist without punishment or forced intervention.

This activism is happening online, too. Fat activists – especially fat activists of colour – have spent more than a decade carving out space online, spreading messages of radical fat acceptance and critiquing the heavy whitewashing of 'body positivity'. In *Fattily Ever After,* Stephanie Yeboah credits the resurgence of the movement largely to 'black and nonwhite, plus-size users, bloggers and activists' of 'online social platforms such as Tumblr, Livejournal, Yahoo! Messageboards and Blackplanet', who have created online mini communities for fat people to 'celebrate and appreciate their bodies without fear of judgement'.[29]

Gradually, we're moving away from fuzzy, mainstream discussions of 'body positivity' and looking back to radical histories of fat liberation – and again, art played a pivotal role in telling these stories.

In the summer of 1989, almost two hundred women gathered in London for the 'first national fat women's conference',[30] a long-overdue event decades in the making. This wasn't the *beginning* of the radical fat liberation movement – US feminists had formed the Fat Underground almost two decades earlier, and the late 1960s saw New York's Central Park filled with fat activists setting fire to diet books[31] – but it marked the earnest beginnings of a *queer* fat liberation movement.

Details of the ground breaking conference are chronicled in issue 16 of *Trouble & Strife,* a feminist magazine which documented the changing face of the movement. The issue featured a cover image depicting a presumably high-flying business-woman in a chequered power-suit and high heels, dragging a dishevelled-looking man by his tie with her right hand and clutching a briefcase in the other. Inside, there's an extensive report on the conference by a writer named Heather Smith, who explained that the event was the work of the London Fat Women's Group, a collective which gained mainstream visibility after an interview in fellow feminist magazine *Spare Rib.*

Smith gave the opening speech, which 'located fat within a framework of imperialism, capitalism and patriarchy', she recalled. The conference spawned a brilliant, radical document known as the Fat Dykes Statement, which was ballsy, crowd-sourced and punchy, inspired by the bullet-point manifesto styling of the Black Panthers' Ten-Point Program and the Fat Underground's Fat Liberation Manifesto. It's a text which drips with fury: 'Don't assume you're doing me a favour by being in a relationship with me.' 'Don't assume my disabilities are caused by being fat.' 'Don't assume my fat has psychological roots.' 'Don't assume you don't fancy me.'

Decades later, these stories are inspiring radical fat activists to make their own art, especially across Latin America. There's one book in particular that's looked back at fat liberation movements, translating and updating their politics of solidarity. It has the kind of 'fuck you' attitude inherent to these radical movements, embodied by the front cover: a fat, naked body with the head of a furry monster cups its breasts as it snarls, brandishing them almost as weapons. The book in question is a 2014 essay collection entitled *La Cerda Punk*[32] – *cerda* being a reclamation of an insult hurled at fat women, which loosely translates to 'fat pig' – by constanzx alvarez castillo, a Chilean activist, musician, author and artist also known as Missogina.

The last decade has seen fat activist collectives formed all over Latin America, but *La Cerda Punk* – printed in Chile and released by Trio Editorial, an independent press dedicated to publishing disruptive, largely queer and trans authors – was, in many ways, ahead of the curve. It's a book rooted in intersectionality and solidarity, which forges links between fat activism, environmental justice, trans activism and anti-racism. In the acknowledgements, castillo thanks 'feminism for ruining my life, lesbianism for introducing me to pleasure and anarchism, for making sense of existence'. Each essay is a mini-manifesto, introduced with quotes from the likes of Paul B. Preciado, trans scholar and author of *Testo Junkie,* queer disabled activist and performance artist Nomy Lamm, Chilean poet and trans activist Claudia Rodriguez, as well as an array of other activists who embody the book's 'fuck the system' ethos. There's even a double-page spread of musician Beth Ditto bent over at a gig in black leggings and high heels, probably telling the audience to kiss her ass.

Then there's the actual manifesto, led by the tagline: 'Punk will never go on a diet.' It tells us: 'It's not enough to just destroy gender if we don't explode the idea of "normal" bodies.' It's a call to arms, which situates fat liberation within anti-establishment politics, calls for an end to racism, transphobia and capitalist exploitation, and encourages fat activists to 'take out our claws, howl like wolves and leave our space of silence'.

For castillo, finding their voice as a fat activist wasn't exactly easy. In *La Cerda Punk,* they document their search for any kind of history within which they could see themselves represented, but for the most part, the few stories which *did* exist weren't ever written in or translated into Spanish. So, they turned to the internet and to punk fanzines like *GordaZine*, seeking out online communities which allowed them to find and connect with other global movements. Here, they found radical histories of movements like the Fat Underground and the London Fat Women's Group. They discovered blogs and magazines created by fat acceptance advocates, fat people of colour and fat queer people, but castillo found that most of them came from 'countries in the global north', mainly the United States and the United Kingdom. The politics of fatness differ according to context, especially when factors like colonisation and poverty are added into the mix; in that sense, *La Cerda Punk* is castillo's attempt to both document and diversify existing narratives of fat activism, and bring them specifically into a Latin American context.

These stories speak to why art is so effective as activism. Unlike words, visuals have the power to transcend language, to make radical statements for audiences worldwide. When you see an audience of fashion waifs gobsmacked by the sight of a naked, moth-covered Michelle Olley, you know *exactly* what statement is being made; the same can be said of a shit-eating Divine, aiming guns at her audience in a skin-tight red dress. In *Pink Flamingos*, she snarled: 'Filth is my politics, filth is my life.'[33] It's a statement that applies to radical fat art, the kind which gleefully embraces societal notions of fatness as grotesque, *filthy*. Fat liberation leans into these notions of unacceptable bodies; it strips them bare, bends over and orders respectable, mainstream viewers to pucker up.

Treatment Access Campaign

'In South Africa I am oppressed because I am a Black man, and I am oppressed because I am gay. So, when I fight for my freedom, I must fight against both oppressors.'

– Simon Nkoli

In 1985, San Francisco-based AIDS educator Glen Margo contacted the Gay Association of South Africa (GASA) in the hopes of delivering talks about the deadly virus in Johannesburg. He was met first with a positive response and then with an invitation from Dennis Sifris, a doctor who helped establish the country's first AIDS clinic. Margo flew to Johannesburg, where he spoke to a packed crowd of cardiologists and respiratory physicians. Almost all of them were bewildered by this 'hippy' guy with 'homemade sandals' and 'ringlets in his hair'. According to Sifris, interviewed as part of an in-depth *Medical History* journal article, Margo was 'almost laughed off as a joke'.[1]

Yet there had been early AIDS-related deaths in South Africa. A 2014 article[2] published in the *Medical History* journal traces the country's earliest cases back to the deaths of two men: Ralph Kretzen and Pieter Daniël Steyn, who died in August 1982 and January 1983, respectively. Both were flight stewards. In a later assessment of early HIV narratives in South Africa, researchers described public reactions to these deaths as rooted in 'moral panic' and highly influenced by the homophobic narratives of the UK and the US in particular. This was the apartheid era: racial segregation was state-mandated and homosexuality was a crime punishable by up to seven years in prison,[3] one of many anti-gay laws brought to colonised countries by missionaries.[4]

Throughout the 1980s, AIDS was largely treated as a foreign and distinctly homosexual contagion by the South African government. As a result, AIDS prevention efforts fell to gay community advocates in South Africa. Yet these organisations were questionable in their own way, including the aforementioned GASA, which took an apolitical stance on all issues other than homosexuality. In a *Journal of Southern African Studies* article, scholar Daniel Conway explains: 'This apoliticism meant focussing only on white gay rights and operating within the confines of white society, ignoring any critique of apartheid or association with Black South Africans.'[5]

Despite this, there were still activists doing progressive work, like doctors Dennis Sifris and Ruben Sher. They first came together in the late 1970s to study the impact of hepatitis B on the gay male community; when they later heard whispers of a lethal disease similarly sweeping through gay communities, they united to learn more about the mysterious virus. Primarily, they focused on recruiting research volunteers through word of mouth, even if that meant resorting to unconventional tactics. Sifris would take these recruitment drives wherever he could; at times, he would get onstage at gay nightclubs to alert sweaty, dazed club-goers to the project, although the sign-up success rate was, by his own admission, limited. Sher was described as 'neither a fiery activist nor a hardened political creature', but a resolute pragmatist who refused to be cowed by politicisation of the virus. 'It didn't matter if it was a gay issue, a Black issue, or a rich/poor issue,' wrote Sifris, in a memorial article published in the *Southern African Journal of HIV Medicine*.[6] 'People were getting ill. People were dying. There was no need to argue.'

It was only in 1985 that the government announced its first responses to the AIDS crisis, hence Margo's visit. An advisory group on AIDS was established by the Department of Health; naturally, Sifris, with his years of experience and expertise in gay men's health specifically, tried to apply. His application was denied because he belonged to a 'high-risk group', and 'if we have a gay man [within the advisory group], we have to have a prostitute, we have to have a Haitian, and we have to have a Black'. Sifris and Sher continued their activism anyway, playing key roles in the establishment of an AIDS clinic at Johannesburg General Hospital, which quickly built alliances with gay and otherwise progressive organisations involved in HIV activism.

This desire to build coalitions led Sifris and Sher to Simon Nkoli, who throughout the 1980s and early 1990s was affiliated with organisations like GLOW (the Gay and Lesbian Organisation of the Witwatersrand). Activism was on Nkoli's radar from a young age.[7] He was born in Soweto, a South African township which, in 1976, became the site of one of the country's bloodiest uprisings, when Black schoolchildren protested the enforcement of Afrikaans ('the language of the oppressor') in schools.[8] Nkoli took part in the student uprising and, at barely 18 years old, he was already a rising leader within student activist movements; in 1976 alone, he was arrested four times.

Nkoli realised that he was gay as a young adult, but struggled to find anywhere in apartheid-era South Africa that would welcome Black patrons – most of the few gay bars that *did* exist were in white-only areas. But in his teens, he fell in love with a white bus driver named Roy Shepherd, strengthening a flirty romance which began when the two met through a pen-pal magazine. Nkoli's parents reacted to the news with fury, even trying to force him into conversion therapy. Shepherd's family opposed the relationship too, but for them, the issue was Nkoli's skin colour. It was only when their families learned they had penned a joint suicide pact that they relented and reluctantly allowed the relationship to continue. But even when Shepherd and Nkoli both moved to Johannesburg as students, apartheid laws meant that Nkoli had to pose as his lover's live-in servant.[9]

Galvanised by his own life experience, Nkoli became more and more active within anti-apartheid struggle movements and gay liberation groups. In 1980, he took up a prominent role within the Congress of South African Students, which proved easier than ingratiating himself within gay activist circles. Although he tried to make these connections, the white-majority gay lib groups – notably GASA – largely refused to treat apartheid as a struggle worth fighting, shielded from its impact by their almost entirely white membership. Nkoli took matters into his own hands, forming The Saturday Group, the country's first Black gay organisation, but it was to be short-lived; just months after its conception, Nkoli was arrested in the township of Delmas for his role in helping to create a tenants' organisation which would mobilise against and oppose government-imposed rent hikes. It was a brutal day of protests, one which saw police open fire on protestors and launch tear gas into the crowds, using any and all violent methods at their disposal to suppress the disruption.

Nkoli was one of 22 activists detained and thrust into the public spotlight of a high-profile trial in 1984. All eyes were already on the ragtag band of revolutionaries, but these eyes widened considerably when Nkoli spoke openly of his homosexuality. His willingness to do this is still described as a landmark historical moment, most notably because of the reaction he received: despite initially hostile responses, the freedom fighters eventually decided that Nkoli's homosexuality did nothing to lessen his status as a comrade.

The trial – known as the Delmas Treason Trial – became one of the longest in South African history at the time, spanning 240 days in court. Nkoli spent two years detained in prison before being released on bail; during these years, he wrote hundreds of letters to his lover at the time, Roy Shepherd, his 'darling Roy', which have been preserved and documented by South Africa's GALA Queer Archive.[10] They're simultaneously heartwarming and infuriating, offering a glimpse of Nkoli's wit, resilience and tenderness. He's a romantic at heart, requesting romance novels to read inside his cell. Shepherd meets his requests to send clothes, including a 'punk jacket', which Nkoli loves. 'How did you know that I'm punk?' he writes. 'I'm so excited that you didn't buy a suit. I hate wearing suits!' Nkoli's arrest – and high-profile coming-out – made him something of a global figure; in December 1986, he received more than 150 Christmas cards from gay anti-apartheid campaigners in Britain and the Netherlands, a festive gesture of international solidarity.[11]

All the while, Nkoli understood that he was marginalised due to his race *and* sexuality. He gave public speeches which underlined potential links of solidarity between poor, Black and gay communities. He spoke of interconnected struggles, many of which he had personally protested against. His fellow revolutionaries understood that they were all working together for broader benefits, that apartheid was linked to other spheres of discrimination. Nkoli campaigned not just against racism and homophobia, but against poverty, too – and although income inequality in South Africa is still largely divided by race, due in no small part to the generational impact of apartheid, Nkoli extended invitations of solidarity to poor white communities.

Nkoli was eventually acquitted in 1988, and wasted no time leading activist projects which centred Black gay communities, but recognised their positioning within a wider nexus of oppression. In 1990, alongside GLOW member Bev Ditsie, he co-organised the first Gay Pride march in Johannesburg. In an impassioned speech, he said the march represented 'gays and lesbians . . . entering the struggle for a democratic South Africa where everybody has equal rights and everyone is protected by the law: Black and white; men and women, gay and straight.'[12] He founded the Township AIDS Project, an educational project; through GLOW, he provided resources for gay men living in townships, connecting them to HIV resources.

Meanwhile, the anti-apartheid struggle was intensifying and spawning global solidarity networks. In South Africa, white-led gay groups like GASA splintered, due to their refusal to take a firm anti-racist stance. Irish workers went on strike throughout the 1980s, refusing to sell South African products; in 1985, anti-apartheid campaigner Desmond Tutu invited them to South Africa as a show of appreciation.[13] Their strike worked. In 1987, the Irish government implemented a ban on the sale of South African products. Revolutionaries like Desmond Tutu and Nelson Mandela – who later expressed regret for not being more active in the early fight against AIDS[14] – made international headlines, galvanising worldwide support for anti-apartheid campaigners.

Nkoli continued to advocate tirelessly in the years following the landmark 1990 Pride Parade. In 1994, the year in which apartheid laws were finally overturned, he established the National Coalition for Gay and Lesbian Equality (NCGLE, now known as the Lesbian and Gay Equality Project, or LGEP), which connected LGBTQ+ organisations across South Africa and across the continent of Africa more broadly.

Nkoli was proudly radical; there was no room for respectability politics within his activism. One of his fellow organisers described him as 'fantastically subversive' and recalled his Esselen Street office being plastered in 'explicit posters of naked Black men'.[15] Nkoli criticised the moralistic messaging of conservative government initiatives, which encouraged abstinence. He understood that stigma-free, community-led resources were the only way to mitigate AIDS transmission rates; that a community which had long been criminalised for their sex lives weren't about to listen to government officials when they told them to abstain.

Incidentally, the early 1990s marked a turning point in South Africa's HIV history, as heterosexual transmission rates outstripped homosexual rates for the first time. Word was spreading fast that *anyone* could catch the virus, but that the most important determining factors were really race and class, not just sexuality. Low-income Black women slowly became the most heavily impacted demographic. Here, the residual impact of apartheid is obvious: many of these women were blocked from accessing the higher-quality education in white-only schools, which in turn meant they were more likely to live in poverty and rely on sex work to make ends meet. This lack of education extended to sex education, and the government's refusal to even name an AIDS crisis obviously didn't help.

AIDS research – finally being funded, after years of campaigning – was also improving, but this meant that pharmaceutical companies were growing aware that patented drugs could mean big business. At first, antiretroviral medication – which reduces the viral load of HIV patients and significantly lowers the risk of the virus mutating into AIDS – wasn't made available at all in South Africa. When treatment *did* become available, only the patented, super-expensive drugs could be used. South Africa's pharmaceutical industry had essentially blocked any potential competition, with the aid of a corrupt government, meaning that no cheaper, generic alternatives were on the market.[16]

By the time Nkoli died of AIDS-related complications in November 1998, this was the picture: a monthly dose of HIV treatment would set the average patient back R4,500[17] – in today's cash, that's around £200, or $250. Many South African citizens living with HIV didn't even know that drug treatments were available. It simply wasn't on their radar. They had no choice but to prepare themselves to die.

Throughout decades of activism, Nkoli's work and mission had led to kinship with like-minded radicals. Among them was Zackie Achmat, who co-founded the NCGLE with Nkoli in 1994, but their friendship dated back to the mid-1970s. Achmat was also a vehement anti-apartheid campaigner; in 1976, to show solidarity with the Soweto student uprising, he set fire to his school.[18]

Aware of political injustice from a young age, Achmat was raised by his mother and aunt, both of whom were shop stewards for the Garment Workers' Union, which represented textile workers in South Africa. Formed in 1929, the union acknowledged that the struggles of the (mostly) women who worked in the factories couldn't be neatly separated by race or class; again, their defining commonalities were their low pay and social status, which saw their difficulties ignored on a structural level. By the standards of the time, it was a pretty progressive union; women held at least *some* important roles and Eastern European immigrants played a pivotal role in union organising.[19] Achmat was imprisoned sporadically for his activism and, over time, he became affiliated with the African National Congress, the party responsible for leading South Africa out of apartheid.[20]

When Nkoli died, Achmat knew that no tribute to his life or legacy should be sombre or apolitical. So, at Nkoli's memorial event, he delivered a rousing speech which called on mourners to organise and mobilise. Achmat was also HIV-positive; at the time, he had been battling a lengthy, painful bout of oral thrush and noticing the general deterioration of his health. He was prescribed an expensive drug but even with the financial aid of his friends, Achmat said the vital treatment 'nearly bankrupted' him. After that, he started to make it publicly clear that he would refuse to take life-saving antiretroviral drugs until they were freely available in the public sector. Achmat had long been pissed off, but he described Nkoli's death as the 'final straw.'

Just days later, on 10 December 1998 – the date marked annually as International Human Rights Day – Achmat gathered a small, unlikely group of protestors on the steps of St George's Cathedral, a historical building planted in the heart of Cape Town's city centre. In total, there were only about 15 demonstrators, all of them from wildly different backgrounds: one was a medical student; another was a former human rights commissioner; there was a 66-year-old grandmother in their midst, as well as a handful of people battling HIV. By the end of the day, the group had gathered more than a thousand signatures from passers-by, who agreed the government needed to act – and quickly – to ensure HIV medications became accessible.[21]

The transition to democracy had marked hope for some that inequality would decrease, that poverty would no longer be a death sentence. The handful of protestors gathered on the cathedral steps were united by a common belief that poor people deserve healthcare. It shouldn't be a radical statement, but even now – in countries rich and poor alike – it still is.

Achmat's last-minute protest laid the foundations of an organisation that would soon become known as TAC, the Treatment Action Campaign. Their mission and their leaders reflected the diversity of causes aggravating South Africa's AIDS crisis; there was still the issue of homophobia to deal with but, more broadly, the TAC was focused on tackling government corruption, the lethal greed of pharmaceutical companies, and wildly unequal access to life-saving healthcare. Arguably, Achmat's most famous act of protest was to decline antiretroviral medication when it was offered to him, refusing to accept it while others were barred from access by poverty.[22]

During its first decade in particular, the TAC was focused on challenging governmental health policies which weren't evidence-based and which prioritised profits above people. They worked to expose the lies of greedy multinationals, as well as raising awareness among the South African public that AIDS *could* be treated, but that access to this treatment was being denied. International solidarity was a bedrock of the TAC's activism; according to the United Nations, TAC activists forged partnerships with collectives and organisations in 'Brazil, India, Thailand, the United States [and] the United Kingdom', to name a few. They set about gathering affidavits – sworn factual statements – from people living with HIV and healthcare workers across South Africa, combining them with evidence that generic alternatives to the expensive, branded HIV drugs being sold *did* exist. This information was gathered and given to South Africa's Competition Commission, as part of a persuasive – and ultimately, successful – campaign to allow cheaper, generic options to be made available. Through this action alone, the TAC managed to push the price of HIV treatment down from R4,500 to R200.

Just as Nkoli had understood the importance of shared struggle and solidarity, Achmat and the TAC quickly set out to forge partnerships with grassroots organisations across South Africa, leading HIV educational programmes and mobilising communities. They built strategic partnerships with a wide array of organisations: faith-based organisations, labour unions, children's charities and protest medic groups, like Médecins sans Frontières. Achmat also had a legal background; before founding the TAC, he worked as a director of the AIDS Law Project, which advocated for the rights of HIV-positive people on both a structural and interpersonal level.

Before long, the Treatment Access Campaign had galvanised activists across the continent. In August 2002, representatives of HIV organisations from across Africa gathered in Cape Town, at the World Summit on Sustainable Development. One of the most impassioned speeches came courtesy of Milly Katana, a public health specialist and long-time AIDS activist. 'We are angry,' she said plainly. 'Our people are dying. We can no longer accept millions of needless AIDS deaths simply because we are poor Africans.'[23] Like Achmat, she knew that treatment was possible. Katana knew that resources were being hoarded by the same wealthy nations that had long plundered and exploited countries across Africa. As a result, millions of African citizens – even today, it's by far the continent most heavily impacted by AIDS – were being left to die. At that 2002 summit, Achmat and Katana came together with a shared vision: to hold governments and medical sectors to account and to ensure that at least 3 million HIV-positive people would be on antiretroviral treatment by 2005. To realise this vision, they pooled their skills and recruited activists from 21 different countries to form the Pan-African Treatment Access Movement (PATAM).

It's taken decades of work, but the movement has indisputably made gains in terms of access to treatment and HIV education. In a 2021 interview,[24] Tapiwa Kujinga – now director of the PATAM – explained there was 'no framework on access to medicines' back in 2002. Thanks to coalition-based advocacy, he says 'governments have now built a capacity to address HIV/ AIDS.' As well as advocating for the prevention of mother-to-child HIV transmission in countries like Zambia, Kujinga says the coalition also worked hard 'to ensure that the voices of communities would be heard in every President's Emergency Plan for AIDS Relief (PEPFAR) process' – and that community initiatives could access funding for HIV prevention programmes. A 2017 study of AIDS prevalence in South Africa, the home of the Treatment Access Campaign, found that, of the '7.6 million Black Africans estimated to be living with HIV, 62.6 per cent were found to be on treatment'.[25]

The Covid-19 pandemic similarly brought these inequalities to the forefront. There's widespread vaccine inequality even today, and it's largely marginalised groups dying at a disproportionate rate. In the case of the monkeypox epidemic, Western researchers actively ignored[26] the work of African researchers; as the virus spread within increasingly wealthy European countries, these communities were prioritised and, once again, African countries most likely to be impacted were left behind. As for HIV treatment rates across Africa, there are still factors – individual, societal, religious – keeping this number low, and there's still work to be done: the aforementioned report notes that 'access to ARV differs considerably by age and gender,' and that 'there is a need to expand access to treatment among youth.' The fight continues – and still leading these battles is the PATAM, the product of decades of vital, largely queer-led activism.

Even now, there are huge global discrepancies in AIDS mortality rates[27] and a disproportionate focus on stories told through a white, gay lens. There have been attempts to remedy this over the years – Achmat's own story was highlighted in the 2008 book *28: Stories of AIDS in Africa*[28]★ – but Nkoli's legacy is still often diminished, especially within histories of queer activism.

There's still endless work to be done to bring these tales to the forefront, especially as the AIDS crisis played an instrumental role in spawning a new form of radical activism, one which was punchy, distinctly grassroots and rooted in harm reduction. As activists have long argued, silence really *does* equal death. By raising their voices, sacrificing their freedoms and throwing their bodies at the steps of corrupt governments, legions of HIV activists have succeeded in ensuring that, with quick diagnosis and effective treatment, the lethal 'plague' *can* be prevented.

★   28: Stories of AIDS in Africa. Nolen, S (2008)

No Planet, No Future

'When human rights are protected and respected, then climate change mitigation is achieved.'
        — *Victoria Tauli-Corpuz*

No planet, no future.

It's a simple and glaringly obvious statement, but one that bears repeating: without an inhabitable Earth, we're *all* screwed. Despite this fact, a handful of billionaires continue to take the world's future into their hands, extracting endlessly until the Earth has no resources left to give. The communities most impacted by the climate crisis are left to deal with the worst of ecological disasters, while the tycoons causing them are isolated from the consequences.

Much of this vital climate activism is led by Indigenous communities, too often painted solely as *victims* of the climate crisis, which of course, they are: their homelands are routinely destroyed for profit and the effects of climate injustice makes their work either more difficult or impossible. But there's knowledge in these communities, too. 'Indigenous communities are real guardians of the forest', they've routinely claimed in protest, and it's true – they need the forest, but the forest also needs them.

Making these statements has always come with a level of risk, which can be fatal. The Amazon Rainforest, which sprawls across almost 7 million square kilometres and stretches across eight South American countries,[1] has historically been a battleground between Indigenous communities, landowners and corporate interests.[2] Historically, workers within the rainforest have been forced to fight against deforestation and the occupation of Indigenous land. To make matters worse, they've had to lobby for fair wages and resist the exploitation of landowners, who often prefer to pay them in basic goods rather than actual cash. When the workers *are* paid in cash, it's often been far below the standards of a minimum wage.

Inside the rainforest, one of the most reliable ways to make a living has long been rubber-tapping, the process of slicing a groove into the bark of a rubber tree to extract latex. This practice, still a major producer of jobs today, historically brought global trade into Brazil, specifically the Amazonian state of Amazonas, especially as demand for rubber to make war weapons increased at the start of the 20th century. The Brazilian government even started enlisting so-called 'Rubber soldiers' in 1943, as part of an agreement with the United States.[3] The US government promised to pay Brazil $100 for every tapper they enlisted; this promise was swiftly broken, and the workers were instead left to suffer in poverty, exacerbated by near-constant drought conditions.

Whether it was understood in those terms or not, the climate crisis has long driven rights struggles within the Amazon. In 1975, Chico Mendes[4] brought these issues to the forefront. Mendes, born in 1944, started rubber-tapping with his dad at just nine years old, growing up in the business. At 18 years old, he started being educated by Fernando Euclides Távora, a fellow rubber tapper and a vocal activist, who taught

Mendes to read and write by showing him political columns and articles about the state's exploitation of their industry. This lit a political fire in Mendes, who dedicated himself to protecting Indigenous workers whose labour sustained the rubber-tapping industry.

Their deep kinship was brutally destroyed by the 1964 military coup in Brazil, which saw rubber-tapping activists – Távora amongst them – arrested, tortured and killed.[5] Mendes continued to fight and by 1975, he had established the Xapuri Rural Workers' Union, conceived not only to collectivise workers but to protect the Amazon from deforestation.[6] These activists literally put their bodies on the line, standing together to form human blockades known as *empates* (stops), designed to physically block the path of bulldozers and loggers. This risky tactic became a symbol of the rubber-tappers' struggle, partly due to its bravery – Brazil was (and still is) one of the deadliest countries for environmental activists.

Mendes understood the importance of solidarity and the fact that climate justice, class struggle and workers' rights are all deeply interlinked issues.[7] To those in power, that made him dangerous. When he initially reported assassination threats, he was brushed off. Yet his profile continued to rise throughout the late 1970s and early 1980s, and when Mendes reported that landowners had issued death threats in December 1988, he was appointed police protection. The officers were playing dominoes at Mendes's kitchen table when he was shot dead in his back garden by a cattle rancher determined to turn the Amazon land into cattle pastures.[8]

Mendes's legacy lives on in Brazil – the Chico Mendes Extractive Reserve[9] was built on his desire to establish extractive reserves for tappers, Brazil nut collectors and other Indigenous people harvesting nature sustainably – but the assassinations of Indigenous activists (of which there are dozens, sometimes hundreds, every year) continue to go under-reported.

Increasingly, we're talking about the fact that climate justice isn't a single issue; it's deeply intertwined with racial justice, class struggle, workers' exploitation and, of course, colonisation. At the core of the climate crisis is capitalism,[10] and Indigenous communities are fighting to preserve their homelands from being plundered and extracted for profit. Coalition-building has continued over the last few decades, as Indigenous activists have battled for a seat at the tables of global climate conferences, which treat their livelihoods as bargaining chips.

Yet there's still a sort of condescending, paternalistic attitude to Indigenous communities, which has deep, historical roots – just think of the 'civilised' Western explorer setting off on missions to colonise so-called 'barbaric' or 'uncivilised' communities, supposedly for their own benefit. This attitude is exemplified by governmental attitudes to the climate crisis, which ignore the wealth of knowledge possessed by Indigenous communities.

At the 2015 Cop21 climate conference, held that year in Paris, negotiators made clear that they were considering removing 'reference to human and Indigenous rights from the main text of the climate accord', which naturally caused uproar. 'You cannot bargain away human rights,' said Victoria Tauli-Corpuz, the UN Rapporteur for Indigenous Rights. 'When human rights are protected and respected, then climate change mitigation is achieved.'

The climate crisis doesn't exist in a vacuum. For all the talk of melting ice caps and rising sea levels, there are human lives being lost. Often, they're the lives of marginalised people in relatively poor countries. Since 2008, an estimated 24 million people each year have been displaced by natural disasters.[11]

These so-called climate refugees are forced to find new homes but governments are often unwilling to take them in, despite having caused or allowed the conditions that led to their displacement. Border controls are a climate issue. White supremacy is a climate issue.

For the last two decades – but especially over the last few years – there have been growing global calls for a Green New Deal, a near-total policy overhaul. In 2019, US politician Alexandria Ocasio-Cortez teamed up with author and climate activist Naomi Klein and illustrator Molly Crabapple for a video entitled *A Message from the Future*.[12] It's a colourful, engaging art video, which opens with a brief overview of the escalating climate crisis over the last five decades, fuelled by oil tycoons and the lobby groups they created and paid to peddle climate denialism. The video humanises the crisis – Ocasio-Cortez laments the destruction of her family's homeland, Puerto Rico, by Hurricane Maria in 2017[13] – and highlights that politicians have knowingly ignored the crisis for decades, before introducing a potential solution: the Green New Deal.

Before fleshing out what the Green New Deal actually *is*, it's worth journeying back to the United States in the late 1930s. Years of global warfare had devastated economies, but the US had become used to the glitz, glamour and relative wealth of the 'roaring twenties', which came to an abrupt, screeching halt with the disastrous stock market crash of 1929, which led to the Great Depression.[14] Unemployment rates soared (at the height of the Depression, one in four families were jobless) and banks collapsed, leaving families without their life savings.[15] Newly homeless families trekked to the edges of towns and cities, building cardboard shanty towns known as 'Hoovervilles',[16] named after then-president Herbert Hoover, a die-hard Republican.

Corporate greed created the Great Depression. When election time rolled around, Democratic nominee Franklin D. Roosevelt named this fact and responded by pivoting further to the left, launching attacks on big businesses and forming coalitions of poor, rural workers: from labour unions to farming associations, he compelled a spectrum of society's most disenfranchised workers to campaign for a New Deal.[17] Roosevelt's slogans were catchy. He famously said 'the only thing we have to fear is fear itself',[18] and built extensive policies around what he called 'the three Rs' – relief, recovery and reform.[19] They were successful, too – in 1932, Roosevelt beat Hoover. Upon election, Roosevelt's short-term goal was to rebuild the economy. He did so by teaming up with labour unions and migrant workers' organisations, as well as establishing new agencies and programmes. Changes were swift and drastic because they *had* to be.

Grassroots movements fuelled the establishment of Roosevelt's New Deal, driven in no small part by the coalition-building efforts of labour unions, people of colour, poor white people and blue-collar workers. 'It must always be remembered that President Franklin D. Roosevelt rolled out the New Deal in the midst of a historic wave of labour unrest,' writes Naomi Klein in *On Fire: The Burning Case for a Green New Deal.*[20] 'There was the Teamster Rebellion and the Minneapolis general strike in 1934, the 83-day shutdown of West Coast ports by longshore workers that same year, and the Flint auto workers sit-down strikes in 1936 and 1937.' The collective spirit was one of solidarity, with the poorest and most marginalised building strength across their differences to rally against their collective exploitation.

Today, global conditions are similar. There's a long-standing global fight for unionisation,[21] and encouraging examples of key union victories.²² Economies have been decimated by a worldwide pandemic, and there's growing acknowledgement of what Klein calls 'the triple crises of our time: imminent ecological unravelling, gaping economic inequality (including the racial and gender wealth gaps), and surging white supremacy'.

The time is ripe for an updated New Deal – and this time, it *has* to be Green.

Now, back to the future. In the aforementioned video, Ocasio-Cortez uses the imaginary figure of a young girl named Ileana, who grows up as a 'child of the Green New Deal'. Viewers cycle through her illustrated lifetime, which has been transformed by policies like Medicare for All, a federal jobs guarantee and a universal childcare initiative. Ileana takes up newly created jobs, building new, renewable smart grids, taking apart oil pipelines and planting mangroves on the now-liberated land, all the while following the generational expertise of Indigenous communities. After a brief stint as a solar plant engineer, she runs for office in the first cycle of publicly funded election campaigns and goes on to win the same seat that Ocasio-Cortez won back in 2018.

It might sound utopian, but the point is crystal clear: a Green New Deal is far from just an eco-friendly policy overhaul. It's a wide-ranging vision, rooted in the creation of new, sustainable jobs, the redressing of global wealth imbalance, reparations for Indigenous communities whose lands have been extracted for profit, and investment in sectors like education, domestic care and healthcare. 'We stopped being scared of the future,' says Ocasio-Cortez dreamily. 'We stopped being scared of each other.'

Global coalitions are being built around the promise of a Green New Deal.²³ Activists are calling not just for environmental policy change but social change, too. They're reframing the climate crisis as a human rights issue, because don't we all deserve a planet to live on?

Unsurprisingly, the values of solidarity underpin these groups, which span and unite various demographics. A great example of this is the UK's Green New Deal Rising,[24] a fast-growing group of mostly young climate activists. In their sharp, clear manifesto, they underscore that they've grown up 'in a world at the tipping point of climate chaos'[25] driven by corporate greed – the same greed which has seen 'austerity rip apart our communities' and 'the gap between rich and poor get wider and wider'. These activists know that past movements have succeeded; that they 'stand on the shoulders of movements that fought until governments listened, until they built the NHS, until they gave everybody the right to vote and the right to love who they wanted to love.' Many of them know what it's like to be marginalised in other ways, that building solidarity across identity lines is a key tactic needed to win the war against the climate crisis. 'We come from towns devastated by cuts, and we grew up in cities choked by air pollution,' they write. 'We are black, brown and white. Queer, trans and disabled. In school, college and at university. In work and unemployed.'

There's governmental support for the Green New Deal too, evident in the C40 Cities Climate Leadership Group. At the time of writing, mayors in almost 100 member cities[26] are part of C40, meaning they agree to adopt a number of leadership standards which signify their commitment to tackling the climate crisis.

Much like the student activists we met in the first chapter, many leading climate activists – be they Indigenous or not – are young people, the ones whose futures are being directly sacrificed to corporate greed. Pissed-off teens are taking aim at

CEOs and world leaders, who have been historically happy to ignore warning signs in the relentless pursuit of profit. Now, they're being held accountable by the youngsters whose futures have been jeopardised.

Greta Thunberg, a Swedish teenager whose school strikes for climate change went viral back in 2018, has become a sort of climate crisis celebrity, revered on social media for her blunt chastisement of politicians. Much of the coverage has, in some way, centred on her autism – Thunberg's 'superpower'[27] – and her curt, no-nonsense appeals to world leaders, which spread across the web like wildfire. When she's invited to stay in five-star hotels, she declines and camps in a tent outside instead.[28]

There's a broad network of activists doing this work, often taking innovative approaches to getting their voices heard. Singaporean activist Qiyun Woo[29] creates quirky, colourful illustrations containing powerful messages about climate justice as a means to educate young people specifically. In Kenya, teenager Lesein Mutunkei combines his love for football with his passion for climate justice, founding the @trees4goals initiative – for every goal he scores for his football team, he plants 11 trees.[30] Liberian activist Ezekiel Nyanfor has made it his mission to educate other climate activists, creating a free online resource, the Africa Climate Ambassador Toolkit.[31] Many of these young change-makers are fighting to centre the countries currently most impacted by the climate crisis – and that means considering more than just ecology.

Here, global income inequality factors into the equation. According to data from the International Rescue Committee,[32] the majority of the ten countries most at risk from the effects of climate change are spread across Africa, and all but one have been historically decimated by colonisation – only Ethiopia *hasn't* been colonised, although it was briefly under the rule of Italian fascist Mussolini.[33] Extraction-mad billionaires cause the brunt of this damage, draining the Earth's resources and accelerating a climate crisis which is causing chaos in these countries – and they're not exactly pumping cash into these places to help weather the storms. The Lake Chad Basin covers almost 8 percent of the African continent, yet it's dried up significantly. Millions are dying of starvation and displacement, fighting lethal battles to secure access to dwindling resources.[34]

A deadly combination of colonialism, climate injustice and poverty is intertwined in these discussions. Finding solutions for the climate crisis is about more than just eco-friendly initiatives; it's about redressing global inequalities. In this sense, climate justice is a beacon of hope – if truly addressed, it could pave the way for key human rights advancements *and* form blueprints to help other international justice movements to become more intersectional. Though of course, we're not there yet. The climate activism movement has long been accused of being too white, too straight, too middle class – and for good reason. As 'sustainability' has become a buzzword, big corporations have been quick to claim eco-friendly credentials without doing anything concrete to back them up.

It's not uncommon for seemingly progressive values to be used as a smokescreen for far more sinister motives. The term 'pinkwashing' was coined back in 2011, to describe the Israeli government using pro-LGBTQ+ politics[35] to detract from its horrifically violent, decades-long occupation of Palestine.[36] Leftist queer groups have long called bullshit on these state tactics, standing consistently in solidarity with Palestinians, as well as highlighting that queer Palestinians exist – and they're at constant risk of being killed by Israeli forces.

The term 'pinkwashing' spawned an eco-friendly counterpart in the form of 'greenwashing', now commonplace. The term was coined in 1986 by environmentalist Jay Westerveld, who critiqued hotels for asking customers to reuse towels to 'save the environment', all the while doing nothing to actually reduce their energy consumption or waste.[37] It was, as he noted, a money-saving tactic, intended to generate profit and not to genuinely benefit the environment. Capitalism – which, ironically, has been described by countless scholars as the driving force of the climate crisis – has sunk its teeth into sustainability discourse, attaching hefty price tags to so-called 'eco-friendly' products. These costs are sometimes justified (they might be absorbed into buying sustainably-made fabrics, paying workers a living wage, offsetting carbon emissions or funding climate crisis prevention) but the narrative that 'sustainability' has to mean spending a fortune rather than, say, buying from charity shops, composting food waste or learning to customise and mend clothes, has led to widespread critique.

While capitalism has co-opted these conversations, activists in the most impacted countries are left fighting for their voices to be heard. In January 2020, Ugandan climate activist Vanessa Nakate was cropped out of a photograph taken at the World Economic Forum in Davos, Switzerland, leaving Greta Thunberg and three other young white activists in the shot.[38] 'Africa is on the frontlines of the climate crisis but it's not on the front pages of the world's newspapers,' she said in a 2022 interview with the *Guardian*.[39] 'Every activist who speaks out is telling a story about themselves and their community, but if they are ignored, the world will not know what's really happening, what solutions are working. The erasure of our voices is literally the erasure of our histories and what people hold dear to their lives.'

Again, this erasure is tied up in income inequality and global legacies of colonisation. At the Cop26 in Glasgow, held in 2021,

African activists were widely underrepresented. Why? Either they couldn't get accreditation, they couldn't get funding or they couldn't get the required Covid vaccinations.[40] When it comes to the climate crisis, the activists facing the worst current repercussions of environmental pollution on a day-to-day basis are being left out of these conversations.

Worldwide solidarity is the key to redressing the imbalance in these debates and young, coalition-based movements are showing this in spades. September 2019 saw students around the world coordinate a global climate strike: from Bangladesh and Kenya to Cyprus and Poland, millions marched with placards demanding world leaders 'act as if their house were on fire'.[41] Activists borrowed tactics from past direct action movements, like ACT UP; protestors dressed all in black lay around coffins spray-painted with Extinction Rebellion's logo, staging symbolic 'die-ins' to visualise the lethal consequences of the climate crisis.[42] The protests inspired hope and proved the capabilities of activists to build coalitions across borders, but they also sparked the creation of other, more localised, grassroots movements.

One of these movements is the African Climate Alliance (ACA), borne of those initial 2019 climate strikes.[43] When 17-year-old Ruby Sampson heard an international climate strike had been announced, she was travelling across Africa with her family in a truck fuelled by vegetable oil waste and solar power.[44] Galvanised by the strike, she sought out like-minded voices on social media; this became the starting point of the ACA, a South African grassroots group which currently has allies in eight countries outside of South Africa. The ACA's determination resulted in Cape Town's first-ever major climate protest. Initially, organisers took 'the lead from the European climate movement', but it soon became obvious that 'this way of climate organising doesn't fit the South African mould, often excluding those most affected by inequality and climate injustice.[45] So, organisers teamed up with the Youth Climate Council, South Africa's inter-schools coalition of climate justice activists, and set out to spark change across the continent, while engaging an Afrocentric version of the global youth movement.

Global and local coalitions currently make up the world's climate justice movement, which continues to expand. The ACA held regular online meetings throughout the pandemic, and in November 2021, they teamed up with the Vukani Environmental Movement and groundWork to launch a court case against the South African government. Known as the #CancelCoal battle, the fire was lit in 2019, when official plans were unveiled to heavily invest in coal-fired power across South Africa.[46] Not only would this investment further damage the environment, the coalition argued, but 'expert local reports' outlined that the policies would cause unnecessary job losses, as well as having impacts on social, physical and mental health and well-being for people living in South Africa, now and in the future. As evidence, they collated statements from locals whose kids were suffering with severe asthma due to air pollution, as well as energy research reports to prove that shifts to renewable energy plans would be significantly cheaper.

Increasingly, these manifestos and calls to action are centring the human costs of the climate crisis. They're giving voice to the most marginalised, reframing discussions from the abstract (global warming) to the concrete (displacement, inequality) and, in the case of queer climate activists in particular, using witty, innovative ways to push these conversations forward.

If you've ever thought there's nothing sexy about climate justice campaigning, you've clearly never come across *Assuming*

the Ecosexual Position: The Earth As Lover,[47] written by Annie
Sprinkle and Beth Stephens, alongside Jennie Klein. The cover
alone is a smorgasbord of stimuli: high-heeled PVC boots, a
brightly coloured array of flowers in bloom, as well as a decidedly phallic butternut squash. These are all collaged on top of
a portrait of Stephens and Sprinkle; Stephens in a green, leafy
headband, Sprinkle in leopard print, her cleavage decorated by
a gold floral necklace. Ecosexuality represents a newer space in
climate activism, one which reframes queer conversations in
the form of tongue-in-cheek, climate-centric praxis.

So what is ecosexuality? Sprinkle and Stephens offer an expansive, multi-faceted definition. They describe it as a 'new
sexual identity', one adopted by a 'person who finds nature
romantic, sensual, erotic, or sexy, which can include humans
or not'. But in their eyes, ecosexual is also 'an environmental activist strategy' and a 'grassroots movement', and anyone
who adopts this moniker is compelled to 'expand what sex
and orgasm are beyond mainstream definitions'. Better yet, it's
a term in flux – as the closing point of their definition, they
list: 'Other definitions as yet to be determined.' Ultimately,
Sprinkle and Stephens envision the ecosexual movement as 'a
punk-rock, queer, drag, pin-up grrrl version of environmental
activism', in alignment with 'the AIDS activist organisation
ACT UP, sex-positive feminism, ecofeminism, Fluxus performance art, and, sometimes, the hippie movement' – which,
although 'problematic', they credit as a rebellious, anti-
imperialist and environmentalist movement.

Sprinkle belongs to a lineage of tongue-in-cheek, distinctly
queer activism. As an artist, educator and sex worker – she's
been called the 'golden girl of porn' – she's made some pretty
memorable work rooted in sex workers' rights, queerness and
feminism, and always with a sense of humour. In her piece

Anatomy of a Pin-Up Girl,[48] she poses in thigh-high boots, stockings, garters, underwear, a tightly cinched corset and elbow-length gloves; in the comprehensive annotations, she highlights the painstaking labour of performing this ideal femininity, with notes like 'my feet are killing me', 'gloves cover tattoos for a more All-American girl effect', 'corset hides a very big belly' and 'breasts are real but sag, bra lifts breasts'. In 1989, she developed a one-woman show called *Post Porn Modernist*. 'It was kind of the first full-on theatre piece by a sex worker who plays herself,' she explained in a 2019 interview.[49] 'It was performance artsy because I showed my cervix to the audience and did a sex magic masturbation ritual.' When Sprinkle turned her attention to climate justice, she did so with flair – and plenty of light-hearted nods to her horny past. In 2008, the term ecosexual was 'floating around on a few dating sites', but neither Sprinkle nor Stephens could find a definition which encompassed the fullness of their love for nature. So, in the *Journal of EcoSex Research,* they published their own; thus, ecosexuality was born.[50]

Arguably, climate activism has long had a branding problem. The world's wealthiest nations have been largely uninterested in a crisis, which, so far, has wreaked havoc on comparatively poor countries. More people *need* to be invested in these discussions, but the language of climate activism is largely unsexy and intangible. It's all about decarbonisation, fossil fuels, rising sea levels, melting ice caps – terms which feel vague, distant and easy to ignore. The last few decades have seen queer artists and activists, like Sprinkle and Stephens, challenge this framing and try to get people interested in the climate crisis – which, of course, is needed, if the world can mitigate and potentially solve it.

Similarly, YouTuber Natalie Wynn, known as ContraPoints,

has taken an innovative approach to reducing apathy around climate injustice. A leftist YouTube essayist and ex-philosopher, she's built a mammoth following (almost 2 million subscribers on YouTube alone) for her beautifully styled, in-depth videos, which break down complicated topics into bite-size, humorous chunks. In December 2018, she released 'The Apocalypse',[51] a hilarious scripted video in which she plays both Marie, an out-of-touch, rich, right-wing snob, and her catgirl companion, Antoine, a parodic, anime-obsessed 'social justice warrior'. Marie demands smelling salts for her luxurious bath – Antoine says sure, but only if she watches her video essay on the climate crisis. The essay in question is a gloriously deranged recent history, which highlights the ways in which climate campaigner Al Gore, founder and chair of the Climate Reality Project, has been branded as 'fun-ruiner[s], criticising our high-emissions way of life'.

Throughout the video, Marie acts as a mouthpiece for right-wing arguments that dismiss, deny or minimise the climate crisis, which range from 'weather changes sometimes' to the accusation that 'this whole guilt-trip about carbon emissions is just an attack on the American way of life.' Antoine responds to each of these points with facts, logic and a sense of humour, splicing videos of politicians 'throwing a snowball to own the Libs' alongside screenshots of oil companies' record profits and easily understandable arguments about the climate crisis being fuelled by corporate greed. Marie replies: 'How am I supposed to care about rising sea levels when there are Muslims out there? And Mexicans? There could be Muslim Mexicans for all I know.' Wynn's point is crystal clear: marginalised communities are made into scapegoats to distract from the climate crisis, much like when the Mexican Repatriation targeted Mexican-American workers for the stock market crash that led to the formation of Roosevelt's New Deal in the 1930s.

The video ends with Wynn in drag, playing a masochistic, high-femme embodiment of the sea. With her sapphire-rhinestoned lips and twisted aluminium foil headpiece, she urges humans to continue their pollution so that she can rise up, swallowing the world into her 'black pit of wetness'. 'I enjoy your so-called degradation,' she shrieks. 'When you spew your filth all over, oh, it only makes me fucking wet!' Her monologue ends with: 'And that's why I vote Republican!' Antoine turns to Marie: 'You see that? We've got 20 years to stop her, or we're fucked.'

Climate activism has been due a radical makeover, and legacies of queer art and direct activism have been instrumental to this rebranding. These examples are a far cry from the headline-making activists of today, still disproportionately white and sometimes lacking nuance. Extinction Rebellion is a case in point. For years, their overarching goal was to get as many protestors arrested as possible – which, given histories of police brutality against marginalised people, was lacking in intersectional analysis, to say the least.[52]

The more recently formed coalition Just Stop Oil, established formally in early 2022, has been more progressive, already engineering hugely memorable moments. In October, protestors Phoebe Plummer and Anna Holland made headlines for throwing tomato soup at Van Gogh's *Sunflowers*, before gluing their hands to the wall.[53] Their direct action went viral, sparking conversation across the political spectrum and bringing Just Stop Oil – and its mission – into the public consciousness. The success of the action was cemented in early 2023, when youth culture magazine *Dazed* gave the activists a series of spreads, creating high-fashion reinterpretations of their protests.[54]

In theory, all publicity is good publicity when the issues at hand are literally a question of life or death, yet it's undeniably exciting to see the rise of intersectional climate activists like Mikaela Loach, Dominique Palmer, Vanessa Nakate and Gabriel Klaasen, as well as queer activists like Sprinkle and Stephens. Increasingly, the climate crisis is being viewed through new and more expansive lenses, broadening the scope of what remains a vital issue.

Against Borders

'Queer solidarity smashes borders.'
                    – *Lesbians and Gays Support the Migrants*

In November 2015, an estimated 1,500 protestors gathered out-side Yarl's Wood Detention Centre in Bedfordshire, England.[1] They brandished placards reading: NO HUMAN IS ILLE-GAL', 'AIN'T NO BORDER HIGH ENOUGH and END STATE VIOLENCE AGAINST WOMEN – calls to action which drew attendees from around the country to show their support for asylum seekers being held indefinitely.

The protest was a true coalition effort, aided by solidarity groups across the country which provided free transport to and from the centre. The all-women Lips Choir was on hand to create a 'carnival feel',[2] with demonstrators being instructed to sing loud enough that detainees could hear their messages of support and to add to the musical cacophony with their own drums, pans, whistles and sound systems. They kicked the metal fence as they sang. Inside the centre, detained women pressed banners up to the windows. They were able to partici-pate in the protest, as activists called detainees and then held the phones up to loudspeakers, so crowds could hear from them directly. 'There is so much chaos and confusion here,' said one detained woman, unable to access her medication for a month. Another cried as she spoke of her fear of being deported to Nigeria, where her brother had been murdered by terrorist group Boko Haram. 'It is worse than prison because you don't know when you will get out,' said a detainee named Kingsley, a Cameroon native who was detained despite having a valid student visa. 'Something is going wrong.'

Especially over the last two decades, few issues have attracted such widespread consensus and teamwork across the UK as the abuse and mistreatment of immigrants and asylum seekers. Groups like Sisters Uncut, the Black Women Rape Action Project, the English Collective of Prostitutes, Women for Refugee Women and Lesbians and Gays Support the Migrants have collectively organised across class, race and gender lines to build a powerful movement, one which fiercely opposes the UK's horrendous treatment of immigrants.

'Not long ago, LGBT+ people were the "illegals" and queer pubs and bars were being targeted in police raids and subject to state violence,'[3] reads the mission statement of Lesbians and Gays Support the Migrants, inspired in no small part by Lesbians and Gays Support the Miners, the group spotlit in the chapter 'Pits and Perverts'. 'Now, it is homes and workplaces of migrants that are targeted,' they continue, highlighting that 'the state and media' portray migrants – 'particularly Muslim migrants' – as a threat to LGBTQ+ rights, which are presented as 'British' or 'European' values. 'We see through this attempt to pit oppressed and exploited groups against each other,' they state. 'We build on a proud history of queer solidarity to say: no one is illegal.'

The group has made headlines repeatedly over the last decade. In April 2016, they burned fake banknotes featuring the face of Home Secretary Theresa May to protest rules which would deport non-EU workers earning less than £35,000 per year.[4] Almost a year later, a handful of members were arrested as part of the so-called Stansted 15; alongside activists from End Deportations, they lay on the runway of Stansted airport to prevent a chartered deportation flight from taking off.[5] Consistently, they've worked in coalition with other direct action groups like Action for Trans Health; in June 2017, the two organisations teamed up to counter-protest Gays Against Sharia, an Islamophobic faction of the white nationalist English Defence League.[6]

These groups acknowledge that discrimination against migrants – especially migrant women of colour – is wide-ranging, tied to other systemic issues like racism, sexism, domestic violence and poverty. Borders are the antithesis of solidarity. They're brutally policed,[7] politicised to fuel polarisation. Borders buy into the idea that where you happen to be born – an obvious lottery – dictates the rights you receive.

Activists raising awareness of these injustices know how to get their voices heard. British direct action group Sisters Uncut is renowned for its eye-catching, art-driven protests, which draw from movements like the suffragettes. One of their best-known slogans is 'Dead women can't vote,'[8] which they chanted amongst Hollywood stars at the 2015 premiere of *Suffragette*[9] (which, incidentally, was criticised for whitewashing the movement and ignoring women like Sophia Duleep Singh, who raged against the empire after seeing the brutality of life under British rule in India).[10] 'Oh golly,' mouthed Helena Bonham-Carter, as the Sisters Uncut members threw green and purple smoke bombs, before being forcibly removed by the police.

Sisters Uncut work in solidarity with marginalised groups of all descriptions, campaigning for prison abolition, an end to violence against trans people and more. In May 2017, they occupied Holloway Prison's visitors' centre to hold a week-long community festival,[11] its schedule packed full of workshops on women in prisons, state violence against migrant communities and people with disabilities, as well as sessions on yoga, singing and self-defence. Among the groups invited were the Bent Bars Project, a grassroots letter-writing movement showing solidarity with LGBTQ+ prisoners, as well as Movement for Justice by Any Means Necessary, one of the groups defending drag queens across the UK from far-right protests.[12]

These coalition groups of Black, LGBTQ+ and migrant activists regularly intercept immigration raids and share safety and harm-reduction resources, but a frequent target of their protest has been Yarl's Wood, the main immigration removal centre for women in the UK. For two decades, staff have routinely abused these women. NGOs have worked closely with detainees to create in-depth dossiers detailing their treatment, support their legal cases and document the racism and sexism they face inside.[13] But it wasn't until 2015 that the true heinousness of life in the detention centre was exposed thanks to a Channel 4 News investigation, based around a report by Women for Refugee Women. Undercover footage was obtained, which showed the 'racist and aggressive' attitude of staff, who referred to detained women as 'animals' and 'beasties'. Talking about one detained woman, a guard states: 'I'd beat her up.'[14]

In the investigative report, several women – many of whom are sexual assault survivors – spoke of their treatment by male guards in Yarl's Wood. According to the women, guards would routinely make a point of watching the women shower, and they would barge into their rooms with little notice, leaving them no time to cover up if they were naked. Whenever the guards sat down for tea, they would loudly objectify the women, commenting on their bodies. 'There is no dignity, no privacy,' said a woman identified only as Louise.

Serco, the company paid by the government to run the centre, claimed to take all accusations seriously, and said their first concern was always the safety of residents at Yarl's Wood. Historically, this has not been the case. When the UK's Labour government opened Yarl's Wood detention centre back in 2001, a carefully orchestrated press campaign ensued. Journalists were invited to tour the £100 million Bedfordshire facility, which 'looked more like basic student accommodation than anything you would find in a prison', recalled BBC journalist Danny Shaw, with 'soft furnishings, a library and a courtyard'.[15] The centre – the largest in Europe at the time – was built as a face-saving exercise by an ostensibly left-wing government facing critique for its failure to quickly answer asylum claims. Their solution was to introduce Yarl's Wood, billed as 'secure accommodation for women, adult families and, on a short-term basis, men whose cases are being assessed'. According to some of those journalists invited to the opening, their living conditions were 'cushy'. Millions more pounds of public money were ploughed into private contracts. Companies Serco and G4S have been contracted to oversee the centre since 2001; according to a 2016 report by the National Audit Office, the annual contract fees alone cost £10 million of taxpayer funding.[16]

Within just a few months of the well-publicised opening, it became clear that conditions inside the detention centre weren't exactly the cushy, student-pad vibes described to the press. In fact, they were horrific. In February 2002, asylum seekers being held indefinitely set fire to Yarl's Wood in a mass breakout attempt. Detainees smashed CCTV cameras and stormed the control room before lighting the fires – according to a *Guardian* report,[17] 20 refugees escaped the facility but eight were quickly recaptured by police. The chaos caused early stories of detainee mistreatment to trickle out. One 55-year-old woman had been unwell and had asked staff for medical treatment. She was handcuffed in preparation for being taken for treatment but after three days in cuffs, she was still waiting. Seemingly, this was the catalyst for the riot.

The chaos also drew attention to the private contractors' early failures, namely their refusal to install fire-fighting sprinklers, despite being advised to do so a year earlier. 'The early indications are that the conditions at the centre were pretty harsh,' said Mark Littlewood, a representative of human rights group Liberty. 'Sooner or later, it's not surprising an incident like this would occur, which isn't to condone the violence.' Littlewood argued the riot should spark inquiry into 'the treatment of asylum seekers in general. They need to be treated fairly, calmly and justly, not like common criminals.'

This didn't happen. In 2005, Black Women's Rape Action Project teamed with Women Against Rape, the All African Women's Group and Legal Action for Women to begin volunteering with detained women. As well as offering legal aid and resources to cope with trauma, these groups offered a platform for detainees to make complaints about conditions inside. In 2007, the coalition published research 'documenting extensive human rights abuses'. In 2014, they said, these abuses still persisted.[18]

In 2010, it was the protests of detainees themselves which garnered press coverage. According to the *Guardian*, 'at least 50 women'[19] held in Yarl's Wood staged a days-long hunger strike to protest their indefinite sentences, as well as their appalling treatment. 'We have been on hunger strike since Friday protesting about the length of time we have spent in detention here,' said a woman named Aisha, who had, at the time, been inside for three months. The centre was placed on lockdown, leaving women trapped in an 'airless hallway.' Five women on hunger strike fainted but nobody gave them medical attention. 'I had an asthma attack, but no one would come to give me my inhaler,' continued Aisha. 'I'm very weak. But we will stay on hunger strike for as long as it takes.' Almost 20 detained women were 'locked outdoors wearing few clothes', and the detainees locked in communal spaces were left without 'food, water or toilet facilities'.

In February that year, a motion was tabled in Parliament that called on the government to 'carry out an independent investigation into reports of violence, mistreatment and racist abuse from guards', and for a 'moratorium on all removals and deportations of the women who took part in the hunger strike pending the results of that investigation'.[20]

Despite the formation of an all-party parliamentary group on migrants and refugees in 2014, stories of mistreatment have continued – and the last decade of right-wing rule in Britain have only made matters worse. In 2012, then-Home Secretary Theresa May announced her intention to create a 'really hostile environment for illegal immigration'.[21] The effects of these policies have been well-documented, perhaps most comprehensively by Maya Goodfellow in *Hostile Environment: How Immigrants Became Scapegoats*.[22] It started with government-funded vans, brandishing messages ordering immigrants to 'go home or face arrest'. Soon afterwards, the Windrush scandal[23] revealed UK officials had destroyed the landing cards of immigrants promised citizenship in return for rebuilding post-war Britain.

Unsurprisingly, these years of openly hostile immigration policies did nothing to help those detained in centres like Yarl's

Wood. In 2018, news of yet another hunger strike broke. The women on strike described the centre as a form of 'hell' and stated that some women being threatened with deportation 'had been in Britain for more than 20 years, and had partners and children in the country'.

Cuts to legal aid have also had a disastrous impact on the rights of asylum seekers and refugees – one woman, known only as Adesola, explained: 'The lawyer I saw when I came here gave me the wrong advice. I should have applied for asylum straight away, but they didn't because of the money they wanted to take from me.'[24]

This crisis in the treatment of asylum seekers has been largely whipped up by racism, sexism and xenophobia, but increasingly, the appalling treatment of LGBTQ+ asylum seekers in the UK is being documented, too. A 2023 report[25] by Women for Refugee Women surveyed 24 lesbian and bisexual asylum seekers in the UK, with the aid of LGBTQ+ asylum campaign groups Rainbow Sisters and Rainbow Migration. The report featured the story of Anu, who was forcibly circumcised by her parents in Nigeria after being found with her girlfriend, in an attempt to take 'the devil' out of her. After hiding her sexuality from that point onwards, Anu's parents sponsored her to study in the UK in 2012 – and soon afterwards, to appease her family and protect her safety, she married a man. When her student visa ran out, she was quickly detained for six months in the 'lion's den' of Yarl's Wood, where she saw 'women trying to kill themselves'. Anu's claim was rejected and she quickly became ill from stress in continued detention. It was only when Anu contacted an LGBTQ+ support group that she worked up the courage to tell the Home Office about her sexuality. But when she did, the Home Office said 'they did not believe [her]' because she had married a man. 'If I could be accepted as a lesbian in Nigeria, I would not have left,' she explained, 'but . . . I have seen pictures of people being maimed and murdered in Nigeria because of their sexuality . . . similar to what happened to me. If I go back there, my life will be in danger.' Five years after being detained, she still doesn't have refugee status in the UK.

The 24 women interviewed for the research came from countries which criminalise consensual same-sex acts, legislation exported to British colonies by racist and homophobic missionaries. A handful of the women came from Uganda, where the May 2023 signing of the anti-homosexuality bill introduced the death penalty for 'aggravated homosexuality',[26] making the country's laws among the world's most punishing for LGBTQ+ communities. As well as homophobia, many of the women were also victims of gender-based violence, like genital mutilation, forced marriage and 'honour-based' violence. Many of the women were never told they could claim asylum on the grounds of sexual orientation, as they couldn't afford legal aid. Others lacked the mental health support to speak openly about their sexuality, or they had trauma-based fears – and clearly, thanks to stories like Anu's, evidence-based fears – about opening up in asylum interviews.

Several headline-worthy stories have illustrated what campaigners have called a 'culture of disbelief' at the Home Office, as well as key flaws in their official guidance.[27] Deportees have been sent back to countries which criminalise their identities and advised to simply 'pretend to be straight' when they get there. Bisi Alimi, a Nigerian activist now settled in the UK, summarised: 'In Nigeria, people put a tyre around your neck and burn you, and no one cares; or beat you until you die, and no one cares. The Home Office doesn't believe in the impact of threats from non-state actors.'[28]

When LGBTQ+ asylum seekers *are* spared from detention centres and placed in accommodation, they're more likely to face discrimination or violence in this housing, creating a no-win choice between homelessness and abuse. In 2018, the *Guardian* spoke to various sources. 'One intersex person was woken in the night by housemates and their friends demanding to see their genitals, while another transgender asylum seeker said her housemate exposed his genitals while yelling homophobic abuse at her.'[29] Representatives of organisations including Kaleidoscope Trust, Micro Rainbow International, and the UK Lesbian and Gay Immigration Group, shared anecdotal stories of asylum seekers sleeping on kitchen floors to avoid abuse from roommates, and harrowing tales of sexual assault which, when reported to the Home Office, were met with inaction.

Then there's poverty: those waiting for the results of asylum claims aren't legally allowed to work for the first 12 months,[30] and even after that period lapses, they're limited to a short list of largely highly-skilled jobs. They're forced to live on food vouchers alone.

The 2020 Covid-19 outbreak saw Yarl's Wood 'repurposed'[31] as a short-term housing unit for migrants crossing the Channel. Although the number of detainees was necessarily reduced due to the pandemic, the public health crisis ushered in a new wave of human rights abuses, overseen by then-Home Secretary Priti Patel. In June 2021, a court case launched by six asylum seekers and supported by the Joint Council for the Welfare of Immigrants ruled that the 200 detainees held at Napier Barracks were provided 'inadequate and unsafe accommodation',[32] and that the mass Covid outbreak in early 2021 was 'inevitable'. The case revealed that asylum seekers were being 'unlawfully detained in appalling, crowded conditions', and that the 'abandoned, ramshackle military barracks' are 'totally unsuitable sites to house anyone, much less victims of torture and trafficking and people fleeing atrocities'. Yet the UK government continues to buy up barracks and shipping containers in the hopes of transforming them into yet more 'unsuitable' accommodation.

Inside Yarl's Wood, the protests continue. In May 2023, a group of asylum seekers used gym equipment to smash their way out of the centre, resulting in a manhunt for 13 escapees.[33] Activists have continued to frame this unrest as proof that Yarl's Wood is unfit for purpose, a cruel waste of taxpayers' money. Later that month, nationwide protests against detention centres proved there's still a sense of urgency when it comes to standing in solidarity with vulnerable refugees.[34]

Many agree that broader attitudes need to shift for these injustices to end. There's a deeply ingrained belief that refugees need to somehow earn their rights. Despite fleeing violent, abusive or life-threatening circumstances, there's an expectation that they then still need to prove themselves of being worthy as if their human rights are conditional.

Someone who knows this better than most is Sarah Mardini. In 2015, she and her sister, Yusra, were two of many refugees fleeing the civil war in Syria. As the choppy waves of the Aegean Sea threatened to swallow their tiny, overcrowded boat whole, the two sisters jumped into the water, tied themselves to the vessel and swam three hours to shore, dragging the boat with them.[35] They managed to save the lives of all 18 refugees on board. Mardini and her family were granted political asylum in Germany, but these experiences encouraged her to help migrants making the potentially lethal journey across to Lesvos, Greece. Despite doing literally life-saving work, Mardini was arrested alongside fellow activists Seán Binder and Nassos Karaktisos in 2018 for spending their summer on the lookout for boats in distress. They were eventually acquitted, although someone without Mardini's high profile would potentially have met a different fate.

As we've seen throughout this book, it's not unusual for tangible, sometimes life-saving acts of solidarity to be criminalised – whether it's the Black Panthers having their survival programmes trashed by the FBI or environmental activists being detained for preserving our planet, standing up for the most marginalised often comes with a price. The last few years alone have seen people across Europe prosecuted for providing food, warmth and shelter to starving refugee families, giving them lifts to safety and helping them pass safely through snowy forests. In February 2018, a Swiss minister named Pastor Norbert Valley was accosted by police and subsequently charged with 'facilitating the illegal stay' of someone whose asylum claim had been rejected because his home country of Togo was 'not at war'.[36] The man attempted suicide after receiving the decision. Valley was ordered to pay a fine of €1,000, which he successfully appealed. Activists stood outside the court brandishing placards reading 'SOLIDARITY IS NOT A CRIME'. As Valley stated: 'There are hundreds who are still condemned, who have families. We now must work to change the law.'

In 2016, Nikesh Shukla gathered twenty UK-based writers for a game-changing essay anthology, *The Good Immigrant*. Each story critiques the expectation that immigrants be 'good' in order to be treated with respect; that human rights and fair treatment are conditional upon 'good' behaviour. This isn't a uniquely British phenomenon – in 2019, a follow-up anthology, *The Good Immigrant USA*, similarly detailed these experiences amongst writers of colour in the US – but the most relevant examples can usually be found in apparently heartwarming 'good news' coverage.

A prime example is the case of 'Le Spider-Man'. In 2018, Mamoudou Gassama, an undocumented Malian migrant living in Paris, saw a young child dangling from the balcony of a fourth-floor flat. He scaled the building to save the child, a rescue captured in grainy footage which quickly went viral, earning him his moniker. Days later, Gassama was invited by president Emmanuel Macron to the gilded Palais de L'Elysée, where he was promised 'documents allowing him to stay . . . a fast-track process to gain French nationality . . . a job with the Paris fire and emergency service' and finally, a medal for 'bravery and devotion'. A *Guardian* write-up[37] perfectly encapsulates press coverage of Gassama as the archetypal 'good immigrant': 'In that split second, Gassama, 22, did not think of himself or the threat of discovery and deportation back to Mali,' the news report reads. 'Instead, in an extraordinary feat of strength and bravery that has earned him the nickname "Le Spider-Man", he pulled himself up from balcony to balcony, before lifting the crying four-year-old to safety.'

Is it a good thing that he was offered a job and citizenship? Undeniably, yes. Is it fair that he had to risk his life to receive this offer? Or that the French president framed the offering of citizenship as an act of benevolence by a state perfectly willing to deport 'bad' immigrants? Well, no.

Clearly, not all immigrants and refugees get the same treatment in France. Since 2014, Britain has financially cooperated with France to construct the Calais Border, designed to keep immigrants out.[38] Migrant encampments have cropped up along the so-called Calais Jungle,[39] whose horrific conditions are well-documented. Despite this, the Calais mayor made it illegal in 2017 to feed these starving migrant families.[40] Volunteers offering meals to refugees through the charity Utopia56 were met with violent resistance from police, who 'fired tear gas to prevent volunteers from giving breakfast to about 30 teenagers in a field near the motorway outside the city'. Teenage refugees were detained for visiting a local Catholic centre, where they had been told they could shower free of charge.

Those refugees who aren't deemed 'heroes' are left to rely on the aid of charitable groups, NGOs and human rights activists. Back in Lesvos, an estimated 30,000 refugees have passed through PIKPA, a refugee solidarity camp created by a group named Lesvos Solidarity.[41] In November 2012, volunteers transformed what was once an abandoned campsite just south of Mytilini into a safe haven for those in need, offering them hot meals, legal support, counselling and even medical care. Around 100 families could be housed in secure, modern accommodation at any one point – small houses painted in bright, uplifting colours and decorated with artistic motifs, largely by the refugees themselves. PIKPA was built on the principles of kindness, solidarity and community-building, and it's been maintained by coalition groups across the island.

Amongst the activists plugging lethal gaps in government aid is the Ohana Collective, which organises an annual, almost utopian Queer Ranch Festival.[42] LGBTQ+ performers from around the world make the pilgrimage to Ohana, Lesvos, where they swim in the crystalline sea, pet the collective's adopted goats and dance all night. But in October 2020, one of their members made an impassioned plea to guests drinking colourful cocktails at the Flamingo lesbian bar. 'We are all aware of the unfolding refugee crisis on this island,' they said.[43] 'And yet, we don't seem to be doing anything about it. At best conversational or keyboard activists, we offset our guilt with a like or a mention before getting back to our ouzos, daiquiris and lesbian love affairs.'

Just a few weeks before the festival, a huge and mysterious fire had broken out at the Moria refugee camp, an hour and a half away from PIKPA.[44] Lesvos was in a state of emergency, as reports of police brutality and army surveillance emerged. Greek police built a perimeter around Moria to prevent refugees from finding shelter in local villages, forcing families to sleep rough on roadsides and in petrol stations. The morning following the fire, PIKPA volunteers came together in solidarity to cook 'a variety of rice and vegetable dishes'[45] for the refugees forced to flee the blaze. 'The women, themselves refugees from countries like Syria, Eritrea and Afghanistan, also put together small kits containing items like soap, sanitary supplies and clothes.' Small acts of solidarity to keep the refugees clean and fed.

Back at Flamingo Bar, the Ohana Collective announced their decision to team up with PIKPA to ensure the safety of refugees. 'They've been working on this island for eight years, primarily with vulnerable populations,' the Ohana member continued. 'With the money raised tonight, two members of our collective will shop for the necessities – think hand sanitiser, powdered milk, underwear, water – fill a Jeep, and drop them off . . . tomorrow afternoon.' The crowd was encouraged to 'give the cost of a shot or a cocktail – anything you can', but the final lines of the plea were drowned out by raucous cheering. Within half an hour, their donation bucket was overflowing with a total of more than €600. 'Thank you,' said the clearly emotional member. 'We were expecting €100, maybe €200, but this is unbelievable!'

PIKPA was in desperate need of support at the time. As part of its harsh crackdown on refugee rights, the Greek government announced in late September 2020 that it would force the closure of PIKPA by the end of October, forcing its residents out. Despite organisers' best attempts to protect the camp from closure, riot police encircled it on 30 October 2020. 'Residents were woken up in their houses by police,' read a press release from Lesvos Solidarity. 'No official written order was presented at any point, despite lawyers' repeated requests for individualised decisions for transfer to a new place, in respect of national, European and international law.' Despite the eviction, Lesvos Solidarity doubled down on its mission: its members diligently set about building safe, affordable housing, distributing thousands of food packages and blankets, and teaching Greek, English, Arabic, computer literacy and arts to refugees.

Projects like these prove that solidarity is alive and well, a value embedded in the core of leftist, grassroots coalitions. Throughout this book, we've seen historical examples of game-changing collectives, whose political analyses were sharp and intersectional. This spirit of mutual aid and collaboration hasn't gone anywhere but barriers remain – and borders are still one of the biggest. Borders keep us *literally* separated. They ensure that the rights we're given are dictated by where we happen to be born, all the while severing potential ties of international solidarity. State-sanctioned cruelty against refugees and immigrants sadly shows no signs of diminishing, but despite the ongoing, violent prevalence of border policing, activists are building global networks to ensure a safer, more just future.

Trans Fights for Reproductive Rights

'Our bodies are your battlefields.'

— Isabelle Solas

NYC Pride 2022 was set to be a celebration of proud, unapologetic queerness, a statement of defiance in the face of ongoing discrimination. But just days before the parade, a bombshell dropped: Roe v. Wade, which had protected US abortion rights for nearly half a century, had been repealed. After decades of tireless activism, abortion had been re-criminalised.[1]

I was in New York when the news broke. Planned speeches and events were interrupted, weighed down by a newly sombre mood.[2] Speakers took to stages across the city, making impassioned pleas to enshrine reproductive freedoms in law. Many underlined the overlaps between trans and reproductive rights; at their core, both movements are about bodily autonomy. Who should have the right to decide what to do with their body? Why should archaic notions of morality be imposed upon innocent people to block them from making vital decisions about their own lives? The bodies of marginalised people have long been legislated upon by politicians, who usually have no knowledge of what it's like to inhabit those bodies.

That Pride Sunday, the streets of Lower Manhattan were ablaze with colour and thunderous noise. Thousands lined the city's red-hot sidewalks, waiting with anticipation for the march to formally begin. Representatives of Planned Parenthood – best-known for reproductive healthcare but also a valuable provider of trans healthcare – stood at the front of the parade with trans-inclusive abortion rights placards. It was a powerful moment, one which referenced the fact that reproductive justice has always been an intersectional struggle.

According to the Center for Reproductive Rights, unsafe abortions are responsible for an average worldwide death toll of 39,000 per year.[3] This issue to not just limited to the US. Globally, it's not unusual for abortion practitioners to be criminalised for their work.[4] The last few years alone have seen protracted battles for abortion rights in countries like Ireland,[5] Benin[6] and Poland,[7] with varying degrees of success. Criminalising abortion doesn't stop it from happening. Instead, it creates a sense of fatal desperation and leads to hunts for backstreet abortions, which can be lethal.

In 1994, a group of 12 Black women – now known as SisterSong[8] – coined the term 'reproductive justice' to challenge the largely white mainstream feminist movement's sole focus on abortion. Reproductive justice included not only the right to an abortion, but a right to have children *and* to parent those children. When immigrant families are ripped apart by detention laws,[9] it's a reproductive justice issue; when Black women in the UK are four times more likely to die during childbirth,[10] that's a reproductive justice issue; when trans men are coerced into sterilisation in exchange for gender recognition,[11] it's a reproductive justice issue.

These inequalities are entrenched in some pretty dark histories. Planned Parenthood, known for its progressive stances, was founded by a eugenicist.[12] When the first birth control pill was pioneered, poor Puerto Rican women were enlisted as guinea pigs for its earliest trials; three women died during this test phase.[13] Prior to the pill's invention, race and class were key determining factors in who could access abortions. Enslaved women weren't technically mothers in the eyes of the law, they were temporary; their unborn babies were potential assets to be sold, so their access to abortion was policed not only by the state, but by slave-owners.[14] Seemingly, some enslaved women found clandestine ways to induce abortion without attracting attention. Chewing cotton root could induce abortion, as could highly poisonous, potentially lethal substances like turpentine, which women swallowed in order to terminate their pregnancies.

Trans-inclusive discussions of reproductive rights are far newer, largely because society has historically lacked the language. Trans-masculine and non-binary people need access to abortion, yet ongoing sensationalist debates claim medically inclusive language – like 'people with uteruses' and 'pregnant people' – is an attempt to erase cis women from conversations about reproductive rights.[15] This is obviously not the case; the push for inclusive language is a direct response to trans people being failed by healthcare systems, a failure due in part to exclusionary language.[16] Medical misinformation is rife; anecdotally, some trans men have gone through the costly and painful process of having their eggs frozen only to find out that testosterone isn't guaranteed to make them permanently infertile.[17]

In 2017, the European Court of Human Rights officially declared that the compulsory sterilisation of trans people in order to legally change their gender – which, at the time, was mandated by the laws of 22 European governments – was a violation of human rights.[18] A year later, Transgender Europe and ILGA-Europe found sterilisation was still being demanded in the Czech Republic, so they took the government to court and won their case.[19] Some countries have gone a step further than just dropping the legal requirements. In 2018, Sweden became the first country to pay compensation to trans people who were made to undergo sterilisation between 1972 and 2013. Between 600 and 700 victims became eligible to receive compensation of 225,000 SEK (approximately £18,000) as a result.[20] In 2020, the Netherlands followed suit.[21]

In Argentina, the intersectional nature of these struggles has been recognised and capitalised upon by activists, who have worked together to push for collective justice. Their methods have been punchy, attention-grabbing and rooted in harm reduction.

Scour the web and you'll find a radical book with a mind-melting cover. It's a full-sensory attack of vibrant, neon pink, plastered in rainbow stripes and dotted with the trippy, smiley faces most commonly found on LSD tabs. At first glance, it could either be a quirky kids' colouring book or a hallucinogenic history of acid house. In reality, it's neither. The title reads: *Everything You Need to Know about Giving Yourself an Abortion with Tablets* ('*Todo lo que querés saber sobre cómo hacerse un aborto con pastillas*')[22] and there are no individual authors named, just an activist collective: Lesbians and Feminists for the De-criminalisation of Abortion.

This DIY abortion manual was released in 2010; just a year earlier, the collective set up a hotline for people looking to perform at-home abortions. Their pill of choice was misoprostol, a prescription drug designed to prevent stomach ulcers caused by common pain meds. But when combined with mifepristone, a blood pressure medication, it can induce abortion.[23] Whisper networks spread news of these qualities. In a 2011 Argentinian study of its risks, of the 94 respondents who had been exposed to misoprostol, a whopping 81.5 per cent had 'heard about its abortifacient effect through friends, neighbours or relatives'.[24] The results showed that 'women exposed to [the drug] had a significantly higher frequency of abortions', but when it wasn't effective, misoprostol increased the risk of 'major congenital anomalies', like limb defects and lung tissue damage.

It's telling that people sought these abortion pills anyway; as we've always known, criminalising healthcare doesn't make it go away, it just pushes it underground, making it potentially lethal.

In Argentina, there's long been a vocal abortion rights movement. These activists call themselves La Marea Verde[25] – the Green Tide – and they're recognisable by the green handkerchiefs they wave at protests. Throughout the early 2000s, they submitted bills calling on the government to decriminalise abortion – at the time, abortion was criminalised under a 1921 law, and could lead to up to four years' imprisonment. Their calls were consistently ignored, so pissed-off activists decided to take matters into their own hands, hence the DIY abortion book. Through this, they were building on the legacies of initiatives like the US's Jane Collective,[26] which established secret abortion clinics back in the 1960s, before Roe v. Wade achieved decriminalisation.

As the Argentinian movement grew in size and scale, there were calls from within to diversify. Especially in the first few years of La Marea Verde, the focus was solely on cis women, as it had been across the feminist movement in Argentina before that point, as evidenced by the name of the annual feminist conference. First established in 1986, the Encuentro Nacional de Mujeres (the National Meeting of Women) contained little to no mention of trans men or even lesbian women. The messaging of the aforementioned group Lesbians and Feminists for the Decriminalisation of Abortion, in the late 2000s,[27] marked a step forward, proof that coalition-building and finding common interests could work as a political tactic. Lesbian feminists within the group were known for creatively reframing the issues; they took the concept of non-normative desire and extended it to women who desired not to have a child. Building these bridges between lesbians and straight, cis women was a key part of their strategy, but so was the guerrilla distribution of at-home abortion books.

Trans activists similarly played a major role in showing solidarity with abortion rights activists in Argentina. Lohana Berkins was amongst the most vocal of these advocates. Softly spoken and fiercely intelligent, she founded a national trans organisation – ALITT (Asociaciön de Lucha por la Identidad Travesti y Transexual), which went on to spearhead key legal victories. In 2006, the Supreme Court overturned a ruling stating trans people didn't have the legal right to organise and campaign for their rights; four years earlier, Berkins herself made national headlines by enrolling as a school teacher, battling to register with her *actual* name, not her previous name.[28] Anger was a driving force of Berkins's activism, as she alluded to with her signature sign-off: *Furia Travesti* (Transvestite Fury).[29]★ This fury wasn't just directed towards transphobia. Berkins was clear on the importance of solidarity from day one, understanding that struggles for justice are interconnected.

When it came to abortion, she reiterated that the primary issue was one of bodily autonomy. In a famed 2007 speech, she

---

★   activists like Berkins continuously reclaim *travesti*, historically used as a slur

outlined a mission to 'demolish the hierarchies that order identities and subjects, recognising us as black, whores, Palestinians,
revolutionaries, indigenous, fat, prisoners, junkies, exhibition-
ists, *piqueteras, villeras,* lesbians, women and trannies.'[30] Calling
specifically on the need to legalise abortion, she said: 'Although
we [trans women] do not have the ability to give birth to a
child, we do have the courage to conceive another history.'

Berkins is far from the only trans woman who's been on
the frontline of abortion activism in Argentina over the last
few decades. In 2021, Isabelle Solas released the documentary
Our Bodies Are Your Battlefields,[31] an intimate and often hilarious
insight into the lives of the activists of OTRANS, a La Pla-
ta-based activist organisation. Together, the group makes jokes,
shares old stories, pokes fun at politicians on television and, of
course, campaigns for change. OTRANS is led by the charismatic, passionate Claudia Vázquez Haro, who was born in
Peru but moved to Argentina to pursue higher education in the
early 2000s. In 2018, she was one of the women chosen as
an expert speaker at Argentina's National Congress, ahead
of a parliamentary vote to legalise abortion. 'What do trans
femininities and *travestis* have to do with abortion?' she asked,
before making an impassioned plea for solidarity. The vote
failed in 2018, but on 8 March 2019, thousands of protestors
lined the streets of Argentina, demanding the government
legalise abortion.[32]

This continued pressure ultimately paid off in 2020, when
Argentina became the third country in Latin America[33] to
legalise elective abortions. OTRANS was also amongst the
organisations that played a key role in passing Argentina's 2012
Gender Identity Law, which remains comparatively progressive
when compared to other countries' laws.

This legislation represented hope. Clearly, the government

could see that bodily autonomy was a fundamental right, that curbing this autonomy pushed people underground, and that people should have the ability to make decisions regarding their own bodies. Trans activists in particular were quick to highlight these links, aligning themselves with cis feminists to keep pushing for change. *Our Bodies Are Your Battlefields* proves this solidarity wasn't easy, nor was it without its tensions. One scene in the documentary shows Haro's speech in favour of abortion rights being met with applause and cheers, but later, at a protest, she's heckled roughly by the crowd. 'This is how they treat us,' she says, referring to cisgender feminists. Ultimately, though, her speech made waves: in 2019, the Encuentro Nacional de Mujeres was officially renamed the Encuentro Plurinacional de Mujeres, Lesbianas, Trans, Travestis, Intersexuales, Bisexuales y No Binaries.[34] Clearly, Haro's statement that rights movements are stronger when they work in solidarity with one another had made a difference.

In 2014, Tomás Máscolo – a trans activist, socialist and journalist for *La Izquierda Diario* – sat on a panel about abortion within Argentina's trans-masculine community. As part of the panel, he asked a doctor what should have been a simple enough question: 'How do I go about having an abortion if I'm on hormone therapy?' The doctor couldn't answer him.[35] For years, Máscolo had known that trans men were an afterthought within the country's abortion rights movement, but the fact that even a doctor had no idea what to say to him set him out on a mission to learn more. As he suspected, there were little-to-no concrete statistics about trans-masculine people seeking or undergoing abortions. The few studies on Argentina's trans community that did exist were generally skewed towards trans women, and included no questions on abortion or reproductive healthcare. Máscolo illuminated these issues, speaking out about the unsafe conditions of illegal abortions, stories of misgendering and medical mistreatment.[36]

A lot has changed since then. In Marea Verde marches, trans men started holding placards with slogans painted in the movement's signature green: *LOS VARONES TRANS TAMBIÉN ABORTAMOS* ('Trans guys have abortions too').[37] Throughout the late 2010s, public visibility of trans men within reproductive rights movements was heightened. Men spoke about being misgendered by health professionals at fertility clinics, and shared the harrowing stories of their own abortions, with the help of journalists like Máscolo. In 2017, he penned an in-depth article[38] which humanised these men. One was named Álvaro; Máscolo set the scene of him shaking with fear and biting his nails, waiting in an anonymous garage to be seen by a backstreet doctor who had been recommended to him by a friend. Álvaro had only just turned 18 years old, but his boyfriend had wanted to prove to him that his body was 'like a woman's'. He proved it by removing the condom, leaving Álvaro pregnant and in desperate need of an abortion.

As well as relying on the power of storytelling, organisations such as the Frente de Trans Masculinidades (The Trans-Masculinities Front) worked with artists to commission colourful, memorable illustrations, usually with a lick of La Marea's trademark green.[39] The posters featured doodles of trans-masculine folks of all descriptions: some were chubby and hairy, others had visible top-surgery scars; some wore binders and others were chest-feeding young babies. The accompanying slogans varied, but the thread that connected them all was an emphasis on sexual and bodily autonomy. Gradually, the abortion rights movements shifted from the language of 'pro-choice', and instead started to rely on taglines like 'My body is mine.' In 2013, an artist named Effy Beth shared a smiling photo of herself as she sat in an operating room waiting for a gender-affirming surgery. Thanks to the Gender Identity Law, she emphasised: 'I don't have to justify myself. Awake, I can photograph myself in the middle of the procedure, because it isn't illegal. My body is mine. Is your body yours?'

The fight for reproductive and trans justice in Argentina is proof that solidarity is effective, especially when movements work in tandem and navigate difficult conversations along the way. Too often, trans inclusivity is framed as a distraction within reproductive justice movements; there's an implication that the inclusion of trans people must come at the expense of cis women.

As we've seen in this chapter, that's far from true; in the case of La Marea Verde, solidarity across demographics has actively strengthened these calls for justice. Too many of us know what it's like to be blocked from making decisions about our bodies. Throughout history, marginalised communities have seen their bodies become testing grounds, eugenics experiments. It's still not uncommon for intersex babies to be subjected to so-called 'corrective' surgeries, otherwise known as intersex genital mutilation,[40] or for cis women to be subjected to female genital mutilation.[41] NYC Pride became a key platform for these conversations back in 2022, but this intersectional approach isn't just inclusive, it's smart; in the case of Argentina, building these bonds strengthens movements rather than separating them.

Hot Strike Summer

'We are legal, and always have been.'

– OTRAS

In 2023, union membership has never been sexier. This might sound like a strange statement – after all, what's so sexy about collective bargaining and fighting for workers' rights? What's so horny about a picket line? Yet this statement sums up the rebranding of unions, which have long suffered a sort of stuffy, buttoned-up reputation. Over the last decade in particular, that public image has been shifting.

A key marker of this makeover came back in 2014, when an in-depth study led to *The Atlantic* running a headline: 'Union Membership: Very Sexy'.[1] The research[2] in question was conducted by two sociologists, Adam Reich and Daniel Schneider. Both men had been fascinated by existing studies which showed that higher income leads to higher marriage rates. So, they decided to extend this hypothesis by examining whether union membership – which should, theoretically, increase someone's wages – would lead to higher marriage rates, too. Reich and Schneider used 25 years of data to answer their question, and their suspicions of a positive correlation between marriage and union membership rates *did* check out – for men

at least, although the stats for women weren't quite so con-
clusive. 'We argue that membership in a labour union may
increase the marriageability of young men and women,' they
wrote, 'either by helping to secure economic benefits in the
present, or by sending a signal to potential mates about
the stability and certainty of future economic prospects.'

The Atlantic's headline clearly editorialises the findings of the
study – in fact, it's kind of a misnomer, as there's nothing in
the research to indicate that people find union membership sexy
or in any way a turn-on. Yet nine years later, the headline was
being screen-shotted and reposted on Twitter with no context.
Thousands of users retweeted the article headline to endorse
the statement that yes, union membership is very sexy indeed.

In Scandinavian countries like Denmark, Finland, Sweden
and Norway, union membership has remained consistently high
over the last five decades. Statistics collated by NationMaster[3]
indicate that, at the start of the millennium, more than 70 per
cent of workers in Denmark, Finland and Sweden were signed
up to a union. Yet this presence declines rapidly as we get
further down the list. The UK – which had the tenth highest
union membership rate in the world back in 2000, according
to the stats – had just 29 per cent of its workforce signed up to
a union. Although trade union movements remained powerful
in Scandinavia, and union sign-up rates remained consistently high, rates worldwide were largely declining between the
1990s and 2010s.

Seemingly, this started to shift in 2022 – the year of 'hot
strike summer'.[4]

Naturally, the seeds were being planted years prior. In November 2018, the French government announced a fuel tax hike,
which would create a huge financial strain on the country's
citizens. On 17 November, thousands of protestors gathered

from across class, gender and racial lines – a *Jacobin* article[5] described the demonstrators as a coalition of 'poor workers . . . women from working-class households . . . rural youngsters' and more. France has long had a reputation as a politically active country – and for good reason. The excellent 1995 film *La Haine*[6] zooms in on racism and income inequality in Paris, looking at how areas in the *banlieues*[7] – the heavily-stigmatised outskirts of Paris – were systematically starved of resources, surveilled by racist police officers and doomed to repeat cycles of criminalisation. The 2018 movement was broader in focus, taking aim at the capitalist structures which were oppressing French people of all descriptions. To identify themselves, they took to wearing the hi-vis yellow vests of roadside workers. The press picked up on this unofficial uniform and the French protestors became known as *les gilets jaunes* – the yellow vests. Many of these demonstrators weren't officially affiliated with unions; in fact, many were critical of just how centrist and resolutely non-radical many French unions were. Yet the *gilets jaunes* sparked a resurgence of the French labour movement, which had long been stagnant. In December 2019, the country was immobilised by widespread strikes[8] in opposition to planned pension reform – and it was all thanks to the political might of these guerrilla protestors.

It wasn't just European workers taking action, either. In January 2019, thousands of Bangladeshi garment workers staged a coordinated strike, barricading highways to prevent traffic from flowing freely. In an interview with news agency AFP, a police official confirmed that 'water cannons and tear gas were fired . . . to disperse huge crowds of striking factory workers',[9] and that more than 50 factories had been forced to shut down operations due to the strikes.

Industrial action had been a long time coming. In 2013,

the collapse of a multi-storey garment factory named Rana Plaza[10] – also in Bangladesh – galvanised a transnational solidarity movement, resulting in the creation of organisations like Fashion Revolution, which demanded transparency and accountability from the global high-street brands enabling exploitation.

Garment workers in the Global South have long been forced to work in dire conditions to constantly supply goods to wealthy Western countries. As well as poor pay[11] and punishingly long work hours, investigations revealed that this predominantly female workforce was regularly subjected[12] to sexual assault and harassment, as well as being forced to work in factories which were structurally unsafe – hence the Rana Plaza collapse.

Some gains have been made since 2013, and it's thanks in no small part to Bangladeshi unions. The aforementioned strikes in Bangladesh led to the government announcing a 'pay rise for mid-level factory workers after meeting manufacturers and unions'.[13] These workers are also increasingly building international links, coordinating actions against global mega-brands. Every year since 2019, unions worldwide have cooperated in a 'Make Amazon Pay'[14] strike on Black Friday, uniting workers from Bangladesh to Japan, Germany to France. 'Unions, civil society, and progressive elected officials will stand shoulder to shoulder in a massive global day of action to denounce Amazon's despicable multimillion-dollar campaigns to kill worker-led unions,' said Christy Hoffman, president of UNI Global Union.

These calls to action have been accelerated by the 2020 Covid-19 pandemic, which devastated global economies, pushing already marginalised workers into further poverty.[15] Worse still is the fact that many of these underpaid workers were designated as 'key workers'[16] and thus forced to risk their lives on the frontlines, while the comparatively sheltered middle classes either worked from home or didn't work at all, often while still being paid. The pandemic thrust inequality into the spotlight. Would homeless people be rehoused for their own safety? What would happen to those of us who had no families to isolate with, no permanent roof over our heads? Soon, research proved the inevitable – that people of colour were most severely impacted by the pandemic.[17]

There were other consequences for marginalised people. Anti-Asian hate crime soared; anyone perceived as Asian on the streets was now more likely to be abused, harassed or verbally assaulted, stigmatised as infectious.[18] In London in May 2020, a Black transport worker named Belly Mujinga was spat on and coughed at by a group of racists. Mujinga later contracted Covid-19, which killed her, although a later inquest into her death refused to take the hate crime into account.[19] Then, in late May 2020, an eight-minute video of George Floyd, an unarmed Black man living in Minneapolis, Minnesota, being murdered by a police officer made global headlines.[20] His grisly death sparked mass protests and galvanised – once again[21] – a global Black Lives Matter movement. None of this was new. As we've seen already in this book, unarmed Black victims have long been killed and brutalised by police forces worldwide. But this time, the world received the news with seemingly unprecedented vigour.

For downtrodden workers, it was yet more proof that the systems designed to supposedly keep them safe – like law enforcement – were actually killing them. Widespread conversations about structural racism ensued, and dedicated campaigners such as Angela Davis and Mariame Kaba gained mainstream attention, as an organised activist movement called to defund the police.[22]

In the UK, the last few years have been chaotic, to say the least. For more than a decade, the right-wing government has been pushing through austerity policies, nudging the poorest and most precarious among us into further poverty.[23] Wages have remained stagnant for years, whereas rapid inflation has caused prices to soar – in October 2022, the annual rate of inflation in the UK reached 11.1 per cent, marking a 41-year high.[24] Growing awareness of a 'cost of living crisis'[25] has lit a fire underneath workers nationwide, sparking a wave of collective organising in the UK, buoyed largely by unions, who have had some of their strongest showings in recent history.

This is the context behind 'hot strike summer'. Workers of all descriptions are pissed off. They increasingly understand that their shitty pay packets are thanks to CEOs skimming profits and dodging taxes. So now, these conversations are being taken to the streets.

The summer months of 2022 saw hundreds of thousands[26] of UK workers marching to, demand better pay and working conditions. Workers may have been furious, but their shared attitude was pretty punk in its 'fuck you' messaging. Some strikes had an air of jubilant chaos, while others showed a steely determination by workers to have their voices heard. Nurses took to picket lines in their scrubs, and firefighters donned full uniform to walk alongside them. A handful of protestors wore T-shirts in the NHS's signature sky blue, created by London clothing brand Sports Banger, which fused the NHS logo with a swooping Nike tick.[27] Profits from the sales of these T-shirts had originally gone to providing meals for intensive care workers[28] and local community centres during the pandemic, but when the strikes came around in 2022, Sports Banger created more of these tees, sending them out free of charge to striking healthcare workers as an act of solidarity.[29]

Long-standing tensions were finally bubbling over, and it showed; the numbers were phenomenal. According to the Office of National Statistics (ONS), between June 2022 and December 2022, 2.472 *million* working days were lost.[30] The December figures marked the highest monthly total since November 2011, although it was 'still much lower than the number of days lost in the 1970s and 1980s'.

Despite these enormous figures, union membership in the UK actually declined in 2022[31] – union-busting is still commonplace, and some see trade unions as a relic of the past. Yet popular support for unions seems greater than ever, and those who *are* signed up seem more determined to win than they have been in years. Beyond the statistics, there's a more important takeaway from 'hot strike summer' – union membership is being rebranded as something cool, aspirational and even kinda hot, as the 'hot strike summer' moniker suggests. The striking workers are also achieving their planned mission: to cause chaos, to show just how needed their services are. Even now, national news websites publish regularly updated strike calendars, to let readers know which actions are being planned, and when. It might be a pain in the arse to have your train cancelled, but unions aren't cowing to the tuts of pissed-off members of the public, and they aren't stepping back from their mission.

Much of this rebranding can be credited to the UK movement's public face, Mick Lynch, who became general secretary of the RMT (rail, maritime and transport) union in May 2021.[32] Especially over the last two years, he's fielded endless questions from TV journalists about the disruption that railway strikes would cause, responding in a brilliantly sarcastic fashion, his quick wit and straight-talking, no-bullshit approach to media interviews earning him online praise.[33]

239

These months of coordinated, union-led action have also shone a spotlight on the UK's class system, to the extent that Rishi Sunak, the UK prime minister, accused railway workers of being 'foot soldiers in Mick Lynch's class war'.[34] This right-wing frustration proves that the UK's current wave of working-class solidarity is having a serious impact on those in power.

Despite long histories of union-busting, unions have existed in some form or another for centuries.

In 12th-century Europe, tradespeople and craftspeople of many descriptions started banding together to form what were then known as guilds – merchant guilds for the traders and craft guilds for the artisans. Derived from the Saxon word 'gilden' – which means 'to pay' or 'to yield' – these guilds had multiple benefits for the workers within them.[35] Collectively, merchants shared an agreement to help each other transport goods safely, by travelling together and keeping a lookout for potential thieves. Craftspeople could collectively agree on production standards, reducing the level of competition between them and ensuring that they weren't undercutting each other. Coming together as workers had political benefits, too. Not only could workers share their complaints and identify areas for improvement, they could band together and demand better conditions. To access these benefits, workers were always required to pay a fee into a collective pot. These fees were initially low, but as the guilds grew, workers became richer – and, as a result, the charges for guild membership increased, pricing out lower-income workers in the process.

Naturally, union-busting soon followed. England experienced economic and political turbulence throughout the 1300s; the bubonic plague pandemic killed tens of millions in Europe alone – an estimated 30 to 50 per cent of the European population at the time[36] – and the Hundred Years' War between England and France had all but bankrupted England. In order to rebuild the economy, the government set about imposing and collecting extortionate taxes on England's poorest citizens. Meanwhile, the already-wealthy barons became even richer, as they weren't obliged to pay tax to the king.

Frustrations mounted throughout the 1300s and eventually erupted in May 1381, when a royal official went on a mission to collect unpaid poll taxes from peasants in Brentwood, Essex. The peasants resisted, violently.[37] Protests quickly spread throughout the entire south east of England; court records were burned, and local gaols (prisons) were opened and their prisoners freed. Soldiers were deployed across the country to brutally suppress the protests, and rebel leaders were captured and executed for organising and mobilising the poor.

Academics remain divided as to the true socio-economic impact of the revolt, but what *is* known is that the rebellion dissuaded Parliament from paying for war through taxation of the poor.[38] The collective power of working people had been well and truly proven, so it should come as no surprise that the government began cracking down on workers' guilds later that decade – as part of the 1388 Guild Enquiry, guilds were ordered to detail exactly what they were doing, as well as report how much wealth they had.

Trade unions as we know them now are often traced back to the Industrial Revolution, which lasted roughly between 1760 and the mid-1800s.[39] During this period, new technological innovations changed the everyday jobs of workers, first in the United Kingdom and later around the world. Handmade goods were replaced by mass production, thanks to the creation of large-scale manufacturing processes powered by water and steam.

Around this time, a union movement began bubbling up in the United States: the earliest recorded strike took place in 1768, when journeymen tailors across New York went on strike to protest their wages being reduced.[40] Just a few decades later, shoemakers in Philadelphia, Pennsylvania, formed the Federal Society of Journey Cordwainers.[41] British workers followed suit pretty quickly. In Manchester's People's History Museum in Salford, there's the earliest documented trade union banner in the country, created on behalf of the Liverpool Tin Plate Workers' Society back in 1821.

A lot has changed in the last 200 years, and plenty of these changes are the result of a growing global trade union movement. In 17th-century England, a six-day working week was the norm.[42] For religious reasons, Sunday was given as a day of rest. Workers were usually paid on Saturdays – and many wasted no time taking their hard-earned cash to the pub and spending it on booze. Mondays became known as Saint Mondays[43] because, across the country, employers became used to their workers not attending on Mondays, instead staying at home to nurse their hangovers. Employers naturally abhorred the tradition, as it meant less productivity; religious leaders loathed it too, linking it to bad behaviour, heavy boozing and moral degradation. Not everyone was drunk – some were simply tired and took Monday as a second day of leisure. Whatever the justification, Saint Mondays became a British mainstay.

Religious institutions soon cracked down on so-called Saint Mondays, instead suggesting workers take a half-day on Saturday, to ensure their attendance at church. But workers had tasted the irresistible freedom of two *whole* days off, and trade unions fought consistently to ensure their demands were met. Similarly, today's union members are fighting for a four-day working week, coming together in collective attempts to claw back more of their time from the clutches of capitalism. The four-day week was trialled en masse back in May 2023, with almost 3,000 workers, from brewery employees to bankers, reporting lower levels of stress and burnout.[44] Even the employers themselves were happy; almost all of them pledged to stick to a four-day week after the trial period was over.

Globally, the power of unions and collective bargaining has been proven time and time again. Yet there *are* demographics of workers who are often barred from unionising due to the excessive and unjust criminalisation of their work.

Sex workers fit this bill; as we saw in the chapter 'No TERFs, No SWERFs', they're often forced underground by laws which criminalise their work, leaving them with few or no rights. Yet there are historical examples of game-changing, self-defined prostitutes fighting for union recognition, and the collective mobilisation of sex workers as a combined workforce.

On 10 December 1983, Raúl Alfonsín stood atop a balcony at Argentina's Buenos Aires town hall to give a rousing presidential inauguration speech in which he promised to lead the country into democracy. As crowds gathered in the town square, chanting '*El pueblo unido jamás será vencido*[45] ('A village united will never be conquered') – a popular Chilean protest chant, which later spread across Latin American socialist movements – Alfonsín promised to fight for human rights, to unite the country and to tackle the widespread poverty resulting from the country's economic crisis. Alfonsín's speech is well-documented as the starting point of a new chapter in Argentina's human rights history, but a lesser-known detail is that a 60-something woman named Ruth Mary Kelly was standing somewhere in the first few rows, trying desperately to attract Alfonsín's attention by shouting: 'President, president, I'm a sex worker!'[46]

It wasn't the first time that Kelly had agitated for change – far from it. Through oral histories, her own memoirs and the work of feminist historians, Kelly's trials and tribulations are becoming public knowledge. Increasingly, it's being recognised that her activism – largely within lesbian, sex workers' and labour rights circles – laid the foundations for a sex workers' union in Argentina, among the first in the world.

Kelly was born in Temperley, Argentina, at some point in the mid-1920s (some accounts say 1925, others 1926), but her parents were of Irish and Scottish origin, so Kelly grew up in a household speaking both English and Spanish. In her brilliant, fascinating memoir *Memorial de los Infiernos*, co-written with journalist Julio Ardiles Gray and released in 1972, Kelly speaks openly about being sexually abused multiple times as a young girl: by teachers, authority figures and her own family. At 14 years old, she was locked up in a juvenile correctional facility for young girls in Montevideo, a period Kelly described as the worst nine months of her life. Yet it opened her eyes to injustice, taught her harsh lessons about the world and introduced her to a world full of 'lesbians, thieves, criminals and prostitutes'.

To say the criminal justice system failed Kelly would be a wild understatement. Her teenage years were spent being moved between different correctional and psychological facilities, as her feelings for other women were starting to become known. When she tried to explain that her father had sexually abused her, she was declared clinically insane and held under state supervision in a psychiatric hospital. Throughout these years, Kelly was subjected to electroshock therapy – an old-school, hideously violent form of conversion therapy – and constant surveillance.

After an ill-fated marriage in her early twenties and a sexual experience with a cop in a hotel room, Kelly started to realise she could find solace at sea. 'Maybe I wanted to escape from myself,' she says in her autobiography. 'Maybe I thought a boat would take me far, far away, to other marvellous lands with good men and women, lots of sun and lots of happiness.' Street sex work never took her fancy, so instead she found clients on ships. 'Prostitutes and sailors around the world are part of a very special society,' she wrote. 'Where there are sailors, there are prostitutes. It's not just about sex and money. I'm speaking more generally. There's a type of camaraderie between us, a friendship.' Kelly paints herself as a free spirit of sorts, but also a runaway in search of an adventure, a reprieve from the horrendous memories of her childhood. For decades, sex work enabled her to live this life; first on boats, later in brothels.

By the early 1970s – around the release of her book, which gradually turned her into somewhat of a public figure – Kelly was becoming known as an activist. Throughout her life, she had been a revolutionary socialist; in the late 1940s, she was detained and tortured by the police while pregnant for selling radical leftist magazines. The late '60s Stonewall Riots and the Gay Liberation Front were shaking up global activist circles, and Kelly wasted no time getting involved with the Argentinian Gay Liberation Front – El Frente de Liberación Homosexual (FLH) – formed in August 1971 and designed as a non-hierarchical coalition of gay, lesbian and labour rights groups. Kelly helped found a sub-group named Safo, which centred the lesbians who felt left behind by mainstream feminists.

Increasingly, Kelly was involved with local politicised punks who marched for an end to police brutality, *and* she was fighting for the inclusion of lesbians within the gay rights movement. Defiantly, she referred to herself as a *tortillera* – a dyke. This affiliated Kelly with other radical groups worldwide, who were reclaiming slurs as a symbol of rebellion.

Perhaps the best-known global example is Dykes on Bikes, a lesbian motorbike gang formed in San Francisco in 1976. '[Kelly] didn't say she was gay or a lesbian, she reappropriated the word *tortillera*,' explained historian Deborah Daich,[47] who released a book about Kelly's contributions to Latin American feminism. 'She reappropriated that word in the same way she did with the word "prostitute". She took words designed to stigmatise, to divide and to discipline; she took them and made them her own.'

Kelly's activism continued a long history of Argentine sex workers' resistance. In a 2010 article published in *International Labour and Working-Class History*, scholar Katie Hardy traces this legacy back to the brothels of San Julián; in February 1922, five prostitutes chased a group of soldiers involved in a high-profile massacre out of their brothel with brooms, screaming, 'Murderers, criminals, we will not sleep with you![48] The women were part of a wider wave of workers' resistance – the Rebelde Patagonia – which erupted in 1920 in response to the bloody, continued suppression of rural workers' strikes. In the century since, sex workers worldwide have continued to fight for their rights. Argentina's AMMAR – La Asociación de Mujeres Meretrices de Argentina – was founded in 1994;[49] in 1997, the union became a founding member of RedTraSex, the Latin American and Caribbean Sex Workers' Network, which aimed to foster international solidarity between sex workers, to combine their voices and fight for justice.

Since the 1990s, similar sex workers' unions have been forged worldwide. In 2009, French sex workers formed the Syndicat du Travail Sexuel (STRASS) at a European meeting about prostitution held in Paris. Although sex workers form the backbone of the union, they work closely with the likes of lawyers and sociologists, who help them advocate for the rights of sex workers, with a particular emphasis on migrant sex workers. STRASS is explicitly trans-inclusive, and in the years since its formation, the union has made key progress. In 2017, STRASS made headlines for its long-standing efforts to ensure full medical insurance for sex workers. Speaking to *VICE*, a sex worker using the pseudonym Axelle de Sade explained: 'Most organisations . . . had no interest in protecting prostitutes. An organisation even told me they didn't want to be seen as the health insurance of whores.'[30] Yet after years of campaigning and reaching out to health insurance companies, STRASS managed to convince Mutuelle Prévoyance Interprofessionelle (MPI) to give sex workers 'better reimbursement of gynaecological and psychological care' and even sick leave. Described by the *Libération* newspaper as a historic first for sex workers, unionised workers rejoiced.[31] 'Before, it was impossible to see a dentist or get an eyewear prescription,' said a worker named Juliette. 'We basically couldn't afford to get seriously sick or we would risk losing all our money.' This discrimination placed health workers at serious risk, essentially forcing them to lie in exchange for insurance.

These victories are noteworthy and undeniably encouraging, but it's not all good news; the majority of sex workers in France are migrants, meaning their healthcare access is precarious. In 2016, the so-called Nordic model – which criminalises clients but not sex workers – passed in France[52] and the repercussions were soon felt.[53] Landlords raised their rents, justifying the arbitrary price hikes by saying they were 'taking a risk' in renting out their premises to sex workers. Sex workers' rights NGOs were defunded, whereas organisations which fight for the total abolition of sex work were given extra funding. As part of the law, the French government created a nationwide 'exit programme' for prostitution, through which sex workers can obtain a monthly stipend (roughly €300–400 per month) and migrant sex workers can obtain temporary residence permits. Yet this support often isn't enough to make ends meet; sex workers still need to earn cash. This is hugely difficult, if not impossible; employers can still stigmatise even former sex workers, and the six-month residence permit is often nowhere near long enough to get set up at job centres and find work.

These fights are ongoing, but there's a growing international network of sex workers, as well as more localised chapters, like RedTraSex and the European Sex Workers Rights' Alliance (ESWA). Despite the widespread criminalisation of sex work, unions have found creative ways to advocate for legal sex workers (strippers, erotic dancers, porn performers, online content creators) while simultaneously advocating for decriminalisation.

Plenty of these unions are tech and media-savvy too, using eye-catching taglines and tongue-in-cheek messaging to grab the attention of politically aware youth. Sex Workers' Union, a UK-based branch of the Bakers Food & Allied Workers Union, is one example of this. At the time of writing, the branch has more than 20,000 followers on Twitter, and press secretary Audrey uses the platform frequently to reiterate the union's stance on solidarity. These witty tweets are almost guaranteed to go viral. In February 2023, they tweeted a (now-deleted) statement of solidarity with striking workers at Medieval Times. These performers don heavy, sweaty costumes to flawlessly transport their audiences back in time, yet their acting work has long been undervalued. 'Sex workers know the dangers of jousting and handling swords in unsafe working conditions,' read the tweeted statement of support. 'No worker should be getting lanced without access to protections and safe labour practices. Huzzah the workers!' In November

2022, they tweeted a message of solidarity with striking postal workers, which stated, 'More than anyone, we know the graft of dealing with heavy loads, big packages and full sacks – and we all deserve to do so under safe conditions, with full worker protections.' It's a frankly genius approach to unionisation, which has earned Sex Workers' Union major victories when it comes to challenging strip club bans, fighting for the employment rights of workers and raising awareness of sex workers' demands for decriminalisation. As discourse around 'hot strike summer' continues to strive for humour and accessibility, sex workers are leading the pack in terms of galvanising solidarity.

Popularity and membership rates of trade unions may have fluctuated over the last millennium – and there's evidently still work to be done when it comes to boosting membership – but their purpose has remained largely the same: to fight collectively for fair treatment and better pay. To this day, you can't say the word 'solidarity' without thinking of unions, building global networks rooted in the premise of justice for all. As the world continues to burn, the role of these unions is as important as ever, both to end capitalist exploitation and to ensure the safety, well-being and rights of ordinary, everyday people.

Towards Liberation

'The ultimate, hidden truth of the world is that it is something that we make, and could just as easily make differently.'

– David Graeber

In June 2020, comedian Ziwe Fumudoh announced that she would be interviewing influencer Caroline Calloway live on Instagram. In the midst of a global lockdown, the resulting conversation[1] was an entertaining car-crash, a can't-miss spectacle which offered insight into the discussions of 'allyship' we've been having en masse over the last few years.

First, the context. Ziwe was already a well-known star on YouTube when she made the announcement, thanks largely to a series called *Baited*.[2] The premise is simple: in each episode, Ziwe interviews her mainly white co-workers about race, asking them gloriously sarcastic questions and poking fun at their answers. 'We all feel uncomfortable talking about race,' reads the *Baited* summary. 'It's much easier to pretend it doesn't exist than to acknowledge hard truths. Since Ziwe can't pretend race doesn't exist, she refuses to let her co-workers off the hook either.' It's a funny, incisive and provocative approach to comedy, which sees Ziwe use her academic background in African American studies to make white guests sweat.

Calloway, on the other hand, was known mostly as what Ziwe called – pretty accurately – 'one of the poster children for white privilege'. After amassing an Instagram following of more than 800,000, Calloway advertised a 'Creativity Workshop' in January 2019 and sold tickets for $165 a pop.[3] What was billed as a day full of orchid crowns, eggplant salad and crystal-filled care packages fell apart in spectacular fashion, leading to articles dubbing her a scammer. The final nail in her reputational coffin came in September that year, when *The Cut* published an in-depth essay[4] by a woman named Natalie, who claimed to be a close friend of Calloway's, as well as the ghostwriter of her then-unreleased book. It's a damning portrait, which casts Calloway as a master manipulator, skilled at using her tears and beauty to grift her way to the top. The truth is obviously more complex. Regardless, Calloway became a catch-all avatar for conversations about the whitewashing and memeification of 'wellness'.

By the time their paths crossed in June 2020, the world was in chaos. The brutal murder of George Floyd had sparked a worldwide protest movement – the kind which couldn't be contained or quelled by lockdown rules. The Black Lives Matter movement, founded in 2013[5] by radical Black organisers Alicia Garza, Patrisse Cullors and Opal Tometi, was thrust into the spotlight as attention turned to racial injustice.

In the wake of Floyd's murder, social media proved a highly effective tool for organisers to share meeting locations, communicate with one another and coordinate protests. Many used the #blacklivesmatter hashtag to spread the word, but on 2 June, millions of users posted black squares[6] to their Instagram feeds alongside the hashtag, drowning out the activists

trying to connect with each other. This was never supposed
to happen. The black square post was intended to be limited
to the music industry, as part of a campaign called #The-
ShowMustBePaused.[7] Yet this vital context was lost, as was the
explicit request to *not* use the #blacklivesmatter hashtag, but
to use #blackouttuesday instead. Seemingly well-intentioned
white people were accidentally burying vital information.

This energy was short-lived; within just three weeks of the
protests breaking out, how-to articles were explaining how to
overcome 'allyship fatigue'.[8] It didn't take long for anti-racism
to slip down the global priority list. As this sense of urgency
died down, Ziwe's Instagram became a place for vital discussions to continue and shed light on the phenomenon of
performative allyship – 'doing the work' to look progressive,
with little long-term investment in dismantling oppressive
structures. Ziwe's razor-sharp, hilarious interviews dug deeper
into the shallowness of what people thought of as 'allyship'.
In her interview with Calloway, Ziwe pointed out that Calloway had shared a list of Black authors to read and pointedly
asked: 'How many of these books have you read?' Calloway
replied: 'Honestly, of the nine books that I recommended on
my Instagram, I've read four. But I've ordered the other five
from Black bookshops, so I would like my ally cookie now.'
Ziwe smiled. 'There are no cookies in this game.'

Although comedic, Ziwe's interviews illuminate the trans-
actional connotation that allyship's newest definition seems
to have acquired. In December 2021, Dictionary.com named
'allyship' word of the year, defining it as 'the status of being an
advocate for the inclusion of a marginalised group of which the
advocate is not a member'.[9] The etymology of the term 'ally'
is traced back to a Latin verb, which means 'to bind', but the
word 'allyship' was first recorded in English in the late 1840s,

meaning 'the state of being associated with another or others for a common purpose', a definition that 'differs from allyship's current meaning', the entry notes.

Here, a personal disclaimer: the purpose of this essay isn't to shit on allyship altogether. Doing *something* is better than doing nothing, and even if people are donating money and reading marginalised authors solely for social media clout, those acts are still valuable. A donation is a donation, no matter the motive. What's interesting to me is the way that definitions of allyship have changed over time. The *original* definition of allyship — rooted in the sense of fighting for a 'common purpose' — sounds pretty much the same as solidarity. It's about identifying shared goals and uniting for the broader pursuit of justice. It's about mutuality, whereas the framework of allyship reiterates difference.

Arguably, the language of allyship is also the language of corporations. In the wake of Floyd's death, in a frenzied desire to self-educate, white people began buying books about race en masse. Yet the book which seemingly benefitted most was *White Fragility,* written by a professor named Robin DiAngelo. In July 2020, the *New York Times* ran an in-depth feature[10] on anti-racism training which prominently featured DiAngelo, described by writer Daniel Bergner as '63 and white, with greying corkscrew curls framing delicate features'. Throughout the summer of 2020, DiAngelo's inbox was filled with requests from corporations desperate to hire her for diversity and equality seminars — global companies like Nike, Amazon, Facebook, Goldman Sachs, Netflix and more. DiAngelo's training sessions were newsworthy not just for their content but for their delivery. In a 2020 book review for *The Atlantic,* linguistics professor John McWhorter reported that white attendees of DiAngelo's seminars 'regularly tell her — many while crying, yelling or storming toward the exit – that she's insulting them and being reductionist'.[11] The *New York Times* article describes her as similarly frank; she warns the audience: 'I will not coddle your comfort.'

The popularity of DiAngelo's book over countless others, many of which are written by authors of colour, is telling. First, today's definition of 'allyship' is reliant on distance. It's always been the case that allies aren't members of the demographics they're advocating for, but now, there's an implication that allies are fighting against systems which don't impact them *at all.* As Emma Dabiri writes in *What White People Can Do Next,* today's framing of antiracism is 'generally devoid of analysis of class or capitalism, which it seems to have largely replaced with interpretations of interpersonal "privilege"'.[12] Dabiri writes of a 'martyrdom' intrinsic to current discussions of allyship, which partly explains the success of DiAngelo's *White Fragility.* There's an almost self-flagellatory tone to these conversations. In his review, McWhorter paraphrases DiAngelo's insistence that 'you must not ask Black people about their experiences and feelings, because it isn't their responsibility to educate you'. This insistence is echoed in countless allyship infographics shared on social media, which state bluntly: 'Google is free.' And it is! But, in DiAngelo's school of thought, McWhorter continues that 'consulting books and websites' will have you accused of 'holding actual Black people at a remove, reading the wrong sources, or drawing the wrong lessons from them'. Basically, he concludes: 'If you are white, make no mistake: You will never succeed in the "work" she demands of you. It is lifelong, and you will die a racist just as you will die a sinner.' Black readers don't fare much better. 'Few books have more openly infantilised . . . or simply dehumanised us,' writes McWhorter, who describes *White Fragility* as a 'book about how to make certain educated white readers feel better about themselves'.

This final critique hits at the crux of today's definitions of allyship. Ultimately, it's about making people feel less guilty. For corporations and influencers, declarations of allyship are good for business; as DiAngelo herself says of the corporate diversity training seminars she hosts, they allow companies to say: 'We heard DiAngelo speak,' as though paying her absolves them of all accountability in perpetuating discrimination. It's a framework which gestures limply at unity, all the while relying on a definition which underlines difference.

Throughout *Shoulder to Shoulder,* we've seen the power of coalition-building in action. Long before the language of allyship, people have been coming together to fight for justice, to advocate for each other's rights. Perhaps the biggest issue with the framing of allyship is that it's described as a journey, the lure of being declared a true ally just a few workshops away.

In 2009, Cuban American scholar José Esteban Muñoz published the influential *Cruising Utopia: The Then and There of Queer Futurity.*[13] In the book's opening lines, he sketches a lyrical, affirming definition of queerness as 'the warm illumination of a horizon imbued with potentiality'. It's a statement that's simultaneously powerful and optimistic, one which refutes any kind of goal-orientated mentality. 'Some will say that all we have are the pleasures of this moment,' he writes, 'but we must never settle for that minimal transport; we must dream and enact new and better pleasures, other ways of being in the world, and ultimately, new worlds.'

Muñoz represents a school of thought rooted firmly in optimism, one which refuses to entertain the idea that the world we live in *now* is all we'll ever get. This is the driving ethos of abolitionism. The word 'abolish' might conjure images of destruction and tearing down, but abolition as a school of thought is all about building *new* structures. It's about looking at the hellscape around us, and choosing to believe that there *are* alternative ways of doing things. It's a movement rooted in hope; in fresh beginnings; in honest acknowledgements that current systems are broken, and that doing things differently requires a radical re-evaluation of the 'normal' we've been conditioned to accept as the only possible default.

In 2023, renowned abolitionist Mariame Kaba and Movement Memos founder Kelly Hayes teamed up to write a book called *Let This Radicalize You,* which Hayes describes as a 'resource for organisers who are new to movement work'.[14] It's an insightful and engaging read, one which Kaba says is 'really clear-eyed about the reality of the problems and the ongoing calamities our world faces', yet one which also acknowledges that 'good and bad things happen in parallel'.

This hope can be hard to retain in today's age of social media, one defined by doom-scrolling and the endless absorption of shitty news, interrupted by the occasional wholesome animal meme. Worldwide, a whopping 6.92 billion[15] of us – 86.34 per cent of the global population – have a smartphone, which usually means we also have access to social media. Yet these platforms, most of which are designed around the infinite scroll, are custom-built for addiction, modelled on slot machines and casino roulette wheels.[16] 'In the online economy, revenue is a function of continuous consumer attention – which is measured in clicks and time spent,' said Natasha Schüll, the author of *Addiction by Design,* in a 2018 interview.[17] So, what gets our attention? Bad news. In a 2023 study conducted by Harvard researchers, academics sifted through 105,000 headlines and 370 million story impressions to 'determine how emotional language affected news consumption'.[18] Their findings showed that 'negative language in news headlines increased the likelihood' of clicks; essentially, that 'sadness, not anger, seemed to be the main emotion driving those clicks'.

This latter point is crucial: whereas sadness is immobilising, anger is incendiary. Fury galvanises movements.

In the introduction, I wrote about the accusations of failure levelled at activist movements. The underlying message is: if we're doomed to fail anyway, why bother trying? People in power have everything to gain from a world immobilised by sadness, a society which sees solidarity and coalition-building as pointless endeavours. Yet throughout the pandemic, the impossible sometimes *became* possible. In 2020, the UK government temporarily housed tens of thousands of previously unhoused people in hotels[19] and private rentals, proving that people don't *have* to die on the streets. Local mutual aid groups were rapidly established; before we knew it, plenty of us were donning face masks and doing grocery shops for people we had never met.

Much like in the era of Roosevelt's New Deal, the world saw that swift and drastic change is possible. Yet despite calls to move towards a more accessible, more just post-pandemic future, the momentum behind demands for radical overhaul slowly faded.

It's no coincidence that the Black Lives Matter movement gained its greatest traction yet during this tumultuous period. When the horrific video of George Floyd's murder circulated online, protestors across the globe took to the streets in the midst of a pandemic to show solidarity with Black communities. In 2021, more than twenty cities across the US actually followed activists' demands to defund the police, investing those saved dollars into housing programmes and food access schemes.[20] In Minneapolis, the city of Floyd's murder, a small team of mental health responders have been introduced in a pilot programme, heeding the call of abolitionists to create a viable alternative.[21] There's still endless work to be done – obviously, it shouldn't take the murder of an unarmed victim for governments to make change – but these are small victories. 'In my organising experience, I have experienced countless losses, but there have also been some magnificent wins, so I know that these are possible,' says Kaba, in conversation with Hayes. 'If we fight, we might lose. But if we don't fight, we're definitely going to lose.'

Abolition centres this spirit of optimism, the belief that there's scope to centre utopia within activism. It tells us not to just look at what's already been done, but rather at what we can do from this point onwards. As this book has – hopefully – proven, there *has* been excellent work done worldwide, especially over the last century. We've seen rainbow coalitions, AIDS activist movements, and alliances formed between trans and reproductive rights activists, some of which have made real, tangible gains. We've also seen that these coalitions are hard to sustain; egos, conflict and burnout all get in the way, the inevitable difficulties that come with working together. Yet minimising these stories, these links between marginalised activists, does us all a disservice, because they represent hope and community, even if their work is messy, complex and ongoing.

It *is* possible to dream of a world rooted in community care, in solidarity and mutual aid. Disability collectives have long reframed care as something nurturing and enriching, rather than a necessary evil. In *Care Work: Dreaming Disability Justice*,[22] Leah Lakshmi Piepzna-Samarasinha writes of being inspired by Loree Erickson's 'care collective'. Erickson, a 'queer femmegimp porn star academic', took matters into her own hands after being failed repeatedly by the state, which refused to adequately fund her care. When she *was* able to hire the occasional care attendant, they were 'homophobic and unsupportive', Piepzna-Samarasinha explains. So, Erickson fired her attendants and instead wrote a friendly callout for help, which she distributed amongst friends, encouraging them to share it with their friends, too. Erickson has lived in this way for 15 years; her care collective has aided her move to Toronto and, in return, they've been given the 'chance to build community, hang out with Loree, and have fun – not as a chore'. Piepzna-Samarasinha, in collaboration with countless other other queer, disabled activists of colour, have continued this work of building care collectives, both offline and online. Their calls to reframe care have been influential, and they speak to the core of an abolitionist movement rooted in collectivism and kindness, rather than individualism and the old systems we know to be broken.

It's not accidental that acts of solidarity are criminalised. We're discouraged from standing in solidarity with one another because it's politically useful to people in power, who have more to gain by keeping us divided. Global histories of union-busting prove that coalitions are a perceived threat. As Dabiri underscores in *What Can White People Do Next?*, the concept of whiteness was built and rooted in supremacy to shatter potential bonds of solidarity between European and African workers. In the earliest days of sexology, homosexuality had to become something that you *are* rather than something that you *do* because it needed to be framed as some kind of innate, inherent deviance – the sinful *yang* to the pure, conventional *yin* of heterosexuality. It had to set us apart as some mythical *other*, one worthy of criminalisation.

These threads are all connected. If queer theory teaches us

nothing else, it's that binary and oppositional thinking does all of us a disservice. Activists and scholars have long seen and called out the division sown by 'single-issue' thinking; in the words of Audre Lorde, 'There is no such thing as a single-issue struggle because we do not live single-issue lives . . . our struggles are particular, but we are not alone.'

Yet in today's world of capitalism and 'self-optimisation', we're encouraged to work on ourselves and ourselves only. In *Trick Mirror,* Jia Tolentino writes of a 'market-friendly and mainstream' feminism which has 'greatly over-valorised women's individual success'.[23] To an extent, the same can be said of the mainstream framing of most social justice issues. When Barack Obama was elected into the White House, *NPR* pondered whether or not his election signified a 'post-racial America'.[24] Margaret Thatcher is sometimes held up as a steely feminist icon, despite personally overseeing the decimation of millions of working-class livelihoods.[25] Katherine Araniello's hilarious send-up of the 2012 Paralympics advert made the salient point that celebrating 'superhuman' disabled athletes does nothing to improve the daily lives of disabled communities across the UK, whose lives have been endlessly worsened by austerity policies.

When activism is reduced to single-issue struggles and individual success stories, we lose sight of the broader fact that our struggles are, and always have been, more interconnected than we might have initially believed. Instead of focusing on difference, as allyship would encourage us to do, solidarity tells us to lead with kindness and empathy, to build long-term partnerships. These partnerships become communities, and they can be pretty damn joyous – communal meals, mutual aid and broad, loving networks can dull the day-to-day hardships of life.

At the risk of sounding like a Hallmark card, hope can be a lifeline in even the shittiest of circumstances. Too often, activism is framed as something goal-orientated and reactive, a temporary burst of anger designed to stamp out some new, horrific atrocity. In reality, resistance is a daily project. Centuries of deeply ingrained discrimination won't disappear overnight; untangling and surviving these webs of oppression is an ongoing process. Since moving back to Sheffield in 2020, I've found myself enmeshed in mutual aid networks, grassroots initiatives and leftist groups dedicated to feeding their communities, fundraising constantly and supporting those who need it most. There are letter-writing initiatives, intended to create brief moments of solace for people in prison. There are communal kitchens, volunteer projects dedicated to casework for queer asylum seekers, DIY collectives throwing euphoric parties to raise cash and forge new links between like-minded locals. These grassroots efforts are ongoing, and despite the bleak circumstances facilitating their existence, they can be pretty damn life-affirming. It sounds clichéd, but there's joy to be found in resistance.

I don't mean that we should cling to naïve optimism or advocate for constant positivity – when the odds are stacked against you, there's nothing more infuriating than someone trying to assure you that things aren't *that* bad. Because sometimes, they are. Sometimes, things are really shit. Yet no matter how dire the circumstances, there's an ongoing need to do what we can to ensure our collective survival in that moment; to maintain hope that the world can be better.

As we're often reminded, progress isn't linear; sometimes we go forward, sometimes not. Yet there's solace to be found in the likes of abolitionists like Kaba, who remind us that both gains *and* losses are made constantly. All we can do is strive to make tomorrow better than today, not just for ourselves, but for others. In the spirit of past activists, coalitions and change-makers, we can stand shoulder to shoulder and march collectively towards a kinder future.

Endnotes

Definitions of 'solidary'
1. 'Solidarity', Collins Dictionary Online, collinsdictionary.com
2. 'Solidarity', Britannia Online, britannica.com

Introduction
1. 'The forgotten history of the world's first trans clinic', scientificamerican.com
2. 'Cruising in Berlin's famous Tiergarten', xtramagazine.com
3. 'Magnus Hirschfeld: Berlin's third sex', rixfordeditions.com
4. *Magnus Hirschfeld: The Origins of the Gay Liberation Movement.* Dose, R (2014)
5. 'File: Mann Hirschfeld was jede frau vom wahlrecht Wissen muss.djvu', commons.wikimedia.org
6. 'The early 20th-century ID cards that kept trans people safe from harassment', atlasobscura.com
7. 'Burning sexual subjects: books, homophobia and the Nazi destruction of the Institute of Sexual Sciences in Berlin'. Heike, B. In: *Book Destruction from the Medieval to the Contemporary*, eds. Partington, G. and Smyth, A (2014)
8. 'LGBTQ institute in Germany was burned down by Nazis', teenvogue.com
9. *Racism and the Making of Gay Rights*, Marhoefer, L. (2022)
10. 'One of the world's first gay rights activists was racist and sexist', xtramagazine.com
11. 'Anna Walentynowicz, Polish provocateur who spurred Communism's fall, dies at 80', newyorktimes.com
12. 'The Gdansk agreement', jstor.org
13. *Coalition Politics: Turning the Century*, Johnson Reagon, B. (1983)
14. '(1977) The Combahee River Collective statement', blackpast.org
15. 'The right used to mock identity politics: now it's all it has', independent.co.uk
16. 'Before wokeness, there was "political correctness"', inthesetimes.com
17. 'Woke is not a right-wing myth', spiked-online.com

18. 'How AIDS activists used "die-ins" to demand attention to the growing epidemic', history.com
19. '*Pose*'s "condom over the house" scene really happened – here's how', out.com
20. *Against Equality,* Conrad, R. (2014)
21. '18 November 2003: Section 28 bites the dust', stonewall.org.uk
22. 'How Subarus came to be seen as cars for lesbians', theatlantic.com
23. *What White People Can Do Next: From Allyship to Coalition,* Dabiri, E. (2021)
24. 'The problem with the internet's obsession with queerbaiting', them.us
25. 'Homosexual/heterosexual: first print uses of the terms by Daniel von Kászony (1868–1871), Janssen, D., *J Homosex* 68(14): 2574–2579 (December 2021)
26. 'Map of countries that criminalise LGBT people', humandignitytrust.org
27. 'The colonial project of gender (and everything else)', O'Sullivan, S., *Genealogy* 5(3): 67 (2021).
28. 'Close to 2,000 environmental activists killed over last decade', e360.yale.edu
29. 'Five years later, the mystery of Marielle Franco's assassination has not been solved', jacobin.com
30. 'Almost half of human rights defenders killed last year were in Columbia', the-guardian.com
31. 'Black Trans Lives Matter protest: Why we're marching', bbc.co.uk
32. 'Global mapping of sex work laws', nswp.org
33. 'Sex work is work – and its laborers are officially unionizing', vice.com
34. *The Queer Art of Failure,* Halberstam, J. (2011)
35. 'Supreme Court overturns Roe v. Wade', npr.org
36. 'After Roe fell: Abortion laws by state', reproductiverights.org

Fighting a Working-class War

1. 'Community connection: Cherry blossom bloom dates in Washington, D.C.', epa.gov
2. *Working-Class War: American Combat Soldiers & Vietnam,* Appy, C. (1993)
3. 'Taking to the streets against the Vietnam War: A timeline history of Australian protest', labourhistorymelbourne.org
4. 'Mar. 03, 1965 – Police stops anti-Vietnam demonstration', alamy.com
5. 'Malcolm Browne: The story behind the burning monk', time.com
6. '"I have chosen the flaming death": The forgotten self-immolation of Alice Herz', Coburn, J., *Peace & Change* 43(1): 32–60 (2018)
7. 'Teach-ins helped galvanize student activism in the 1960s', thenation.com
8. 'The four stages of the antiwar movement', nytimes.com
9. '50 years on: The anti-Vietnam War protest in London', magnumphotos.com
10. *How We Get Free,* Taylor, K.-Y. (2017)
11. 'African-American involvement in the Vietnam War: Malcolm X and the nation of Islam', aavw.org
12. 'SNCC statement on Vietnam, January 6 1966', snccdigital.org

13. '"Violence was inevitable": How 7 key players remember the chaos of 1968's Democratic National Convention protests', time.com
14. *Street Fighting Years*, Ali, T. (1987)
15. 'In France, the protests of May 1968 reverberate today – and still divide the French', npr.org
16. Vanguard Magazine Vol. 1 No. 7 (May 1967), https://www.digitaltransgenderarchive.net/files/3r074t94h
17. *Transgender History*, Stryker, S. (2017)
18. '(1982) Audre Lorde, "Learning from the 60s"', blackpast.org

Building a Rainbow Coalition
1. *Black Panthers*, Varda, A. (1968)
2. '"Discredit, disrupt and destroy": FBI records acquired by the Library reveal violent surveillance of Black leaders, civil rights organizations', lib.berkeley.edu
3. *Judas and the Black Messiah*, King, S. (2021)
4. 'The Black Panther Party's deep Alabama roots', al.com5.
5. '(1966) The Black Panther Party Ten-Point Program', blackpast.org
6. 'Black Panther Party', vault.fbi.gov
7. 'The radical origins of free breakfast for children', eater.com
8. 'How the Black Panthers' breakfast program both inspired and threatened the government', history.com
9. 'Black Panther Party's free medical clinics (1969–1975), blackpast.org
10. 'Working together to reduce Black maternal mortality', cdc.gov
11. 'Bending the bars of Empire from every ghetto for survival', Heynen, N. *Annals of the Association of American Geographers* 99(2): 406–422 (2009)
12. 'Free Huey movement', pbs.org
13. *An Autobiography*, Davis, A. (1974)
14. 'Detroit's star activist adds BLM rally to her 50 years of rebellion', theguardian.com
15. 'Unity of the Black Panthers and Brown Berets', chicagoleader.com
16. 'The Brown Berets, as explained by founding member Dr David Sanchez', teenvogue.com
17. 'Fifty years of Fred Hampton's Rainbow Coalition', southsideweekly.com
18. 'Young Patriots and Panthers: A story of white anti-racism', redneckrevolt.org
19. 'When Black Panthers aligned with Confederate Flag-wielding working-class whites', the conversation.com
20. 'Revolutionary hillbilly: An interview with Hy Thurman of the Young Patriots Organization', redneckrevolt.org
21. *The Women's House of Detention*, Ryan, H. (2022)
22. 'Daughters of Bilitis', glbtqarchive.com
23. 'Picket in front of US Army building, first ever US gay rights protest', nyclgbtsites.org

24. ' "The beginning of a conversation": What it was like to be an LGBTQ activist before Stonewall', time.com

25. 'Diana Davies photographs', digitalcollections.nypl.org

26. '"All of us are unapprehended felons": Gay liberation, the Black Panther Party, and intercommunal efforts against police brutality in the Bay Area', Leighton, J., *Journal of Social History* 52(3): 860–885 (2019)

27. 'Angela Davis on abolition, capitalism and the politics of coming out', advocate.com

28. *Soul on Ice*, Cleaver, E. (1965)

29. 'The genius of Jean Genet', nybooks.com

30. 'Jean Genet and the Black Panther Party', Sandard, R., *Journal of Black Studies* 16(3): 269–282 (1986)

31. 'Jean Genet's May Day Speech, 1970: "Your Real Life Depends on the Black Panther Party"', socialtextjournal.org

32. 'Genet emerges as an idol of the Black Panthers', nytimes.com

33. '(1970) Huey P. Newton, "The Women's Liberation and Gay Liberation movements"', blackpast.org

34. 'The incredible true adventure of five gay activists in search of the Black Panther Party', harpersbazaar.com

35. 'Street transvestite action revolutionaries: Lavender & Red part 73', workers.org

36. 'Joy, rage and activism: The gendered politics of affect in the Young Lords party', Soares, K., *Journal of Women in Culture and Society* 46(4) (2021)

37. 'The Black Panther solidarity committees and the voice of the Lumpen', Höhn, M., *German Studies Review* 31(1):133–154 (2008)

38. 'The British Black Panther Party 1968–1973', blackpast.org

39. 'Hooligans and gangsters? A look at the Teddy Boys of the 1950s', britishnewspaperarchive.co.uk

40. 'A brief history of the Teddy Boys', rs21.org.uk

41. 'Exploring the Notting Hill race riots of 1958', britishnewspaperarchive.co.uk

42. 'Notting Hill Carnival 2002', theguardian.com

43. 'Fighting Sus! Then and now', irr.org.uk

44. 'Speaking out: Civil liberties in Britain', bl.uk

Making Mischief

1. 'Comment: 9 féministes ont lance le MLF le 26 août 1970 sous l'arc de triomphe', huffingtonpost.fr

2. 'Women's strike for equality', nytimes.com

3. 'What ecofeminist Françoise d'Eaubonne can teach us in the face of the climate emergency', versobooks.com

4. *Le Corps Lesbien*, Wittig, M. (1973)

5. 'Arcadie: sens et enjeux de l'homophilie en France, 1954–1982', Jackson, J., *Revue d'Histoire Moderne & Contemporaine* 4(53):150–174 (2006)

6. 'Exploring LGBTQ history in Paris', kent.ac.uk

7. 'Les aventures d'une alliance objective', Chauvin, S., *L'Homme & La Société* 4(158):111–130 (2005)

8. 'Was there something queer about May 1968? The FHAR and Guy Hocquenghem', autonomies.org

9. *The Screwball Asses*, Hocquenghem, G. (2009)

10. 'Sociology and the Gay Liberation Front – Bob Mellors at LSE', lse.ac.uk

11. '1945–51: Labour and the creation of the welfare state', theguardian.com

12. 'About the NHS birthday', england.nhs.uk

13. 'Cabinet Papers: Post-war nationalisation', nationalarchives.gov.uk

14. 'Trade unionism, workplace and politics in post-war Britain – and inferences for Canada', Spencer, B., *Labour/Le Travail* 28: 187–217 (1991)

15. 'GLF at Highbury Fields', Islington.humap.site

16. '"We're not ugly! We're not beautiful! We're angry!" The feminists who flour-bombed the 1970 Miss World pageant', independent.co.uk

17. 'The first Black Miss World looks back on her tumultuous win 50 years later', time.com

18. 'What happens when drag queens and beauty queens collide', elephant.art

19. '"We danced naked in Hyde Park – and then changed the world": The inside story of UK Pride, 50 years on', theguardian.com

20. 'The story of Gay Liberation Front in Britain', artsandculture.google.com

21. 'How workers battled to kill the bill in 1971', socialistworker.co.uk

22. 'Freaking London's Jesus festival', rollingstone.com

23. 'How a "zap" campaign helped gay people enter the news dialogue', journalism-history.org

24. 'Mark Segal: Making his own road to LGBT equality', epgn.com

25. 'How the Pride march made history', nytimes.com

26. 'Brixton Faeries', unfinishedhistories.com

27. 'A radical history of 121 Railton Road, Lambeth', libcom.org

28. 'Olive Morris and a legacy of transient politics', manchesterhistorian.com

29. 'Olive Morris, Squatters' Handbook', boroughphotos.org

30. 'Brixton Faeries: Made possible by squatting', youtube.com

31. 'Stories from Railton Road', brixtonadvice.org

32. 'Remembering Pearl Alcock, Black bisexial shebeen queen of Brixton', gal-dem.com

33. South Africa's historic speakeasies are still thriving', vogue.com

34. 'Love at first fight! Queere Bewegungen in Deutschland', schwulesmuseum.de

35. '50 Jahre Tuntenstreit: Geschichte queerer Kern-Konflikte', siegassaeule.de

No TERFs, No SWERFs

1. *Significant Contemporary American Feminists: A Biographical Sourcebook*, Scanlon, J. (1999)

2. *A Vindication of the Rights of Whores*, Pheterson, G. (1989)

3. Fischer, Anne Gray, "Forty Years in the Hustle: A Q & A With Margo St. James," *Bitch Media*, February 2013

4. 'Remembering Margo St James, a pioneering sex worker organizer', jacobin.com

5. 'Remembering Margo St James, patron saint of sex work', foundsf.org

6. *Revolting Prostitutes*, Mac, J. and Smith, M. (2018)

7. 'Getting it on at the Hookers' Ball', digitaltransgenderarchive.net

8. 'Obituary: Margo St James, pioneer of the sex workers' rights movement', nswp.org

9. 'St James Infirmary', stjamesinfirmary.org

10. 'The mothers who fought to radically reimagine welfare', npr.org

11. 'A rare look at the radical lesbian movement of the 1970s', wmagazine.com

12. 'Gay liberation in New York City, 1969–1973', outhistory.org

13. 'Kvennafridagurinn – The day Icelandic women went on strike', loc.gov

14. 'The day Iceland's women went on strike', bbc.co.uk

15. *Prostitutes: Our Life*, Jaget, C. (1980)

16. 'International Sex Workers' Day', nswp.org

17. '200 Prostitutes of Lyons in siege at church', nytimes.com

18. 'La revolte des prostituees – English script translation', maggiemcneill.files.wordpress.com

19. '100 years of the sex workers' rights movement', tenderloin museum.org

20. 'The mysteries of Mary Magdalene', historyextra.com

21. 'Nick Kristof and the holy war on Pornhub', newrepublic.com

22. 'Closure of Soho brothels raises risks for women, says local priest', theguardian.com

23. 'No Nordic model', nonordicmodel.com

24. 'On the game and on the move', azinelibrary.org

25. 'A brief history: The English Collective of Prostitutes', prostitutescollective.net

26. 'Prostitutes of New York (PONY)', nswp.org

27. 'On the game and on the move', azinelibrary.org

28. 'New York repeals "walking while trans" law', npr.org

29. 'There used to be tens of thousands of prostitution arrests in NYC. Now? About 100', gothamist.com

30. 'English Collective of Prostitutes' occupation of Holy Cross Church', bl.uk

31. 'From the archive: The spreading taint of suspicion', theguardian.com

32. 'Met Police "four times more likely' to use force on black people', bbc.co.uk

33. *Sex, Race and Class: The Perspective of Winning*, James, S. (2012)

34. *The Service*, Miren, F. (2021)

35. 'Facts about sex work', prostitutescollective.net

36. 'Trans solidarity! Decriminalise sex work now', digitaltransgenderarchive.net

37. ' "Social workers aren't always available – I am": trans activists in Tbilisi', opendemocracy.net

38. 'Sex worker community responses', nswp.org

39. 'Statement: The Soho raids – what really happened', prostitutescollective.net

40. 'West End extra: Colourful protest after sex workers are evicted from flats', prostitutescollective.net

Piss on Pity

1. 'Our history', riglobal.org
2. 'The origins and history of Disabled Peoples' International (DPI), 1945–1985', central.bac-lac.gc.ca
3. *From Stories to History: The Trek of People with Disabilities to Actualiza Self-Advocacy in Tanzania*, Rutachwamagyo, K. (2022)
4. 'Participation of People with Disabilities: An International Perspective', Miller, K., *Selected Papers from the 1980 World Congress of Rehabilitation International* (1980)
5. 'About us', disabledpeoplesinternational.org
6. 'Oral History Center: Disability rights', lib.berkeley.edu
7. 'Hans Asperger aided Nazi child euthanasia, study says', nytimes.com
8. 'Vic Finkelstein obituary', theguardian.com
9. 'Vic Finkelstein: A personal journey into disability politics', disability-studies.leeds.ac.uk
10. 'Disability, socialism and autonomy in the 1970s: case studies from Denmark, Sweden and the United Kingdom', Rydström, J., *Disability and Society* 34(9–10) (2019)
11. 'Fundamental principles of disability', disability-studies.leeds.ac.uk
12. 'Overlooked no more: Kitty Cone, trailblazer of the disability rights movement', nytimes.com
13. 'The 1977 504 sit-in', disabilityrightsflorida.org
14. 'Black Panther Party calls for the Section 504 regulations to be signed', longmore-institute.sfsu.edu
15. '"Butterfly Brigade" memories: SF survivors of anti-LGBTQ+ violence recall group's power', cbsnews.com
16. 'The International Year of Disabled Persons 1981', un.org
17. 'Ian Stanton' (draft obituary), disability-studies.leeds.ac.uk
18. 'On the Block Telethon protest', the-ndaca.org
19. 'Block Telethon 1992: The day we pissed on pity', medium.com
20. 'How the Nazi regime's pink triangle symbol was repurposed for LGBTQ Pride', time.com
21. 'DAN Timeline (1993–2011)', tonybaldwinson.files.wordpress.com
22. 'Psychiatric Survivor Pride day: Community organizing with psychiatric survivors', Finkler, L., *Osgoode Hall Law Journal* 35(3–4): 26 (1997)
23. 'How an insane asylum shaped this Toronto neighbourhood', housecreep.com
24. '"Transgender" could be defined out of existence under Trump administration', nytimes.com
25. 'Many try to return to normal from COVID, but disabled people face a different reality', npr.org
26. 'Mad Pride Paris 2015', youtube.com

27. https://www.bl.uk/learning/timeline/item106472.html [Note: the British Library website is still down following the cyber attack]

28. 'Mad Pride parade bed push', torontomadpride.com

29. 'Mad Pride rises in Mexico', madinamerica.com

30. 'Mad studies and Mad Pride on the rise in Latin America', madinamerica.com

31. 'Meet the "lunatics" fighting for psychiatry abolition at Mad Pride', theface.com

32. 'Making mad history: Mad Pride 2022', freedomnews.org.uk

33. 'Piss on Pity: Disabled artists versus charity', disabilityarts.online

34. 'Katherine Araniello: An obituary for SickBitchCrips, the queen of mischief', disabilityarts.online

35. 'Katherine Araniello: Pity (2013), pissonpityexhibition.wordpress.com

36. 'Damien Hirst homecoming announced for Yorkshire sculpture festival', the-guardian.com

37. 'Piss on Pity zine catalogue', pissonpityexhibition.wordpress.com

38. 'Loree Erickson is the porn star academic championing disabled porn', melmagazine.com

Dispatches from the AIDS crisis

1. 'Gay History – May 18, 1981: Dr Lawrence Mass becomes the first person to report about AIDS', back2stonewall.com

2. 'Rare cancer seen in 41 homosexuals', nytimes.com

3. 'Homophobia and HIV/AIDS: Attitude change in the face of an epidemic', Ruel, E., and Campbell, R. T., *Social Forces* 84(4):2167–2178 (2006)

4. 'AIDS virus invaded US from Haiti in 1969 – study', reuters.com

5. 'Trump baselessly claims Haitian immigrants entering the US "probably have AIDS" and letting them come in "is like a death wish"', businessinsider.com

6. 'HIV is a story first written on the bodies of gay and bisexual men', Ayala, G. and Spieldenner, A., *Am J Public Health* 111(7):1240–1242 (2021)

7. 'Aids: Origin of pandemic "was 1920s Kinshasa"', bbc.co.uk

8. 'Experiencdes of COVID-19-related anti-Asian discrimination and affective reactions in a multiple race sample of US young adults', Hamh, H. C., *et al*, *BMC Public Health* 21:1563 (2021)

9. 'Boy's 1969 death suggests AIDS invaded US several times', nytimes.com

10. 'Case shakes theories of AIDS origin', chicagotribune.com

11. 'Chlamydia', who.int

12. 'Fifty years of HIV: How close are we to a cure?', theguardian.com

13. 'Inaugural address 1981', reaganlibrary.gov

14. 'Word AIDS Day: "Never forget all those who were forsaken"', attitude.co.uk

15. 'Bob Jones III apologises for 35-year-old call to kill gays', nbcnews.com

16. 'The bigotry of gay-blood-donation bans', theatlantic.com

17. 'Remembering Dr Joseph Sonnabend, early pioneer on AIDS', amfAR.org

18. 'How AIDS remained an unspoken – but deadly – epidemic for years', history.com

19. 'Current trends mortality attributable to HIV infection/AIDS – United States, 1981–1990', cdc.gov

20. '*It's a Sin*: The woman who inspired Russell T. Davies' AIDS drama', bbc.co.uk

21. 'Barbara Vick interview', lambdaarchives.org

22. 'Barbara Vick interview', lambdaarchives.org

23. '*It's a Sin* tells the true story of Britain's shameful response to the AIDS epidemic', esquire.com

24. 'Antiretroviral drug discovery and development', niaid.nih.gov

25. 'The "L" in LGBT, and why order matters', theforeword.org

26. 'Homosexual/heterosexual: first print uses of the terms by Daniel von Kászony (1868–1871), Janssen, D., *J Homosex* 68(14): 2574–2579 (December 2021)

27. 'Vagrancy Act 1824', legislation.gov.uk

28. 'Know your rights: A guide for sex workers', prostitutescollective.net

29. 'The Contagious Diseases Acts and the prostitute: How disease and the law controlled the female body', Baker, K., *UCL Journal of Law and Jurisprudence* 1(1):88–119 (2012)

30. 'Irish outcry over teenager's underwear used in rape trial', bbc.co.uk

31. 'Making sense of Erykah Badu's comments on slut shaming and school uniforms', i-d.vice.com

32. 'Women prostitutes in the AIDS era', onlinelibrary.wiley.com

33. 'Black sex workers' history is Black history', poz.com

34. 'Carol Leigh, who sought a new view of prostitution, dies at 71', nytimes.com

35. *Working: My Life As A Prostitute*, French, D. (1988)

36. 'Our philosophy', calpep.org

37. 'Nonoxynol-9 for preventing vaginal acquisition of HIV infection by women from men', Wilkinson, D., *et al*, *Cochrane Database Syst Rev* 2002(3) (2002)

38. 'Evaluation of the 100% condom programme in Thailand', data.unaids.org

39. 'Empower Foundation', nswp.org

40. 'Mr Condom', faceofaids.ki.se

41. 'Presentes: 40 años de visibilidad LGBTIQ+ en Guadalajara', sc.jalisco.gob.mx

42. 'Ex Convento del Carmen, entre historia y cultura', ntrguadalajara.com

43. *A Comedian and an Activist Walk into a Bar: The Serious Role of Comedy in Social Justice*, Borum, C. and Feldman, L. (2020)

44. 'Senator Helms's callousness towards AIDS victims', nytimes.com

45. 'In memory of Jesse Helms, and the condom on his house', poz.com

46. 'The sodomy offence: England's least lovely criminal law export?', Kirby, M., *Human Rights, Sexual Orientation and Gender Indentity in the Commonwealth* (2013)

47. 'Dressing up in power: Tom of Finland and gay male body politics', Lahti, M., *J Homosex* 35(3–4): 185–205 (1998)

48. 'Safe sex in the 1970s: Community practitioners on the eve of AIDS', Blair, T. R., *Am J Public Health* 107(6): 872–879 (2017)

49. 'Untucking the queer history of the colourful hanky code', out.com

50. 'A long-nosed cartoon figure wearing a brown all-in-one suit with a speech bubble

exclaiming thanks for latex...', wellcomecollection.org.

51. 'A heterosexual couple, a gay couple, and a lesbian couple with a latex glove, condom and lubricant...', wellcomecollection.org

52. 'Heterosexual HIV diagnoses overtake those in gay men for first time in a decade', tht.org.uk

Pits and Perverts

1. 'Summer in the city', *Gay Times*, issue 72, 1984

2. '1980s', tht.org.uk

3. 'Miners' strike: 1984–1985', archiveshub.jisc.ac.uk

4. 'Solidarity and sexuality: Lesbians and Gays Support the Miners 1984–5', Kelliher, D., *History Workshop Journal* 77:240–262 (2014)

5. 'Ashton, Mark Christian (1960–1987), oxforddnb.com

6. 'Out and proud for the miners', tribunemag.co.uk

7. 'E27–29: Lesbians and Gays Support the Miners', workingclasshistory.com

8. 'Section 28 protesters 30 years on: "We were arrested and put in a cell up by Big Ben"', theguardian.com

9. '9 Oct 1987: Speech to Conservative Party Conference', margaretthatcher.org

10. 'I was a gay teacher under Section 28 – let's not go back there', labourlist.org

11. '2nd February 1988: Lesbians abseil into House of Lords to protest Section 28', gayinthe80s.com

12. 'Mike Jackson of Lesbians and Gays Support the Miners: "I didn't come out – I exploded"', newstateman.com

13. 'All out! Dancing in Dulais', youtube.com

14. '18th century Molly Houses – London's gay subculture', britishnewspaperarchive. co.uk

15. 'From gay conspiracy to queer chic: the artists and writers who changed the world', theguardian.com

16. 'Pits and Perverts', bl.uk

17. 'Rising cost of living in the UK', commonslibrary.parliament.uk

18. '30 years ago, the conversations we had about Section 28 were the same as the ones we have about trans rights today', independent.co.uk

19. '2022: The year trade unions came back', tribunemag.co.uk

No Fats, No Femmes

1. 'Darkness and light: the life and death of Alexander McQueen', sbs.com.au

2. 'Archive, 1996: Alexander McQueen, the bull in a fashion shop', theguardian.com

3. 'VOSS – Remembering Alexander McQueen's S/S 2001 show', gatamagazine. com

4. 'Fashion flashback: McQueen's Asylum show', vogue.co.uk

5. 'Diary entries by Michelle Olley on Appearing in VOSS, spring/summer 2002', blog.metmuseum.org

6. 'Skin whitening: What is it, what are the risks and who profits?', edition.cnn.com

7. 'Diet pills global market report 2023', globenewswire.com

8. 'Addressing weight stigma and fatphobia in public health', publichealth.uic.edu

9. 'Maintenance of lost weight and long-term management of obesity', Hall, K. D., *Med Clin North Am* 102(1): 183–197 (2018)

10. 'Fat bias at the doctor's office takes a serious toll', northcarolinahealthnews.org

11. 'Overweight adults', ethnicity-facts-and-figures.service.gov.uk

12. 'Obesity and African Americans', minorityhealth.hhs.gov.uk

13. 'Obesity among Black women in food deserts', Gailey, S. and Bruckner, T. A., *SSM Popul Health* 7 (2019)

14. 'Optimising health equity through para sport', Fagher, K. *et al*, *British Journal of Sports Medicine* 57: 131–132 (2023)

15. 'Eating disorders and disordered eating behaviours in the LGBT population: a review of the literature', Parker, L. and Harriger, J., *Journal of Eating Disorders* 8: 51 (2020)

16. '"I am divine": The icon's 7 most heavenly moments', queerty.com

17. 'Pink Flamingos (1972) by John Walters', cinematary.com

18. 'That time thousands of callers complained about Divine's "obscene" performance on Top of the Pops', queerty.com

19. 'Unpicking the history of gay male beauty standards', dazeddigital.com

20. 'Sex, sin and sausages: the debauched brilliance of Leigh Bowery', theguardian.com

21. 'Stock image ID 125657c: "Blitz" designer collection fashion show at the Albery Theatre, London, Britain, 1986', shutterstock.com

22. 'The fierceness of "Femme, Fat and Asian"', theatlantic.com

23. 'The handsome undercover cop smiles. Is he entrapping gay men or cleaning up a park?', latimes.com

24. 'Dating, disclosure and the transgender panic defense', transworldview.com

25. '"But where are the dates?" Dating as a central site of fat femme marginalisation in queer communities', *Psychology & Sexuality* 13(1) (2022)

26. 'Shame and HIV: Strategies for addressing the negative impact shame has on public health and diagnosis and treatment of HIV', Hutchinson, P. and Dhairyawan, R., *Bioethics* 32(1): 68–76 (2018)

27. 'A life exposed', nytimes.com

28. 'Review of *Sara Baartman and the Hottentot Venus*', Durbach, N., *Biography* 32(4): 858–860 (2009)

29. *Fattily Ever After*, Yeboah, S. (2020)

30. *Trouble & Strife*, issue 16, troubleandstrife.org

31. 'The rebellious history of the fat acceptance movement', centerfordiscovery.com

32. *La Cerda Punk*, alvarez castillo, c. (2014)

33. '"Filth is my politics, filth is my life": Rebuilding queer identity through Pink Flamingoes', varsity.co.uk

Treatment Access Campaign

1. 'Two tales about illness, ideologies and intimate identities', Tsampiras, C., *Med Hist* 58(2): 230–256 (2014)

2. 'Two tales about illness, ideologies and intimate identities', Tsampiras, C., *Med Hist* 58(2): 230–256 (2014)

3. 'The progression of LGBTIQ+ rights in South Africa (part 1)', schindlers.co.za

4. 'African sexuality and the legacy of imported homophobia', stonewall.org.uk

5. 'Queering apartheid: The National Party's 1987 "Gay Rights" election campaign in Hillbrow', Conway, D., *Journal of South African Studies* 35(4): 849–863 (2009)

6. Sifris, Dennis. "Remembering Ruben Sher." *Southern African Journal of HIV Medicine*, no. 28, spring 2007, p.7.

7. 'Simon Nkoli', sahistory.org.za

8. 'The Soweto uprising, 1976', michiganintheworld.history.lsa.umich.edu

9. 'Simon Nkoli', sahistory.org.za

10. 'Till the time of trial: The prison letters of Simon Nkoli', gala.co.za

11. 'LGBT activists in the anti-apartheid struggle', antiaparthaidlegacy.org.uk

12. 'Simon Nkoli, queer South African freedom fighter', thegavoice.com

13. 'How 11 striking Irish waters helped to fight apartheid', irishtimes.com

14. 'Mandela's stance on HIV set him apart from his ANC successors', theconversation.com

15. 'Two tales about illness, ideologies and intimate identities', Tsampiras, C., *Med Hist* 58(2): 230–256 (2014)

16. 'Cheaper antiretrovirals to treat AIDS in South Africa', Zwi, K., *BMJ* 320(7249):1551–1552 (2000)

17. 'A decade of fighting for our lives', un.org

18. 'The birth of the Treatment Action Campaign', sahistory.org.za

19. 'Separation for unity: The garment workers' union and the South African clothing workers' union 1928 to 1936', Witz, L., *Social Dynamics* 14(1) (1988)

20. 'Zackie Achmat: Profile', theguardian.com

21. 'The birth of the Treatment Action Campaign', sahistory.org.za

22. 'Zackie Achmat is the iconic AIDS crusader you don't know about', afropunk.com

23. 'New African movement for HIV/AIDS patients launched at Summit', thelancet.com

24. 'Tapiwa Kujinga, Director of PATAM: In Zimbabwe, civil society is involved in every aspect of the response to AMR', reactgroup.org

25. 'The HIV epidemic in South Africa: Key findings from 2017 national population-based survey', Zuma, K., et al, *Int J Environ Res Public Health* 19(13): 8125 (2022)

26. 'Monkeypox in Africa: the science the world ignored', nature.com

27. 'Fact sheet: Global HIV statistics', unaids.org

28. *Stories of AIDS in Africa.* Nolen, S. (2008)

No Planet, No Future

1. 'Amazon: Facts', worldwildlife.org
2. 'Slave labor in the Amazon: Risking lives to cut down the rainforest', news.mongabay.com
3. 'Tapping the Amazon for victory: Brazil's "Battle for Rubber" of World War II', repository.library.georgetown.edu
4. 'Chico Mendes: The Amazon's first climate-change activist', onetribeglobal.com
5. 'The life of Chico Mendes at a glance', blogs.ntu.edu.sg
6. '1977–88: Brazilian rubber-tappers campaign against deforestation', libcom.org
7. 'Socialist ecology: The life and death of Chicho Mendes', workersliberty.org
8. 'Brazil salutes Chico Mendes 25 years after his murder', theguardian.com
9. 'In famed Chico Mendes reserve, Brazil nut harvesters fight to save the forest', news.mongabay.com
10. 'How capitalism is a driving force of climate change', pitjournal.unc.edu
11. 'The refugees the world barely pays attention to', npr.org
12. 'A message from the future with Alexandria Ocasio-Cortez', youtube.com
13. 'The facts: Hurricane Maria's effect on Puerto Rico', mercycorps.org
14. 'Stock market crash of 1929', federalreservehistory.org
15. 'Great Depression facts', fdrlibrary.org
16. 'Hoovervilles and homelessness', depts.washington.edu
17. 'President Franklin Delano Roosevelt and the New Deal', loc.gov
18. 'The inauguration of Franklin D. Roosevelt', nps.gov
19. 'America's Great Depression and Roosevelt's New Deal: Relief programs', dp.la
20. *On Fire: The Burning Case for a Green New Deal*, Klein, N. (2019)
21. 'Global labor unions and federations', alfcio.org
22. 'Ten times workers won in 2022', tribunemag.co.uk
23. 'Global Green New Deal', c40.org
24. 'Green New Deal Rising', gndrising.org
25. 'Our story', gndrising.org
26. 'About C40', c40.org
27. 'Is autism a superpower', theguardian.com
28. 'Teen activist tells Davos elite they're to blame for climate crisis', edition.cnn.com
29. 'Qiyun Woo', explorer-directory.nationalgeographic.org
30. 'This teenager in Kenya is hoping to attract FIFA's attention – but not for his football skills', edition.cnn.com
31. 'West African climate activists at the forefront of the movement for climate justice', climaterealityproject.org
32. '10 countries at risk of climate disaster', preventionweb.net
33. 'The defense of Ethiopia from fascism', daily.jstor.org
34. 'Drying Lake Chad Basin gives rise to crisis', un.org
35. 'Pinkwashing', Blackmer, C. E., *Israel Studies* 24(2):171–181 (2019)
36. 'Israel's occupation: 50 years of dispossession', amnesty.org

37. 'The troubling evolution of corporate greenwashing', theguardian.com

38. 'Photo-cropping mistake leads to AP soul searching on race', apnews.com

39. '"Africa is on the frontlines but not the front pages": Vanessa Nakate on her climate fight', theguardian.com

40. '"I have a voice": African activists struggle to attend UN climate talks in Egypt', theguardian.com

41. 'Protesting climate change, young people take to streets in a global strike', nytimes.com

42. 'Extinction Rebellion activists stage die-in protests across globe', theguardian.com

43. 'African Climate Alliance', climateculture.earth

44. 'Ruby Sampson', giraffe.org

45. 'Youth lead protest at parliament (Cape Town) calling for climate action and environmental justice', greenbuildingafrica.co.za

46. 'Youth-led #CancelCoal climate case launched against government's plans for new coal-fired power', cer.org.za

47. *Assuming the Ecosexual Position: The Earth as Lover,* Sprinkle, A. and Stephens, B. (2021)

48. 'Anatomy of a pin-up photo', lesbianartandartists.tumblr.com

49. 'Sexologist Annie Sprinkle isn't covering anything up', interviewmagazine.com

50. *The Journal of Ecosex Research* 1(1)

51. 'ContraPoints: The Apocalypse', youtube.com

52. 'Does Extinction Rebellion have a race problem?', theguardian.com

53. 'Just Stop Oil activists throw soup at Van Gogh's Sunflowers', theguardian.com

54. 'Art attack! The unstoppable uprising of young climate activists', dazeddigital.com

Against Borders

1. 'Protestors demand closer of UK detention centre', aljazeera.com

2. 'Hundreds protest to demand closure of Yarl's Wood immigration centre', theguardian.com

3. 'Who we are', lgsmigrants.com

4. 'Activists burn £35,000 in fake bank notes at Home Office to protest Theresa May's new immigration rules', independent.co.uk

5. 'Stansted runway closed after anti-deportation protesters block flight," guardian.co.uk

6. 'Lesbians and Gays Support the Miners to counter far-right Gays Against Sharia Manchester protest', thepinknews.com

7. 'Spanish minister defends police accused of brutality at Melilla border', theguardian.com

8. 'Dead women can't vote: Why we chained ourselves to parliament', huckmag.com

9. 'Why I protested with Sisters Uncut at the *Suffragette* premiere', independent.co.uk

10. 'With "Sophia", a forgotten Suffragette is back in the headlines', npr.org

11. 'Services not sentences: Sisters Uncut occupy Holloway Women's Prison', gal-dem.com

12. 'Movement for Justice', facebook.com

13. 'Dossier calling for Yarl's Wood closure chronicles decade of abuse complaints', theguardian.com

14. 'Yarl's Wood: Undercover in the secretive immigration centre', channel4.com

15. 'Yarl's Wood: Years of misery and controversy', bbc.co.uk

16. 'Yarl's Wood Immigation Removal Centre', nao.org.uk

17. 'Asylum centre wrecked by fire', theguardian.com

18. 'Submission to the All-Party Parliamentary Group on Migrants & on Refugees: Inquiry into immigration detention, 1 October 2014 – Black Women's Rape Action Project and Women Against Rape', detentioninquiry.files.wordpress.com

19. 'Yarl's Wood women on hunger strike "locked up and denied treatment"', theguardian.com

20. 'Hunger strike at Yarl's Wood Immigration Removal Centre', edm.parliament.uk

21. 'UK governments past & present have emboldened far-right anti-migrant attacks', newarab.com

22. *Hostile Environment: How Immigrants Became Scapegoats*, Goodfellow, M. (2019)

23. 'What was the Windrush scandal, and what compensation has been paid to those affected?' standard.co.uk

24. '"It's like hell": Yarl's Wood women launch hunger strike against their indefinite detention and imminent charter flight', independent.co.uk

25. 'See us, believe us, stand with us', refugeewomen.co.uk

26. 'Uganda's president signs repressive anti-LGBT law', hrw.org

27. 'Beyond Belief: Our new report reveals a Home Office culture tainted by prejudice', freedomfromtorture.org

28. 'LGBTQ asylum seekers are still being let down by the Home Office', vice.com

29. 'Protect LGBTI asylum seekers in Britain, private firms told', theguardian.com

30. 'Guidance: Permission to work and volunteering for asylum seekers', gov.uk

31. 'The re-purposing' of Yarl's Wood and the invisibility of women in immigration detention', refugeewomen.co.uk

32. 'The use of Napier Barracks to house asylum seekers: regret motion,' lordslibrary.parliament.uk

33. 'Police make six more arrests in hunt for immigration centre escapees', itv.com

34. Nationwide protests against detention centres', notohassockfield.org.uk

35. 'Refugee, volunteer, prisoner: Sarah Mardini and Europe's hardening line on migration', thenewhumanitarian.org

36. 'Switzerland: Authorities must drop absurd charges against priest who showed compassion to asylum-seeker', amnesty.org

37. '"Spider-Man" of Paris to get French citizenship after child rescue', theguardian.com

38. 'Irregular migration: A timeline of UK-French cooperation', commonslibrary.parliament.uk

39. 'Life, death and limbo in the Calais "Jungle" – five years after its demolition', theguardian.com

40. 'Calais mayor bans distribution of food to migrants', theguardian.com

41. 'About Pipka Camp', lesvossolidarity.org

42. 'The Festival', queerranchfestival.org

43. 'The power of queer community: How the isle of Lesbos is coming together to aid refugees', gomag.com

44. 'Moria migrants: Fire destroys Greek camp leaving 13,000 without shelter', bbc.co.uk

45. 'Do not close Pipka down, replicate it', aljazeera.com

Trans Fights for Reproductive Rights

1. 'Supreme Court overturns Roe v. Wade, ending right to abortion upheld for decades', npr.org

2. 'Pride march in New York infused with new sense of urgency', nytimes.com

3. 'The world's abortion laws', reproductiverights.org

4. 'Almost every country criminalises abortion in some circumstances', bmj.com

5. 'Ireland votes to repeal the 8th amendment in historic abortion referendum – and marks a huge cultural shift', theconversation.com

6. 'Benin parliament votes to legalise abortion', reuters.com

7. '"I will do the same again": Activists continue fight against Poland's strict abortion laws', theguardian.com

8. 'Reproductive justice', sistersong.net

9. 'The secret history of the US government's family-separation policy', theatlantic.com

10. 'Black women four times more likely to die in childbirth', bbc.co.uk

11. 'Reproductive injustice, trans rights and eugenics', Radi, B., *Sex Reprod Health Matters* 28(1):1824318 (2020)

12. 'Our history', plannedparenthood.org

13. 'The first birth control pill used Puerto Rican women as guinea pigs', history.com

14. *Women, Race & Class*, Davis, A. (1981)

15. 'Is the word "women" being erased from the abortion rights movement?', nbcnews.com

16. 'For many pregnant trans people, competent medical care is hard to find', pbs.org

17. 'Transgender fertility study sheds light on testosterone's impact', nbcnews.com

18. 'Human rights victory! European Court of Human Rights ends forced sterilisation', tgeu.org

19. 'Legal victory for trans people – European human rights body slams forced sterilisation in the Czech Republic', ilga-europe.org

20. 'Sweden to pay compensation to trans victims of sterilisation', gaytimes.co.uk

21. 'Netherlands to compensate trans victims of forced sterilisation', reuters.com

22. 'Todo lo que querés saber sobre cómo hacerse un aborto con pastillas', clacaidigital. info

23. 'Mifepristone and misoprostol administered simultaneously versus 24 hours apart for abortion', Creinin, M. D. et al, *Obstet Gynecol* 109(4): 885–94 (2007)

24. 'Misoprostol teratogenicity: a prospective study in Argentina', Barbero, P., et al, *Arch Argent Pediatr* 109(3): 226–31 (2011)

25. 'La Marea Verde', amnesty.org

26. 'Code Name Jane: The women behind a covert abortion network', nytimes.com

27. 'Shadow report to the committee on the convention on the elimination of all forms of discrimination against women', www2.ohchr.org

28. 'Argentinian trans activist dies', windycitytimes.com

29. 'Lohana Berkins, furia travesty, siempre', agenciapresentes.org

30. 'How trans activists changed Argentina', redpepper.org.uk

31. *Our Bodies Are Your Battlefields*, dir. Solas, I. (2021)

32. 'Buenos Aires, epicentor del 8m en América Latina', elpais.com

33. 'Argentina legalises abortion in landmark moment for women's rights', theguardian.com

34. 'El Encuentro Nacional de Mujeres debate cambiar de nombre', pagina12.com.ar

35. 'Cuerpos que importan', pagina12.com.ar

36. '"We can conceive another history": Trans activism around abortion rights in Argentina', Fernández Romero, F., *Int J Transgend Health* 22(1–2): 126–140 (2021)

37. '"Los varones trans tabién abortamos": una realidad invisible en Argentina', fundacionreflejosdevenezuela.com

38. 'Darios de un trans – Romper el tabú: embarazo y abort en hombres trans', laizquierdadiario.com

39. '"We can conceive another history": Trans activism around abortion rights in Argentina', Fernández Romero, F., *Int J Transgend Health* 22(1–2): 126–140 (2021)

40. 'Why intersex genital mutilation needs to stop', teenvogue.com

41. 'Female genital mutilation', data.unicef.org

Hot Strike Summer

1. 'Union membership: Very sexy', theatlantic.com

2. 'Marrying ain't hard when you got a union card? Labor union membership and first marriage', Scheider, D. and Reich, A., *Social Problems* 61(4):625–643 (2014)

3. 'Trade union membership: Countries compared', nationmaster.com

4. 'Everything you need to know about hot strike summer', novaramedia.com

5. 'France's strikes show the unions are alive', jacobin.com

6. *La Haine,* Kassovitz, M. (1995)

7. 'The Paris Banlieue: Peripheries of inequity', Angélil, M. and Siress, C., *Journal of International Affairs* 65(2):57–67 (2012)

8. 'Grève du 5 décembre: au moins 806 000 manifestants en France, du jamais-vu sous l'ére Macron', leparisien.fr

9. 'Bangladesh garment workers clash with police as strikes roll on', guardian.ng

10. 'Bangladesh factory collapse toll passes 1,000', bbc.co.uk

11. 'Garment worker pay at 45% gap from living wage, report finds', businessoffashion.com

12. '80% of garment workers in Bangladesh have experienced or witnessed sexual violence and harassment at work', actionaid.org

13. 'Bangladesh strikes: Thousands of garment workers clash with police over poor pay', theguardian.com

14. 'Strikes and protests in over 35 countries to make Amazon pay', progressive.international

15. 'Poverty and inequality surge across Europe in the wake of Covid-19', ox.ac.uk

16. 'The Future of Work Podcast: Why are key workers undervalued?', voices.ilo.org

17. 'Why ethnic minorities are bearing the brunt of Covid-19', lse.ac.uk

18. 'COVID-19 pandemic and anti-Asian racism and violence in the 21st century', Lim, H. et al, *Race and Justice* 13(1): 3–8 (2023)

19. 'Belly Mujinga's family still seeking answers two years after death', theguardian.com

20. 'How George Floyd was killed in police custody', nytimes.com

21. 'Herstory', blacklivesmatter.com

22. 'Defund the police', blacklivesmatter.com

23. 'UN poverty envoy tells Britain this is "worst time" for more austerity', theguardian.com

24. 'Rising cost of living in the UK', commonslibrary.parliament.uk

25. 'The cost of living crisis', crisis.org.uk

26. '"Hot strike summer": Hundreds of thousands of UK workers are going on strike', teenvogue.com

27. 'Sports Banger's NHS T-shirts are the epitome of grassroots philanthropy', elephant.art

28. 'The social gathering hero of 2020: Jonny Banger', thesocial.com

29. '"Up the Workers" white T-shirt', shop.sportsbanger.com

30. 'People in work', ons.gov.uk

31. 'Trade union membership, UK 1995–2022: Statistical bulletin', assets.publishing.service.gov.uk

32. 'General secretary', rmt.org.uk

33. 'Mick Lynch round-up: best moments of the week', leftfootforward.org

34. 'Sunak claims workers are "tired of being foot soldiers in Mick Lynch's class war', standard.co.uk

35. 'The trade unions of the Middle Ages', phm.org.uk

36. 'The bright side of the Black Death', americanscientist.org

37. 'Wat Tyler and the Peasants' Revolt', historic-uk.com

38. 'The Peasants' Revolt and the Government of England', Ormrod, W. M., *Journal of British Studies* 29(1): 1–30 (1990)

39. 'Trade unions in the British Industrial Revolution', worldhistory.org
40. 'Strike of the journeymen tailors: They cry for more', nytimes.com
41. 'The cordwainers protest: A crisis in labor relations', Quimby, I., *Winterthur Portfolio* 3: 83–101 (1967)
42. 'How workers won the weekend', tribunemag.co.uk
43. 'Saint Monday', tribunemag.co.uk
44. 'What is the four-day working week and how close are we to getting it in the UK?', bigissue.com
45. 'Union songs', unionsong.com
46. 'Tres las huellas de Ruth Mary Kelly: Feminismos y prostitución en la Buenos Aires del siglo XX', ri.conicet.gov.ar
47. *Tras las Huellas de Ruth Mary Kelly*, Daich, D. (2019)
48. 'Incorporating sex workers into the Argentine labor movement', Hardy, K., *International Labor and Working-Class History* 77: 89–108 (2010)
49. 'Asociación de Mujeres Meretrices de Argentina (AMMAR)', escr-net.org
50. 'How French sex workers are organizing for health care and labor rights', vice.com
51. 'Sante les travailleurs et travailleuses de sexe seront enfin couverts', liberation.fr
52. 'France adopts the Nordic model', feministcurrent.com
53. 'How the Nordic model in France changed everything for sex workers', opendemocracy.net

Towards Liberation

1. 'Ziwe interviews Caroline Calloway', ziwe.com
2. 'Baited with Ziwe', avclub.com
3. 'Caroline Calloway's "Creativity Workshop" taught me nothing about creativity, but a lot about scamming', wmagazine.com
4. 'I was Caroline Calloway', thecut.com
5. 'Herstory', blacklivesmatter.com
6. 'This is why millions of people are posting black squares on Instagram', forbes.com
7. 'How Blackout Tuesday became a social media moment', nytimes.com
8. 'How to reject allyship fatigue and keep doing the work of anti-racism', greatist.com
9. 'Dictionary.com's 2021 word of the year is...', dictionary.com
10. '*White Fragility* is everywhere – but does anti-racism training work?', nytimes.com
11. 'The dehumanizing condescension of *White Fragility*', theatlantic.com
12. *What White People Can Do Next*, Dabiri, E. (2021)
13. *Cruising Utopia*, Muñoz, J. (2009)
14. 'Let this conversation with Mariame Kaba radicalise you', truthout.org
15. 'Six billion smartphones on Earth, but who will fix them', ifixit.com
16. 'Social media copies gambling methods "to create psychological cravings"', theguardian.com
17. 'Sick of the attention economy? It's time to rebel', forbes.com

18. 'Lessons learned: A negative headline makes it more likely you'll click', hsph. harvard.edu

19. 'UK hotels to become homeless shelters under coronavirus plan', theguardian.com

20. 'These US cities defunded police: "We're transferring money to the community"', theguardian.com

21. 'After two years, the future of Minneapolis's mental health response program is uncertain', startribune.com

22. *Care Work: Dreaming Disability Justice*, Piepzna-Samarasinha, L. (2018)

23. *Trick Mirror*, Tolentino, J. (2019)

24. 'Are we living in a post-racial America?', npr.org

25. 'Margaret Thatcher: A feminist icon', theguardian.com

Acknowledgements

There are so many people I'd love to thank. I've been shitting a brick in case I miss someone – which I *obviously* will – but here goes anyway.

Mum, for showing me what strength looked like from a young age and making me laugh like nobody else can. Grandad, for always being at the other end of the phone and never, ever judging me. Eli, for making these last few years the best of my life. Alice, for putting up with my shit for the last decade and being such a wonderful friend. Hannah, Shami, Claire, Wemmy – you've all made Sheffield feel like home, and I love you for it. The excellent folks at Juno Books, for the endless pep talks, book proofs and M&S biscuits! Lewis, Jeanie, Rose, Marj, Vikram, Ayoola; everyone that kept me sane during the years of chaos in London. I'll always be grateful.

Holly, for being a fantastic agent and believing in this book even when my own confidence waned. Katie, for championing this work – and my voice – so fiercely and choosing to publish it. The team at Trapeze Books, for working so tirelessly to make this book the best it can be possibly be. Juno Roche, for showing me that queer, working-class writers can do *excellent* things when we put our minds to it, and for being the closest thing to a mentor I've ever had.

Finally, the writers and revolutionaries I admire: Emma Dabiri, Frankie Miren, Anna Sulan Masing, Emma Garland, Shon Faye, Angela Davis, Dan Glass, countless others. The world is a better place with your words in it.

About the Author

Jake Hall is an author and journalist who has been writing about intersectionality and queer culture for over a decade and who has written extensively for publications like *British Vogue*, *The Independent*, *Pink* News, *Dazed*, *i-D*, *VICE*, *Refinery29* and *Slate*. Their first book, *The Art of Drag*, published in 2020 and has become an award-winning success. As a working-class queer kid from Doncaster, Jake has always been interested in the experience of marginalised groups and their aim is to uncover histories that have long gone untold.

CREDITS

Trapeze would like to thank everyone at Orion who worked on the publication of *Shoulder to Shoulder*.

Agent
Holly Faulks

Editorial
Katie Packer
Serena Arthur

Copy-editor
Liz Marvin

Proofreader
Tara O'Sullivan

Editorial Management
Jane Hughes
Charlie Panayiotou
Lucy Bilton
Claire Boyle

Audio
Paul Stark
Jake Alderson
Georgina Cutler

Contracts
Dan Herron
Ellie Bowker
Alyx Hurst

Design
Nick Shah
Jess Hart
Joanna Ridley
Helen Ewing

Photo Shoots & Image Research
Natalie Dawkins

Finance
Nick Gibson
Jasdip Nadra
Sue Baker
Tom Costello

Inventory
Jo Jacobs
Dan Stevens

Production
Paul Hussey
Katie Horrocks

Marketing
Yadira Da-Trindade

Publicity
Sharina Smith

Sales
Jen Wilson
Victoria Laws
Esther Waters
Tolu Ayo-Ajala
Group Sales teams across
Digital, Field, International
and Non-Trade

Operations
Group Sales Operations team

Rights
Rebecca Folland
Tara Hiatt
Ben Fowler
Alice Cottrell
Ruth Blakemore
Ayesha Kinley
Marie Henckel